Handbook of Roman Catholic Moral Terms

HANDBOOK *of* ROMAN CATHOLIC MORAL TERMS

James T. Bretzke, SJ

Georgetown University Press
Washington, DC

Library of Congress Cataloging-in-Publication Data

Bretzke, James T., 1952–
    Handbook of Roman Catholic moral terms / James T. Bretzke.
        pages cm
    Includes bibliographical references.
    ISBN 978-1-62616-003-3 (pbk. : alk.paper)
    1. Christian ethics—Catholic authors—Dictionaries. I. Title.
    BJ1249.B625 2013
    241'.04203—dc23   2013002928

This book is printed on acid-free paper meeting the requirements of the American National Standard for Permanence in Paper for Printed Library Materials.

20 19 18 17 16 15 14 13   9 8 7 6 5 4 3 2   First printing

Dedicated to the memory of my parents,

Carl Frederick Bretzke and Mary Adelaide Hoch Bretzke

Contents

Preface

Purpose and Scope of This Handbook

Ideally, a handbook of this sort should be clear, concise, and comprehensive. Yet I have discovered that these three Cs often pull in different directions, so the final product is a best-effort compromise in producing a quick reference and starting point for further investigation of many of the key concepts and topics in both fundamental and applied Christian ethics in the Catholic moral tradition. While the focus is on the Catholic moral tradition, this book is meant to be neither an exhaustive encyclopedia of moral theology nor a compendium of the current official position of the Church on the terms and their underlying debates. Terms such as "grace," while obviously foundational to theology and employed several dozen times in this text, have no separate entry since they are either sufficiently well-known or more complete resources can be easily found elsewhere. In order to include a greater number of terms, other sacrifices have had to be made in the depth and breadth that many of the terms deserve, and unfortunately, other worthy concepts on the original list had to be left on the cutting room floor.

How to Use This Handbook

To reduce explicit and repetitive references to terms that appear elsewhere in the text, the following conventions are employed. A term that includes other terms with separate independent entries is indicated by **bolding** the other term that can be found elsewhere in this book. At the end of an entry, other related terms that are helpful in fleshing out a fuller understanding of the term are indicated by **See also,** followed by the additional terms shown *in italics*. Several entries also include one or more bibliographic suggestions indicated by ***For further reading***. A bibliography of reference aids is included at the end of the text. For example, the brief entry on marriage includes bolded terms that have their own definitions that augment this important term: **Augustine, canon law, covenant,** *debitum, Gaudium et spes,* **historical development, impediment,** *remedium concupiscientiae,* **responsible parenthood, Tradition,** and **Vatican II.** The entry concludes with the "see also" listings for ABC, AIH, birth control, gender, inseparability principle, natural family planning, privilege (Pauline and Petrine), and safe sex, and it concludes by suggesting a couple of general works under **"For further reading."** To give as many research leads as possible, different bibliographic references among related items are suggested rather than repeating the same texts over again.

Acknowledgments

I would like to thank Richard Brown and the staff of Georgetown University Press for their invaluable assistance in bringing this project to completion, as well as to the three anonymous referees for their corrections and suggestions for expansion of the terms covered. I am also very grateful to the dean of the Boston College School of Theology and Ministry Rev. Mark Massa, SJ for supporting my sabbatical application that allowed me to undertake this project and for supporting Kevin Dowd as my research assistant, whose very meticulous proofreading and editorial suggestions have certainly greatly improved the original manuscript. The bulk of my sabbatical was spent in the Jesuit Community of Marquette University, and I am very grateful to them for their interest and support in my daily writings. Several colleagues have helped me along the way as well, although deficiencies in the final outcome are my responsibility alone. Finally, I am especially grateful to the life and example given me by my parents, Carl and Mary Bretzke. Although they both died well before I became a Jesuit, I have come to realize how much we owe to our family, and so it is with humble gratitude that I dedicate this work to their memory. I pray that they are smiling down on their only son from above.

Abbreviations

N.B. Documents are indicated in **bold**.

ABC	abstinence, be faithful, condom use
AG	***Ad gentes***, Vatican II "Decree on Missionary Activity in the Church"
AHCD	advance health care directive
AID	artificial insemination by donor
AIDS	acquired immune deficiency syndrome
AIH	artificial insemination by husband
ANH	artificial nutrition and hydration
ARCIC	Anglican–Roman Catholic International Commission
ART	assisted reproduction technologies
ASPD	antisocial personality disorder
CC	***Casti connubii***, 1930 encyclical of Pius XI
CCC	***Catechism of the Catholic Church*** (1992, 1997)
CDF	*Congregatio pro doctrina fidei* (Congregation for the Doctrine of the Faith)
CIC	***Codex iuris canonici*** (*Code of Canon Law*, 1983)
CTSA	Catholic Theological Society of America
CUA	Catholic University of America (Washington, DC)
CV	***Caritas in veritate***, 2009 encyclical of Benedict XVI
DH	***Dignitatis humanae***, Vatican II "Declaration on Religious Liberty"
DS	***Denzinger-Schönmetzer*** (***Enchiridion Symbolorum et Definitionum*** [***Handbook of Creeds and Definitions*** in Latin and German])
DV	***Dei verbum***, Vatican II "Dogmatic Constitution on Divine Revelation"
EN	***Evangelii nuntiandi***, 1975 apostolic exhortation of Paul VI
ERD	***Ethical and Religious Directives for Catholic Health Care Institutions***
FC	***Familiaris consortio***, 1981 apostolic exhortation of John Paul II

FR	*Fides et ratio*, 1998 encyclical of John Paul II
GIFT	gamete intrafallopian transfer
GS	*Gaudium et spes*, Vatican II "Pastoral Constitution on the Church in the Modern World"
HCPoA	health care power of attorney
HG	*Humani generis*, 1950 encyclical of Pius XII
HIV	human immunodeficiency virus
HV	*Humanae vitae*, 1968 encyclical of Paul VI
ICSI	intracytoplasmic sperm injection
ID	*Indulgentiarum doctrina*, 1967 apostolic constitution of Paul VI
IVF	in vitro fertilization
LG	*Lumen gentium*, Vatican II "Dogmatic Constitution on the Church"
MCS	minimally conscious state
NARTH	National Association for Research and Therapy of Homosexuality
NCCB	National Conference of Catholic Bishops (since 2001, the USCCB)
ND	*Neuner-dupuis (Enchiridion symbolorum et definitionum [Handbook of Creeds and Definitions])*
NFP	natural family planning (e.g., Billings method or the rhythm method)
OA	*Octogesima adveniens*, 1971 apostolic letter of Paul VI
OCD	obsessive-compulsive disorder
PA	*Pastor aeternus*, Vatican I "Dogmatic Constitution on the Church"
PAS	physician-assisted suicide
PDE	principle of double effect
PEG	percutaneous endoscopic gastrostomy (aka feeding tube)
PGD	preimplantation genetic diagnosis
PH	*Persona humana*, 1975 CDF "Declaration on Certain Problems of Sexual Ethics"
PP	*Populorum progressio*, 1967 encyclical of Paul VI
PT	*Pacem in terris*, 1963 encyclical of John XXIII
PVS	persistent (or permanent) vegetative state
QA	*Quadragesimo anno*, 1931 encyclical of Pius XI
RP	*Reconciliatio et paenitentia*, 1984 apostolic exhortation of John Paul II
SALIGIA	*superbia, avaritia, luxuria, invidia, gula, ira,* and *acedia* (the seven capital sins)

SCE	Society of Christian Ethics
SCG	*Summa contra Gentiles*, Thomas Aquinas
SpirEx.	*Spiritual Exercises* (the actual text of Ignatius of Loyola)
SRS	*Sollicitudo rei socialis*, 1987 encyclical of John Paul II
ST	*Summa theologiae*, Thomas Aquinas
S.T.D.	Doctor of Sacred Theology (ecclesiastical terminal degree)
STDs/STIs	sexually transmitted diseases or sexually transmitted infections
USCCB	United States Conference of Catholic Bishops (before 2001, the NCCB)
VD	venereal disease
VS	*Veritatis splendor*, 1992 encyclical of John Paul II
WCC	World Council of Churches

A

ABC (**abstinence**, be faithful, **condom use**) is the acronym for a public health program used widely in sub-Saharan Africa, which is ravaged by **HIV/AIDS**. Since condom use is specifically recommended, this program has been contested by public health officials, theologians, and even popes and bishops. While the exhortation to abstain from sexual relations and to remain faithful to one's spouse in marriage alone could in theory prevent the further spread of HIV/AIDS virus, many people realistically argue that condoms have to be included in comprehensive public sexual health protocol. Bishop Kevin Dowling of South Africa has said a number of times that "abstinence before marriage and faithfulness in a marriage is beyond the realm of possibility here. The issue is to protect life. That must be our fundamental goal." However, other bishops and **Benedict XVI** assert that condoms alone can never resolve the HIV/AIDS pandemic. No doubt this *status quaestionis* will continue until a reliable HIV vaccine and cure for AIDS are found. *For further reading*, see John Coleman, "Bishop Kevin Dowling: AIDS and Condoms" *America*, June 9, 2009, with reader responses (http://america-magazine.org/content/all-things/bishop-kevin-dowling-aids-and-condoms); Mary Jo Iozzio with Mary M. Doyle Roche and Elise M. Miranda, eds., *Calling for Justice throughout the World: Catholic Women Theologians on the HIV/AIDS Pandemic* (New York: Continuum, 2008); and Cardinal Theodore McCarrick, "Pastoral Letter on HIV/AIDS," *Origins* 33 (June 19, 2003): 81; 83–86. **See also** *compromise with evil, lesser evil, marriage, safe sex, sexual ethics, STDs,* and *tolerance.*

Abomination (Old Testament). See **Holiness Code**

Abortion as a moral concept refers to the elective and direct termination of fetal life that otherwise would be viable if the pregnancy were to continue to its normal conclusion. The Catholic Church has always held abortion to be a serious **intrinsic evil**, with a *latae sententiae* **canonical penalty** of **excommunication** for those who procure an abortion (*CIC* #1398). However, it is important to distinguish a **direct abortion** from other foreseen terminations of fetal life, such as an **ectopic pregnancy**, which is judged to be **indirect** in terms of both the **moral object** (*finis operis*) and the accompanying **intention** of the agent (*finis operantis*) and morally licit if **proportionate reason** is present. The **USCCB**'s *Ethical and Religious Directives for Catholic Health Care Services* (*ERD*) at #47 states that "operations, treatments, and medications that have as their direct purpose the cure of a proportionately serious pathological condition of a pregnant woman are permitted when they cannot be safely postponed until the unborn child is viable, even if they will result in the death of the unborn child."

Since the 1973 US Supreme Court decision of *Roe v. Wade*, which gives the legal right to abortion, many hold as a basic tenet of **feminist ethics** of reproductive choice that termination of a pregnancy is the sole, elective decision of the woman herself. The effort to recriminalize abortion remains a hot-button political issue and, while some argue that no Catholic politician or voter should ever support any piece of legislation that contains pro-choice or abortion provisions, **John Paul II** in his 1995 *Evangelium vitae* outlines situations in which elected officials (and by extension voters) "could licitly support proposals aimed at limiting the harm done by such a law and at lessening its negative consequences at the level of general opinion and public morality. This does not in fact represent an illicit cooperation with an unjust law, but rather a legitimate and proper attempt to limit its evil aspects" (*EV* #73). *For further reading*, in addition to *Evangelium vitae*, see also **CDF**, *Questio de abortu* ("Declaration on Procured Abortion") November 18, 1974; John R. Connery, *Abortion: The Development of the Roman Catholic Perspective* (Chicago: Loyola University Press, 1977); John T. Noonan Jr., ed., *The Morality of Abortion: Legal and Historical Perspectives* (Cambridge, MA: Harvard University Press, 1970). **See also** *canonical penalties*, *direct and indirect*; *double effect principle*; *ectopic pregnancy*; and *finis operis and finis operantis*.

Absolutes (moral absolutes) hold that some **moral norms**, usually expressed as either **prescriptions** or **proscriptions**, are universally binding both in time and space. Such moral choices admit no legitimate exception, regardless of when or where (i.e., **circumstances**) or **intention**. These moral absolutes are grounded in either **God**'s *lex aeterna* (eternal law) such as the **Decalogue** or **natural law**. Absolutes that express proscriptions are termed **intrinsic evils**, and absolutes that express prescriptions are usually cast as duties according to **deontology**. **Thomas Aquinas** expressed the foundational moral absolute that grounds all the rest: *Bonum est faciendum et prosequendum, et malum vitandum* ("The good is to be done and fostered, and evil avoided" *ST I-II*, Q. 94, art. 2). **Discernment** of what constitutes a genuine moral absolute has been the locus of much **casuistry** over the centuries as well as considerable moral debate, especially since the promulgation of **Paul VI**'s 1968 *Humanae vitae*, which holds that the prohibition of artificial **birth control** is absolute, although the practice of **NFP** was morally permissible under certain circumstances (see *HV* #14–16). Much of this debate centers on just how we can discover with certainty the level, universality, and moral rectitude of the various moral norms. These debates grow out of larger debates such as **physicalism** versus **personalism** and the **classicist and historical worldviews**, and the epistemological competency of the **magisterium** to pronounce definitively (e.g., *de fide definita*) on concrete moral norms. **John Paul II**'s 1993 *Veritatis splendor* charged that some contemporary moral theories, especially those connected with **consequentialism, utilitarianism**, and **proportionalism**, effectively denied the possibility of moral absolutes, although this latter charge is sharply contested by many **revisionist moral theologians**. In the ensuing debates, unfortunately, it is often overlooked that the manualist moral tradition never held that *every* moral norm is necessarily absolute. Thomas Aquinas observes that some norms are generally true but allows for certain legitimate exceptions (*lex valet ut in pluribus*). As we descend further to the concrete application in **practical reason** due to **contingency and fallibility, concrete material norms** will be necessarily less certain and less universal than those more general and abstract norms arrived at through **speculative reason**. *For further reading* from a variety of perspectives, see Charles E. Curran and Richard A. McCormick's *Readings in Moral Theology, No. 1: Moral Norms and Catholic Tradition* (New York: Paulist Press, 1979); John Finnis, *Moral Absolutes: Tradition, Revision, and Truth* (Washington, DC: Catholic University of America Press, 1991); Josef Fuchs, "The Absolute in Moral Theology," ch. 1 in *Moral Demands and Personal Obligations* (Washington, DC: Georgetown University Press, 1993), 15–29; Bernard Häring, "Traditions, Laws, Norms and Context," ch. 7 in *Free and Faithful in Christ: Moral Theology for Priests and Laity*, vol. 1 (Slough, UK: St. Paul Publications, 1978), 302–77; and William E. May, *Moral Absolutes, Catholic Traditions, Current Trends, and Truth* (Milwaukee, WI: Marquette University Press, 1989).

Absolution is the prayer given by the priest for the **forgiveness** of sins following confession in the **sacrament of reconciliation**. Over the centuries various formulas have been used, such as the indicative *ego te absolvo* ("I absolve you . . .") or the precatory "May God Almighty have mercy on us and forgive us our sins." The **Council of Trent** taught that the prayer of absolution is not only a statement of God's mercy on our sins but also a juridical act by which those sins were actually forgiven (see *DS* #1685, 1709; *ND* #1628, 1649). For absolution to be sacramentally effective, **contrition** and a firm purpose to amend one's life (**conversion**) are also required. The prayer of absolution recited in the penitential rite in the Eucharist is not the sacrament of reconciliation but a sacramental rite.

Abstinence is the voluntary forgoing of something or some activity that normally has pleasurable aspects and to which one otherwise would have rights so that one could practice **asceticism**, pursue some higher spiritual goal, aid the **cardinal virtue** or **temperance**, or conform oneself to the regulations of the Church. For example, **canon law** currently calls Catholics over the age of seven to abstain from meat on Ash Wednesday and Good Friday. Sexual abstinence, sometimes also termed **continence**, was also the traditional counsel given to couples who wished to practice **birth control**, or given as a penitential practice for a limited period of time such as during Lent.

Acculturation and enculturation are two key concepts of **cultural anthropology** that must be distinguished from **inculturation**, although recognition of their dynamics is critical to the successful process of inculturation. Enculturation is also sometimes termed "**socialization**" and is the process by which an individual becomes truly a part of his or her own "native" **culture**. This process takes place not at birth but in the early years of childhood and involves both formal and informal processes of learning the native culture, including its principal belief system, mores, symbols, dominant images, and so on. Acculturation is what happens when enculturated individuals or groups of individuals from different cultures come into sustained contact that results in change on both parts. Acculturation can occur positively or negatively in terms of moral values, for example, in a deeper appreciation for another culture's positive moral sensitivities, or negatively occurring much in the same way as close contact with "bad examples" of moral living, inculcation of consumerist values, and so on. As with culture itself, these related processes of enculturation and acculturation are dynamic and thus are both ongoing and open-ended to a definite extent. **See also** *culture and inculturation*.

Acedia. See **capital sins**

Acquired knowledge and virtues require **human experience**, cooperation, and effort to develop. These are contrasted with the **infused virtues** (or **theological virtues**) of faith, hope, and **charity**. **See also** *infused knowledge and infused virtues*, and *virtues*.

Action *in se* refers to the moral object (***finis operis***, as contrasted with just the physically observable nature of the action), which by definition includes a basic consideration of the **fonts of morality** (action *in se*, **circumstances**

and **intention** [*finis operantis*]). *In se* in Latin references the whole context of the action, which in this usage presumes the circumstances and intention. **See also** *actus hominis and actus humanus, direct and indirect, double effect principle*, and *intrinsic evil*.

Actual sin is personal real **sin** containing all three required elements, namely sinful matter, **sufficient knowledge** that the matter is indeed sinful, and **sufficient consent** or **freedom** to do the sinful act. The term is synonymous with **formal sin** and contrasted with **material sin**, which may involve sinful matter but lacks sufficient knowledge, consent, or both to make the action actual sin.

Actus hominis and *actus humanus* are two Latin terms that highlight the distinction between simple human activity and activity that has moral agency. *Actus hominis*, usually translated as "act of man," designates a whole range of human activities from automatic biological functions such as respiration to involuntary, inconsequential, or totally unintended actions. Choosing one color shirt over another color shirt or accidentally bumping into another person would both be classed as an *actus hominis* and would not carry moral meaning. *Actus humanus* is translated as "human act" in the *Catechism of the Catholic Church* and refers to moral acts that have the three requisite **fonts of morality**, namely a **moral object**, an **intention** done in **freedom**, and in concrete **circumstances**. Some contemporary moral theologians like to broaden *actus humanus* to include virtually all human choices, but this goes beyond the **manualist tradition**'s use of these terms and its key distinction. **See also** *finis operis and finis operantis* and *intrinsic evil*.

Address to the Italian Midwives is the 1951 **occasional allocution** of **Pius XII** that expressed for the first time in papal teaching the legitimate possibility of a couple to practice **birth control** for "serious motives" of **responsible parenthood**, even for the duration of the **marriage**. The method used had to be either total **abstinence** from sexual relations or the practice of a form of what today is called **NFP** but at the time was termed the **rhythm method**. This address was an important **development of moral doctrine** of the **magisterium**'s **sexual ethics** from **Pius XI**'s 1930 **encyclical** *Casti connubii*, later confirmed by **Paul VI**'s 1968 encyclical *Humanae vitae*.

Adikia (αδκια, unrighteousness) is one of the three principal terms used in the New Testament to denote **sin**. The other two terms are **hamartia** ('αμαρτια, missing the mark) and **hubris** (ύβρις, **pride**). Of these three *adikia* comes closest to the Latin for sin, *peccatum*, though the latter connotes a stronger notion of crime than the Greek terms. *Adikia* must also be understood in the corresponding Greek term for righteousness (δικαιοσύνη, *dikaiosune*), which in the New Testament refers to **God**'s standards and demands of judgment, which may differ from human conceptions (see Mt. 3:15). The Christian call to Gospel righteousness involves not only a **conversion** (*metanoia*, μετανοια) from wrongdoing but also a commitment to God's kingdom values, which often go more deeply than human **justice** or fairness.

Adultery. See **fornication and adultery**

An **advance health care directive** (AHCD), colloquially known as a living will, outlines in advance the medical care decisions individuals wish to be made on their behalf should they be unable to indicate or make these decisions at the necessary time, thus providing them with a greater possibility of **death with dignity**. The AHCD usually spells out a number of possible medical scenarios in some detail, including the termination of procedures, drugs, therapies, and so on, that can be considered **extraordinary means**, and it often includes designating a trusted individual as a health care proxy with power of attorney (HCPoA) who then has the legal rights and responsibilities to make these decisions on the patient's behalf. **Ordinary means** of health care would always be morally obligatory, but specifying in an AHCD the conditions for the exclusion or termination of extraordinary means is a legitimate exercise of bioethical **autonomy** and as such is explicitly recognized by the Church in a variety of documents such as the ***Ethical and Religious Directives for Catholic Health Care Institutions (ERD)*** and through the papal **magisterium** (see **John Paul**'s 1995 **encyclical** *Evangelium vitae* #65 and his November 2004 **occasional allocution** given to the 19th International Conference of the Pontifical Council for Health Pastoral Care), as well as in the CDF's 1980 "Declaration on **Euthanasia**," *Iura et bona*, and its 2007 ***Responsum ad dubium*** on **artificial nutrition and hydration (ANH)**.

Advertence means awareness of one's actions, traditionally used in the **sacrament of reconciliation** to help assess the penitent's **culpability** for sinful actions. If, due to lack of attention, impaired judgment, distraction, and so on, one was unable to advert to the actual action performed, this would be important in judging the effect of the action on the agent himself. Since **sufficient knowledge** logically precedes **sufficient consent** to committing a **sin**, factors that diminish the knowledge likewise diminish the culpability or responsibility for one's bad actions.

Aeterni Patris (Eternal Father) is the 1879 **encyclical** of **Leo XIII** that mandated the use of **Scholasticism**, especially **Thomas Aquinas**, in the study of Christian philosophy.

Affirmative action is the umbrella term given to private- or public-sector policies that consciously seek to benefit underrepresented or historically discriminated groups, thereby trying to rectify injustices that have arisen from **patriarchy, racism, white privilege**, and other forms of systemic discrimination. **See also** *feminism and feminist ethics, liberation theology, political correctness*, and *restorative justice*.

Agape, eros, and philia are the ancient Greek terms for three types of **love**. Agape is **charity** toward others, often involving some sort of self-sacrifice. Eros refers to the Greek god of love (the Roman counterpart is Cupid [Latin, *cupiditas* for "eager desire" or "passionate longing"]). Eros refers primarily to aspects of love that relate to sexual desire, although eros goes beyond this. *Philia* refers to fraternal affection and charity. Of the three, agape was viewed as most in line with Christian charity, whereas eros was seen as the most problematic, especially since sexual desire was identified closely with **lust** and **concupiscence**. While this Greek tripartite conception of love continues to play an important role in Christian theology, aspects of agape have been critiqued for promoting a form of **charity** that insufficiently considered the demands of **justice** in situations of **social sin and structural evil**. Likewise, uneasiness with eros could lead to a false sense of **asceticism** and denial or repression of the legitimate role of the **body** and pleasure in **sexual ethics** and human relationships.

AID (artificial insemination by donor). See **artificial insemination** and **reproductive technologies**; **see also** *Dignitas personae* and *Donum vitae.*

AIDS (acquired immune deficiency syndrome). See **HIV/AIDS, STDs, ABC, condom use**, and **safe sex**

AIH (artificial insemination by husband). See **artificial insemination** and **reproductive technologies**; **see also** *Dignitas personae* and *Donum vitae*

Allocutions (occasional and papal) refer to an address by a member of the **magisterium**, often the pope, on some particular occasion such as a meeting or congress. Often, such allocutions are not written by the hierarch himself but rather are composed by someone connected with the particular gathering.

Thus, these speeches usually are not as rigorously vetted as teachings that rank higher in the "manner" criterion outlined in the **character, manner, and frequency criteria** of *Lumen gentium* #25, which help discern the proper level of **authority** that documents possess, and thus determine the corresponding level of *obsequium religiosum* that is expected on the part of the faithful. Examples of some well-known papal **occasional allocutions** on moral matters are **Pius XII's** 1951 **Address to the Italian Midwives** and **John Paul II's** 2004 speeches on **ANH** for **PVS** patients in March and his subsequent speech in November on forgoing **extraordinary means**, which many considered to be a corrective nuance on some interpretations of the earlier address. **See also** *charism of office, in forma communi and in forma specifica*, and *infallibilism*.

Always Our Children: A Pastoral Message to the Parents of Homosexual Children and Suggestions for Pastoral Ministries was originally released by the **NCCB** (today the **USCCB**) in October 1997. After strong complaints from some bishops, such as Fabian Bruskewitz, then of Lincoln, Nebraska, who called the practical advice offered in the letter for parental patience and acceptance of gay children not only misguided but actually "evil" in some aspects, and blunting the **magisterium**'s teachings on **homosexuality**, the letter was then slightly revised to avoid any misunderstandings of the original text and reissued in July 1998 with the approval of the CDF. The core text, though, continued to counsel parents to show love and acceptance both of themselves and their gay children and to try to help them maintain a spiritual life in the Church. It does not counsel the controversial practice of **reparative therapy. See also** *Persona humana* and *pastoral letters*.

Amendment (firm purpose of) is expressed in many traditional formulas of the various acts of **contrition** prayed by the penitent in the **sacrament of reconciliation**, often coupled with the phrase "to avoid the **occasions of sin**" to indicate the individual's willingness to turn from **sin** by changing one's life through **conversion**. A sincere desire for amendment in one's life (traditionally termed "firm purpose of amendment") is necessary for sacramental **absolution**, but this need not be an absolute promise or prediction that these same sins will never again be committed in the future.

Americanism. See *Testem benevolentiae nostrae*

Analogy (Greek, ἀναλογία analogia, "proportion" or "correspondence") refers to the relation between two terms that are both similar and dissimilar to some degree. While an analogy helps in identifying similarities and solving variables such as "A is to B as C is to D," a moral argument based solely on analogy is fraught with internal limitations and weaknesses that reside in the dissimilar aspects of the two terms being compared. While certain similarities can be expressed as "A is to B as C is to D," these are not strict equivalences, and there will also likely be important aspects in which A, B, C, and D are also dissimilar from one another. An argument drawn from an analogy thus will be true only insofar as the two terms in fact are similar in their key attributes. In theology, three traditional uses of analogy are the analogy of being (*analogia entis*), the analogy of faith (*analogia fidei*), and the analogy of scripture (*analogia scipturae*). The analogy of being is grounded in **God**, who, as the fullness and perfection of all reality, is the prime analogue for all creaturely goodness. The analogy of faith (see Romans 12:6) holds that an individual biblical passage must be interpreted within the larger context of the whole faith that the Church holds (see *DS* #3016, 3283). The analogy of scripture further specifies that a particular biblical passage, especially if it seems ambiguous or unclear, must be interpreted in accord with the message and interpretation of other biblical texts that deal with the same issue or theme and not reduced to simplistic **proof-texting**.

Angelic Doctor (Doctor Angelicus) is the common title used for **Thomas Aquinas** (1225–74).

Anger (*ira*), a strong **passion** listed as one of the **capital sins**, can be countered through the **cardinal virtues**, especially **temperance** and **prudence**, as well as by **charity** and **forgiveness**. The Bible, though, gives ample testimony to the righteous anger of **God** and Jesus. Modern psychology has shown that repressed or untreated anger can easily turn into depression as well as erupting into more violent and inappropriate forms of expression. Some liberation theologians and feminist ethicians, such as **Beverly Wildung Harrison**, hold that anger can function as a virtue for women and others oppressed as a means to **restorative justice**. *For further reading,* see Beverly Wildung Harrison, "The Role of Anger in the Work of Love: Christian Ethics for Women and Other Strangers," ch. 1 in *Making the Connections: Essays in Feminist Social Ethics* (Boston: Beacon Press, 1985), 3–21.

Anglican Communion is the term chosen by the first **Lambeth Conference** of 1867 for the association of Anglican and Episcopalian churches in communion with the Church of England, whose symbolic head is the **Archbishop of Canterbury**. It is the third-largest Christian communion, after Roman Catholicism and the Eastern Orthodox Churches. Over the years, a number of **ecumenism** initiatives with the Roman Catholic Church, most notably ARCIC, the Anglican–Roman Catholic International Commission, established in 1970, produced statements on the Eucharist, ordination,

authority, and ministry, although these reports have not yet found unanimous agreement by all of the member churches and other tensions have arisen from issues such as **women's ordination**, **birth control** and **sexual ethics**, especially **homosexuality**.

ANH (artificial nutrition and hydration) is required when a patient cannot take normal nourishment (food or liquids) without some sort of medical assistance, such as a **PEG tube** (percutaneous endoscopic gastrostomy, aka feeding tube). The use and especially the discontinuation of ANH is hotly debated, and despite a number of magisterial directives and statements, we cannot arrive at a simple and clear directive that fits all possible cases from, for example, lock-jaw to long-term **PVS (persistent/permanent vegetative state)**. **See also** *advance health care directive, ordinary and extraordinary means*, and *Responsum ad dubium*.

Annulment and dissolution are the juridical findings in **canon law** determining that one or more of the necessary elements for a valid sacramental **marriage** were either missing or defective such that even though the marriage may have appeared to be valid, it was in fact not. Both an annulment (technically called a decree of nullity) and a dissolution free both parties from the bonds of their marriage, and if they are not bound by some other union or obligation, they are free to marry within the Church. However, any children born of this union are still considered legitimate. While sometimes dubbed "Catholic divorce," an annulment both in civil and canon law is a finding that no marriage existed in fact, and therefore "divorce" would not even be legally possible. The Church holds that a *ratum et consummatum* (validly ratified and consummated) marriage is indissoluble until the death of one of the parties. In centuries past, the grounds for annulment were interpreted quite strictly, but following **Vatican II**, a more expansive application has been taken by many diocesan marriage tribunals that evaluate annulment petitions. The principal grounds for an annulment are the defects of lack of free consent due to reservations (*CIC* #1102), force or fear (*CIC* #1103), lack of **intention** to contract a lifelong monogamous relationship open to children (*CIC* #1096 and #1101), and psychological incapacity to fulfill the obligations of marriage (*CIC* #1095, a section sometimes dubbed the "loose canon," which states that those incapable of contracting marriage include "§1/ those who lack the sufficient use of reason; §2/ those who suffer from a grave defect of discretion of judgment concerning the essential matrimonial rights and duties mutually to be handed over and accepted; §3/ those who are not able to assume the essential obligations of marriage for causes of a psychic nature"). Some sixty thousand annulments are granted annually, two-thirds of them coming from the United States, and although this number has leveled off in recent years, there is ongoing discussion around the understanding of free and informed consent for marriage and the legitimacy especially of a broader application of the "psychic grounds" criterion enunciated in *CIC* #1095 §3. **See also** *privilege (Pauline and Petrine)*.

Anthropology is the study of the nature of the **human person**, especially in society and **culture**. **See also** *ensoulment* and *imago Dei*.

Antinomianism comes from two Greek words: *anti* (ἀντί), meaning against, and *nomos* (νόμος), meaning law. In **Christian ethics** this term was used against **legalism** and the perceived **works righteousness** position of Roman Catholicism, which stressed following the **Decalogue** and the **natural law** in addition to performing good works. Coined by Martin Luther to stress his position that humans are saved by **God** through faith (i.e., *sola fide* or **justification by faith alone**) and not through following the law, although Luther himself argued against an extreme form of antinomianism in his 1539 tract *Against the Antinomians*. The expression today is also used colloquially to refer to individuals who resist forms of established **authority** or law.

Antisocial personality disorder. See **sociopath**

Apostolic Signatura, with institutional roots going back to the fourteenth century, today is roughly equivalent in the Holy See's legal administrative structure to the US Supreme Court, except that the highest legal authority is the pope, rather than the US Constitution (see *CIC* #1442). The Signatura adjudicates any controversies that might arise among the other offices of the Vatican curia or other tribunals in the Catholic Church and acts as a court of review over decisions or sentences handed down by the **Roman Rota** (see *CIC* #1443–1445). **John Paul II**'s 1988 apostolic constitution *Pastor bonus* set the current structure of the Signatura, and its head (or prefect) is usually a cardinal, or becomes a cardinal at a future consistory convoked by the pope.

Apostolos suos, **John Paul II**'s 1998 apostolic letter on the theological and juridical nature of episcopal conferences, mandated unanimous consent of the members of a bishops' conference, such as the **USCCB**, or a *recognitio* from the Holy See for **pastoral letters** on doctrinal matters issued in the name of a bishops' conference. This requirement has curtailed the practice of bishops' conferences writing pastoral letters, although individual bishops may still issue them *motu proprio* (on his own authority) as an exercise of their **ordinary magisterium**.

Appetite is the desire for something, and **inclination** is the corresponding direction to pursue that desire. If the object of the desire and inclination is good, then the corresponding **free will** guided by **reason** can be a strong motivating force (or passion) to realize goods in our lives, strengthen our moral **character**, and aid us in the pursuit of the **virtues**. However, if the object desired is bad or if the will and reason do not play their proper roles, then the appetite can prove a hindrance to our moral striving. **Thomas Aquinas** divided the sense-based appetites into two powers, the concupiscible (such as instincts leading to either pursuit or avoidance), or the irascible (such as instincts evidenced in competition, aggression, or defense). While the vocabulary connected with "appetite" was widely used in Scholasticism, contemporary language tends to prefer the term "inclination." **See also** *concupiscence* and *habit*.

Aquinas. See **Thomas Aquinas**

***Arcanum Divinae Sapientiae* (*Hidden Design of Divine Wisdom*)**, the 1880 **encyclical** of **Leo XIII** on Christian sacramental **marriage**, decries **divorce** and attempts of the state to regulate marriage civilly—a domain that should reside with the Church alone. There is no mention of **birth control** in this encyclical.

The **Archbishop of Canterbury**, Primate of England, is the symbolic head of the **Anglican Communion** (although King Henry VIII's 1534 *Act of Supremacy* established the monarch rather than the pope as official head of the Church of England). The archbishop is appointed by the British prime minister and sits or chairs most of the church's key committees, such as the decennial **Lambeth Conference**, and plays a central role in ceremonies such as royal weddings and the monarch's coronation. Although the archbishop does not have the same level of authority in the Anglican Communion as the pope has in Roman Catholicism, he is respected as the spiritual leader of Anglicans around the world and is a key figure in **ecumenism** with Roman Catholicism.

Aristotle (Ἀριστοτέλης, Aristotélēs) (384 BCE–322 BCE) was a Greek philosopher whose comprehensive system of thought has most influenced the development of Western philosophy. A student of Plato and a teacher of Alexander the Great, Aristotle's metaphysics and his *Nicomachean Ethics* (Ἠθικὰ Νικομάχεια) were used extensively by **Thomas Aquinas** and countless others to address the questions of what constitute human moral nature, right living, politics and community life, authentic happiness, **virtue**, and so on.

Arregui, Antonio, SJ (1863–1942), taught at the University of Deusto in Bilbao (1904–15; 1918–19). He was succeeded by **Marcelino Zalba, SJ** (1941–62), who later went to the Gregorian in Rome, and together they formed a very influential approach to the **manualist tradition** immediately prior to **Vatican II**. Arregui's well-known moral compendium, *Summarium theologiae moralis. Ad recentem codicem iuris canonici accommodatum. Editio tertia decima iuxta recentissimas declarationes Pontificiae Commissionis ad Codicis canones authentice interpretandos* (Westminister MD: Newman Bookshop, 1944), is an example of the popularity of this sort of **moral manual**. It went through fourteen editions by the time of his death in 1942, and a further ten posthumously (revised by Zalba). **See also** *casuistry*, *canon law*, and *manualist tradition*.

ART (assisted reproductive technology) is the common acronym for a wide variety of **reproductive technologies**, including IVF and AIH.

Artificial contraception. See **birth control, contraception,** *Humanae vitae*, and **Pontifical Commission on Births**

Artificial insemination refers to those **reproductive technologies** in which the sperm is inserted directly into the vagina by artificial means, usually to overcome some issue, such as high acidity in the woman's cervical secretions or low sperm count in the male, that prevents normal conception from occurring or in cases in which the woman has no male partner but wishes to become pregnant. Used extensively for many years in livestock breeding with no moral problem, a number of issues arise when this practice is used in human reproduction. The two main types of human artificial insemination are AIH (with the husband's sperm) and AID (with the sperm of a donor), both of which are condemned by the **magisterium** in the **CDF**'s 1987 *Donum vitae* and its 2008 *Dignitas personae*, since both AIH and AID use **masturbation** to obtain sperm, which violates the **inseparability principle** that prohibits any separation of the **procreative and unitive dimensions** of the marital relations, even if the ultimate aim is conception rather than **contraception**. Since AIH is quite different from more problematic reproductive technologies such as **IVF**, many Christian ethicists accept the moral possibility of AIH while most concede that AID is much more problematic since it introduces a third party into the parenting relationship and involves other difficult issues with **genetics** and **responsible parenthood**.

Asceticism refers to spiritual and corporal practices of mortification, self-denial, **temperance**, or training such as fasting, wearing uncomfortable clothing such as hair shirts, and the like. It can indicate a belief that the body is weak and prone to **sin** and needs to be reined in, punished, and trained so that the individual can see spiritual progress or perfection. Positively, asceticism can be a means of training one's self to be better able to value the things of the world in their proper perspective. Some forms of monastic asceticism could suggest that a truly committed Christian disciple should abandon the world (*fuga mundi*) and deny the more physical aspects of worldly life in his or her *sequela Christi*. These beliefs also strengthen the notion of a spiritual elite superior to everyday Christians who would marry, have children, and make a life in the world.

Assent gives agreement or submission of either the intellect or the will to some perceived desire, choice, or **authority**. The intellect gives assent to an argument or proposition that appears to be convincing in **reason** and cannot be commanded simply by external force or authority. Similarly, the will responds to that which is considered good or desirable. Genuine assent always requires **freedom**, and coercion compromises or even destroys the necessary freedom involved in true consent. In moral theology, assent is tied to a range of other concepts such as **advertence**, *credenda and tenenda*, **conscience**, **dissent**, formal and material distinction in **causality**, **intention**, and *obsequium religiosum*. **See also** *actus hominis and actus humanus* and *fonts of morality*.

Assisted suicide. See **suicide and assisted suicide**

Athematic choice. See **fundamental option theory**

Attrition. See **contrition (perfect and imperfect)**

Augustine of Hippo (November 13, 354–August 28, 430) was a convert to Christianity, then a bishop and an important early theologian. His writings on **just war**, **marriage**, and **sexual ethics** have strongly influenced moral theology ever since, both positively and negatively. His spiritual autobiography *Confessions* recounts his own struggles with **chastity** in his youthful prayer to God: "Grant me chastity and continence, only not yet." This undoubtedly affected his views on sexual desire, which he termed **concupiscence** and the transmission mode for **original sin**. *For further reading*, see John Mahoney, "The Legacy of Augustine," ch. 2 in *The Making of Moral Theology: A Study of the Roman Catholic Tradition* (Oxford University Press, 1987), 37–71.

Authority is crucial to the stability or order of any institution, the Church included. In moral theology, "authority" can refer to an external body such as the secular government or the Church's **magisterium**, or to an internal voice like **conscience** or **reason**, or a corpus that exerts some special claim such as scripture and **Tradition**. Depending on the type of authority involved, the moral **discernment** over the proper response will differ. For example, if the government has posted a speed limit on a highway of 55 mph, normally we would respect that, although in the case of a medical emergency we might invoke *epikeia* to justify driving a heart attack victim to the hospital at a higher speed. The magisterium's three *munera* (singular *munus*) of teaching, governing, and sanctifying—each has its proper authority and appropriate mode of exercising that authority. For example, the authority of teaching (*munus docendi*) functions best when that which is being proposed for acceptance is done with arguments that internally convince those being taught of the teaching's correctness and importance.

Some divide authority into two basic types, absolute and dialogic. Absolute authority is coercive, either through a logical reasoning process, such as $2+2 = 4$, or though physical or mental force, such as holding a gun to a victim's head in a robbery. In both cases, while one could resist or refuse the authority claim, to do so would seriously compromise one's physical or mental well-being. In Western philosophy, the principle of noncontradiction is an example of absolute authority, for example, something cannot be both "A" and "Not-A" in the same way, same time, and same place. While some claim that the only valid response of a proper *obsequium religiosum* to any and every magisterial teaching is to accept it in this absolute character, this absolutist view is neither enunciated in the **moral manuals** nor by the magisterium itself. Dialogic authority, on the other hand, invites either implicitly or explicitly a consideration of the truth claims being made in order that these may be verified, accepted, and put into appropriate action. Most teaching aimed at genuine learning would involve the exercise of dialogic authority since the goal is for those being taught to see for themselves the intrinsic truth or worth of what is being proposed. Force that coerces acceptance of authority often hinders full acceptance, as Milton observed in *Paradise Lost*, "who overcomes by force hath overcome but half his foe." *For further reading*, see Joseph A. Selling, "Authority and Moral Teaching in a Catholic Christian Context," in *Christian Ethics: An Introduction*, edited by Bernard Hoose (Collegeville, MN: Liturgical Press, 1998): 57–71; Francis A. Sullivan, "The Authority of the Magisterium on Questions of Natural Moral Law," in *Readings in Moral Theology, No. 6: Dissent in the Church*, edited by Charles E. Curran and Richard A. McCormick (New York: Paulist Press, 1988), 42–57.

Autonomy (bioethical principle) is distinguished from the concept of **moral autonomy**. In **bioethics**, autonomy refers to the right of the individual to make health care decisions for himself, and to designate a proxy (e.g., through an **AHCD**) to make these same decisions if he should become incapacitated or otherwise would desire to hand this decision-making power over to another. This notion of autonomy is one of the four foundational principles along with **beneficence**, **nonmaleficence**, and **justice** in the bioethical theory termed **principlism**. **See also** *death with dignity, euthanasia,* **Evangelium vitae,** *ordinary and extraordinary means,* and *vitalism.*

Autonomy (moral), from the Greek words *nomos* (νομος, law) and *auto* (αυτο, self), means that the individual first **discerns** and then applies the law to herself or himself. It does not mean that the individual somehow "invents" the individual moral law. **Primacy** and **sanctuary of conscience** are key to autonomy since obedience to this moral voice is the locus of all moral **goodness** and badness for the **human person**. The *Catechism of the Catholic Church* expresses the authentic notion of moral autonomy in this command: "A human being must always obey the certain judgment of his conscience. If he were deliberately to act against it, he would condemn himself" (*CCC* #1790). Thus, no one should be forced to act contrary to her or his conscience, presuming, of course, the prior obligation both to form and inform one's conscience. Here Church teaching and **authority**, as well as the other **fonts of moral theology**, such as scripture and reflection on **Tradition** are important aids. Nevertheless, even in the case of a malformed or poorly informed **erroneous conscience**, the individual is obliged to follow that conscience. The opposite of moral autonomy is **heteronomy**, and if the properly formed and informed conscience is not the ultimate moral authority to be obeyed, then whatever is posited as that ultimate moral authority would of necessity be outside of the person. The Catholic moral tradition since **Thomas Aquinas** has held to the notion of moral autonomy over heteronomy or **Voluntarism**. Since **Vatican II**, a debate has arisen regarding the proper understanding of moral autonomy, especially in reference to **scripture and ethics** and the role of the **magisterium** as a moral teacher. These competing schools are often referred to as the **Moral Autonomy school and Faith Ethics school** (or *Glaubensethik* school). Certainly, in cultures that place especially high values on individualism and personal freedom, the notion of autonomy can be abused to sanction whatever an individual desires.

Avarice. See **capital sins**

B

Bad faith. See **good faith and bad faith**

Balasuriya, Tissa, OMI. See **liberation theology**

Barth, Karl (May 10, 1886–December 10, 1968), remains one of the most important Protestant theologians of the twentieth century. Barth never took a doctorate but taught in Germany until he was forced to return to his native Switzerland after joining his disciple **Dietrich Bonhoeffer** in the Barmen Declaration of the Confessing Church, which opposed Hitler. Extreme disillusionment with World War I and the liberal Protestantism of theologians such as Harnack and Schliermacher led to his groundbreaking 1918 *Epistle to the Romans*, arguing that **God's divine sovereignty** as revealed in Jesus's cross always stands in tension with **culture** and human accomplishments. His multivolume *Church Dogmatics* (1925–55) outlined his major theses on God, **creation**, revelation, and reconciliation. For Barth, there is no real distinction between **law and gospel**, since the former is completely enclosed in the Christological ethics of the latter, whose **divine commands** can only be truly "heard" in unconditional obedience to the Lordship of Jesus Christ. The Bible shows God's basic commands and proper attitudes to inform our obedience, but Barth's **biblical ethics**, which did not hold a strict *sola scriptura* understanding of biblical inerrancy, led to strong critiques from some fundamentalists. On the other hand, Barth's ethic is also criticized as being simply a **theonomy**, in which one's entire moral personhood depends solely on those moments when one is being addressed and responding to the word of God, and there is no ongoing moral **character** or **autonomy** outside of the moments when God is commanding. Barth's ethic pays scant attention to non-Christians or to the **gradualism** that marks most individuals' moral development. *For further reading*, in addition to Barth's own works, see George Hunsinger, *How to Read Karl Barth: The Shape of His Theology* (Oxford University Press, 1993).

Basic Goods theory (or New Natural Law theory) is associated primarily with the moral philosophers Germain Grisez and John Finnis and colleagues. The theory posits eight "basic goods" that, when taken together, "tell us what **human persons** are capable of being, not only as individuals but in community" (Germain Grisez and Russell Shaw, *Fulfillment in Christ: A Summary of Christian Moral Principles* [Notre Dame, IN: University of Notre Dame Press, 1991], 56). Four goods are "reflexive": self-integration, practical reasonableness or authenticity, friendship, and **justice**; three are "substantive": life and bodily well-being, knowledge of truth and appreciation of beauty, and skillful performance and play; the eighth and last basic good is **marriage and family**, which is termed "complex" in that it has both substantive and reflexive aspects. One may never morally act against any of these basic goods; thus, in this view a practice of artificial **birth control** is morally wrong because it is seen as attacking the last basic good of marriage and family. Furthermore, the theory asserts that these basic goods are incommensurable, which means they cannot be weighed against one another as is usually done with resolving a **conflict of duties** using a **hierarchy of values** to help **discern** which is the highest duty or value in this or that particular moral decision. The Basic Good theory is highly critical of **proportionalism**, which it claims attacks the basic goods by employing either **consequentialism** or **utilitarianism**, although others counter that the basic goods theory misconstrues the moral tradition on several fronts including the distinction between **direct and indirect**, the relationship between **moral object** (*finis operis*) and **intention** (*finis operantis*), and the settled **casuistry** around principles of **compromise with evil**, the *minus malum* (**lesser evil**), and the **double effect**. *For further reading*, see Todd Salzman, *What Are They Saying about Catholic Ethical Method?* (Mahwah, NJ: Paulist Press, 2003); John Finnis, *Natural Law and Natural Rights* (Oxford: Clarendon Press, 1980); and Russell Hittinger, *A Critique of the New Natural Law Theory* (Notre Dame, IN: University of Notre Dame Press, 1987).

Beatific vision is the immediate knowledge of and complete union with **God**, which is the state of perfect happiness enjoyed by the angels and the souls in heaven. This also awaits all those who die in a **state of grace** and thus is the *Summum Bonum* for humans that properly orients their moral lives (see *CCC* #1028, 1720).

Benedict XVI—Pope (2005–13), was born **Joseph Aloisius Ratzinger** on April 16, 1927, in Bavaria, Germany. He succeeded **John Paul II** (1978–2005) on April 19, 2005, as the 265th successor of Peter and Bishop of Rome and became the first pope in six hundred years to resign the pontificate, succeeded on March 13, 2013, by the first Jesuit pope, Jorge Bergoglio, who took the name of **Francis**. Benedict's **social encyclicals** *Deus caritas est* (*God Is Love*, 2005), *Spe salvi* (*Hope That Saves*, 2007) and *Caritas in veritate* (*Charity in Truth*, 2009) relate the **theological virtues** of faith, hope, and **charity** to the challenges posed by the concrete world and especially the contemporary global economic order. Pope Benedict has also repeatedly confronted the realities of **secularism** and atheism and has challenged accommodations of a contemporary ethos that he finds overly simplistic and incompatible with the Christian faith. While sharply critical of the **ABC** policy of promoting condom usage for **safe sex** in response to the **AIDS** pandemic in Africa, Benedict excited considerable interest in a book-length interview by seeming to invoke the **lesser evil** principle of the *minus malum* in stating that there "may be a basis in the case of some individuals, as perhaps when a male prostitute uses a condom, where this can be a first step in the direction of moralization, a first assumption of responsibility, on the way toward recovering an awareness that not everything is allowed and that one cannot do whatever one wants. . . . [The Church] does not regard it as a real or moral solution, but, in this or that case, there can be nonetheless, in the intention of reducing the risk of infection, a first step in a movement toward a different way, a more human way, of living sexuality." *Light of the World: The Pope, the Church, and the Signs of the Times—A Conversation with Peter Seewald* (San Francisco: Ignatius Press, 2010), 118–19.

Beneficence is the bioethical tenet of **principlism** to seek to do the patient good and not harm.

Bergmeier case. See **situation ethics**

Biblical ethics is differentiated from **scripture and ethics** in that the latter addresses methodological questions regarding the **exegesis** and use of biblical material for **Christian ethics**, whereas the former seeks to fashion the entire approach to ethics in accord with the patterns and themes found in the Bible, especially the New Testament. While a few Catholic moral theologians such as **Bernard Häring**, CSsR, and Gérard Gilleman, SJ, in the 1950s used biblical themes such as law or **charity** as organizing metaphors, their manuals could not be called a "biblical ethics" in the same sense that characterizes the approach of many Protestant theologians. *For further reading*, see William C. Spohn, *Go and Do Likewise: Jesus and Ethics* (New York: Continuum, 1999); and Thomas Ogletree, *The Use of the Bible in Christian Ethics: A Constructive Essay* (Philadelphia: Fortress Press, 1983; Oxford: Basil Blackwell, 1984).

Biblical interpretation. See **biblical ethics**, **exegesis**, **hermeneutics**, and **proof-texting**

Billings Method. See **natural family planning**

Bioethics (a 1927 neologism coined from the Greek βίος bios, "life," + έθος ethos, "moral behavior, custom") is the fast-growing field in which rapidly developing scientific technology intersects with long-standing **moral principles** connected to myriad issues of health care resources, therapies, drugs, treatment decisions from conception to death, research, experimentation, and so on. It is the subdiscipline of ethics that perhaps most involves the **history and development of moral theology and doctrine**. For example, the **totality principle** has now been revised to allow and commend **organ donation**, which in the past had been strictly forbidden. Vaccines—for example, against smallpox developed by Edward Jenner in 1796 and condemned by Leo XII in1829 as violating **divine sovereignty**—are now routinely accepted by most faith traditions. **Biblical ethics** and the "constancy of **Tradition**" do not completely address complex concrete issues such as those raised by the isolation of stem cells for research (which only dates from November 1998), **reproductive technologies**, genetics, cloning, and so on. New scientific knowledge requires reconsideration of some basic **moral principles**—for example, how to interpret in cases of **emergency contraception** the oft-repeated dictum "life is sacred from the moment of conception" (see *CCC* #2270) in light of the fact that "conception" cannot occur in a "moment" but only when the union of sperm and egg is completed two hours or more after coitus. While moral principles and values remain crucial in bioethical reflection, it will continue to be highly problematic to establish with detailed precision exact applications in each of these areas. *For further reading*, see Tom L. Beauchamp and James F. Childress, *Principles of Biomedical Ethics* (New York: Oxford University Press, 1979, 1983, 1989, 1994); Thomas A. Shannon and Nicholas J. Kockler, *An Introduction to Bioethics*, 4th ed. (Mahwah, NJ: Paulist Press, 2009); James B. Tubbs Jr., *A Handbook of Bioethics Terms* (Washington, DC: Georgetown University Press, 2009).

Birth control is often equated with **contraception**, though more accurately the term focuses not just on avoiding births but also on family planning in accord with **responsible parenthood**, which could use both natural and certain artificial means of **reproductive technologies** and **NFP** to increase the likelihood of conception as well. Although in the traditional theology of **marriage** any attempt to limit or increase family size would be suspected of trying to "play God" and an affront against **divine sovereignty**, this view largely disappeared by **Pius XI**'s **encyclical** *Casti connubii*, and certainly would not be in harmony with **Vatican II**'s treatment in *Gaudium et spes* (see *GS* #51–52), the deliberations of **John XXIII's Pontifical Commission on Births**, **Paul VI**'s 1968 encyclical *Humanae vitae*, or the teachings of their successors. The bibliography on this issue is enormous, but to situate the historical context of the *status quaestionis* at the time *Humanae vitae* was drafted, *for further reading*, see Robert Blair Kaiser, *The Encyclical That Never Was: The Story of the Pontifical Commission on Population, Family and Birth, 1964–1966* (London: Sheed & Ward, 1985, 1987), also published as *The Politics of Sex and Religion*; John T. Noonan Jr., *Contraception: A History of Its Treatment by the Catholic Theologians and Canonists* (Cambridge, MA: Harvard University Press, 1965, 1986); Ambrogio Valsecchi, *Controversy: The Birth Control Debate 1958–1968* (Washington, DC: Corpus Books, 1968); and Leslie Woodcock Tentler, *Catholics and Contraception: An American History* (Ithaca, NY: Cornell University Press, 2004). **See also** *sterilization*.

Body. See **sexuality, gender, sexual orientation, and sexual ethics**

Boff, Leonardo, OP. See **liberation theology**

Bond (marital). See **annulment and dissolution, marriage**, and **privilege (Pauline and Petrine)**

Bonhoeffer, Dietrich (1906–45), was a German Lutheran pastor associated with the Confessing Church, which opposed the state-affiliated Evangelische Kirche (Lutheran Church), which supported the Nazi regime. Along with **Karl Barth** (1886–1968), who influenced his thought deeply, Bonhoeffer is one of the most influential Protestant Christian ethicians of the twentieth century who has also deeply impacted Roman Catholic moral theology, especially in how Christianity should interact with the secular world. Bonhoeffer's major works are his 1937 *Nachfolge*, published in English in 1948 as *The Cost of Discipleship*, and a posthumous work, *Ethics*, compiled and edited by his former student, in-law, and long-time friend Eberhard Bethge from various writings composed and smuggled out while Bonhoeffer was in prison awaiting his execution for his part in the failed plot to assassinate Adolf Hitler. Christological ethics marks Bonhoeffer's major works, especially his call to a radical discipleship obedience in faith to Jesus Christ because He alone is Lord and has purchased our salvation through the "costly grace" of His passion and death; it is this costly grace for which Christians themselves should always strive. The great enemy of the Church is "cheap grace" that would include **works righteousness**, which Bonhoeffer also describes as "the grace which amounts to the justification of **sin** without the justification of the repentant sinner who departs from sin and from whom sin departs. Cheap grace is not the kind of **forgiveness** of sin which frees us from the toils of sin. Cheap grace is the grace we bestow on ourselves" (*Cost of Discipleship*, 45). **See also** *biblical ethics, Constantianism, Proprium, sola scriptura*, and WWJD? *For further reading*, in addition to Bonhoeffer's collected works, see Eberhard Bethge, *Dietrich Bonhoeffer: Theologian, Christian, Man for His Times: A Biography*, rev. ed. (Minneapolis: Fortress Press, 2000).

Bonum (plural *bona*) is the Latin noun for that which is good; it involves a great number of distinctions and subterms that we cannot treat here. **Thomas Aquinas** lists the doing of the good as the foundational principle of the **natural law**. **God** is the fullness or perfection of all goodness, and thus union with God in the **beatific vision** serves for humans as the *Summum Bonum*, and proper **teleology** or end of our nature. Other goods can be instrumental or useful (*bonum utile*) in helping us reach our proper end. That which impedes a legitimate proper end or "good" of a human or a human faculty, such as **procreation**, is termed *contra naturam* and is for this reason **disordered** or sinful. *For further reading*, see the various entries under "*Bonum*" in James T. Bretzke, *Consecrated Phrases: A Latin Dictionary of Theological Terms* (Collegeville, MN: Liturgical Press, 1998, 2003, 2013).

Bonum est faciendum et prosequendum, et malum vitandum ("The good [*bonum*] is to be done and fostered, and evil avoided") is the first or foundational principle or moral **absolute** (i.e., universal moral **precept**) of the **natural law** knowable through **right reason** according to **Thomas Aquinas** (*ST I-II*, Q. 94, art. 2). **See also** *universal moral norm, lesser evil.*

Bonum ex integra causa, malum ex quocumque defectu ("The [moral] **goodness** [*bonum*] of an act comes from its causal integrity [of act plus intention]; **moral evil** comes from any defect [in either act or intention]") is an axiom that underscores the essential importance of the moral **intention** (*finis operantis*) along with the act in itself (*finis operis*) in evaluating ethically a truly human moral act (*actus humanus*). The full aphorism, though, is: *Verum et falsum sunt in mente, bonum et malum sunt in rebus; bonum ex integra causa, malum ex quocumque defectu* (Truth and error exist in the mind, good and evil in things; good demands fullness of being, evil is predicated of any defect). *CCC* #1755 uses this same principle in its definition of a moral act: "A morally good act requires the goodness of the object, of the end, and of the circumstances together. An evil end corrupts the action, even if the object is good in itself (such as praying and fasting 'in order to be seen by men')." The contemporary discussion on the **goodness and rightness distinction**, especially in the thought of **Thomas Aquinas** (see *ST I-II*, Q. 18 and 19), builds on this aphorism and highlights the traditional notion of what happens when one does the "right" thing but for the wrong reasons, such as in the example of giving alms in order to satisfy personal vainglory. This concept is also important in **compromise with evil**, the **double effect** and **lesser evil** (*minus malum*) principles as well as the concept of **intrinsic evil**.

Bonum fidei (good of fidelity). See **marriage**

Bonum prolix (procreative good). See **marriage**

Bonum sacramenti (good of the sacrament). See **marriage**

Brain death. See **states of consciousness: brain death, coma, PVS, MCS, and locked-in syndrome**

Brave sinning. See *pecca fortiter*, *sola fide*, and **works righteousness**

Burden (as criterion in making medical care decisions). See **ordinary and extraordinary means**

C

Cahill, Lisa Sowle (b. 1948), has taught at Boston College since completing her doctorate under **James Gustafson** at the University of Chicago in 1976. A past president of both the CTSA and SCE, she is one of the principal Catholic **feminist** theologians with widely respected work in the areas of **bioethics**, **ecumenical ethics**, **scripture and ethics**, **sexuality**, **gender**, war, **just war**, and **pacifism**. Cahill engages both **Tradition** and the **magisterium**, highlighting both the **history and development of moral theology** and the inconsistencies and "double messages" in these teachings. *For further reading*, see her principal works: *Between the Sexes: Foundations for a Christian Ethics of Sexuality* (Minneapolis: Fortress Press, 1985); *Sex, Gender and Christian Ethics* (New York: Cambridge University Press, 1996); *Family: A Christian Social Perspective* (Minneapolis: Fortress Press, 2000); *Love Your Enemies: Discipleship, Pacifism, and Just War Theory* (Minneapolis: Fortress Press, 1994); *Theological Bioethics: Participation, Justice, and Change* (Washington, DC: Georgetown University Press, 2005); *Genetics, Theology, Ethics: An Interdisciplinary Conversation* (New York: Crossroad, 2005); and *Global Justice, Christology, and Christian Ethics* (New York: Cambridge University Press, 2013).

Calumny and **defamation**, along with **detraction** and **slander**, offend not only against truth but also against **justice** and **charity** by harming the reputation and **human dignity** of an individual (see *CCC* #2477–79). Such offenses can be minor, such as in idle **gossip**, but also can be quite serious with long-lasting effects that are difficult to amend. Calumny, from the Latin *calumnia*, meaning subterfuge or misrepresentation, is a form of **lying** that violates the Eighth Commandment of the **Decalogue** by speech or actions contrary to the truth that may lead others to make false judgments about the person. It is also a **sin** against charity and is closely related to detraction, **rash judgment**, and slander. Detraction involves disclosure of another's faults or failings to another without a valid reason. Defamation and slander can involve both calumny and detraction, whose sinful aim is to destroy another person's reputation.

Often such actions spring from deeper-seated emotions of **envy**, **anger**, or malice and thus are related to the **capital sins**. Those guilty of these actions have an obligation in justice to make **reparation and restitution** as far as possible to restore the reputation of the injured party. **See also** *delectatio morosa*.

Canon law refers both to the body of ecclesiastical and **divine law** that governs the Church and to the discipline of its interpretation that developed over the centuries. The unification project into one code was begun by **Pius X** and completed in 1917 by Benedict XV. **John XXIII** ordered a revision of this code when he called **Vatican II**, and the work was finally completed by **John Paul II** in 1983. *For further reading*, see John Huels, *The Pastoral Companion: A Canon Law Handbook for Catholic Ministry*, 4th ed. (Montreal: Wilson & LaFleur, 2009); and Ladislas Orsy, *Receiving the Council: Theological and Canonical Insights and Debates* (Collegeville, MN: Liturgical Press, 2009). **See also** *annulment*; *canonical penalties*; *Communion (admission to)*; *confidentiality and secrecy*; *crimes and delicts*; *forum, internal and external*; *impediment and irregularity*; *lex dubia non obligat*; *obsequium religiosum*; *odia restringi*; *precept and precepts of the Church*; *privilege (Pauline and Petrine)*; *sexual abuse*; and *suicide and assisted suicide*.

Canonical penalties covered in the 1983 *CIC* in Book VI, "Sanctions in the Church," and Book VII, "Processes," are rather complex, but the section on censures can be summarized as follows. Certain **crimes** and **delicts** carry a penalty of excommunication, interdict, or suspension. Excommunications are either *latae sententiae* or *ferendae sententiae*. A *latae sententiae* is imposed on one who knowingly and willfully commits a particular offense, such as procuring an **abortion** (*CIC* #1398), heresy (*CIC* #1364), or breaking the **seal of confession** (*CIC* #1388). A *ferendae sententiae* must be formally declared by the competent ecclesiastical superior (such as the ordinary or bishop of a diocese) after a canonical warning to cease and desist from the action that is the object of the penalty has been ignored. An interdict is similar to an excommunication, though less severe, and it is inflicted for less serious offenses. For example, the penalty for an attack on the pope is excommunication (*CIC* #1370), whereas an attack on a bishop is punished by an interdict. Interdicts can also be applied to larger groups of individuals such as parishes or even nations, and prohibits the licit celebration of the sacraments for those covered by the interdict. Suspensions are applied only to clerics and can remove the exercise of priestly functions (*a divinas*), of governance and rights or functions of office. These suspensions can only be lifted by the competent ecclesiastical superior and thus cannot be removed in the **sacrament of reconciliation**. *Latae sententiae* is often misleadingly translated as "automatic penalty" but in fact, **canon law** lists a number of situations that either mitigate or even block the imposition of penalties. Some of these conditions are objective (e.g., "insufficient age" or being unaware of the penalty itself), whereas others are subjective (e.g., "imperfect use of reason, force or fear, even if only relative"; see *CIC* #1323 and 1324). As it is difficult to interpret these subjective factors, too often these are laid aside or given insufficient weight. In the application of any penalty, the canonical principle of a strict or narrow interpretation (*odia restringi*, see *CIC* #18) must be observed. **See also** *Communion (admission to)*. **For further reading**, see John Huels, *The Pastoral Companion: A Canon Law Handbook for Catholic Ministry*, 4th ed. (Montreal: Wilson & LaFleur, 2009).

Capacity. See **conscience (faculty of)**, **culpability**, **faculty**, **free will and freedom**, **impediment**, **physicalism and personalism**

Capital punishment is a Catholic moral teaching that has undergone considerable development recently. The *lex talionis* called for capital punishment for capital offenses. In scripture the **Mosaic Law** lists thirty-six capital offenses, and no explicit New Testament passage counters the state's right to execute criminals for serious offenses. Using the principle of **totality** (*ST II-II*, Q. 64, art. 2), **Thomas Aquinas** concluded an individual (as a "part") could be "excised" for the good of the community (the "whole"), and even heresy could be punishable by death (see *ST II-II* Q. 11, art. 3). The death penalty was imposed in the Papal States, and the Vatican City State, from its inception in 1929 until 1969, prescribed the death penalty for anyone who might attempt to assassinate the pope. **John Paul II**, though, substantially modified this teaching both by example in his own public **forgiveness** of his attempted assassin, and explicitly in his 1995 **encyclical** *Evangelium vitae* and subsequent revision of the *Catechism of the Catholic Church*, which states: "The traditional teaching of the Church does not exclude, presupposing full ascertainment of the identity and responsibility of the offender, recourse to the death penalty, when this is the only practicable way to defend the lives of human beings effectively against the aggressor. If, instead, bloodless means are sufficient to defend against the aggressor and to protect the safety of persons, public authority should limit itself to such means, because they better correspond to the concrete conditions of the **common good** and are more in conformity to the dignity of the **human person**. Today, in fact, given the means at the state's disposal to effectively repress crime by rendering inoffensive the one who has committed it, without depriving him definitively of the possibility of redeeming himself, cases of absolute necessity for suppression of the offender today . . . are very rare, if not practically non-existent." (*Evangelium vitae* #56) *CCC* #2267.

Nevertheless, some still maintain that the use of the death penalty is not only allowed but should be exercised by the state as a positive form of **retributive justice**. **Cardinal Avery Dulles, SJ,** said the **magisterium's** teaching against the death penalty is a **prudential judgment** but does not deny the principle that the state still has the right to impose the penalty. Catholics should be attentive to the guidance of the pope and the bishops, but are not bound in conscience to agree with it. Imprisonment without the possibility of parole, which effectively removes the possibility that a criminal can reoffend, coupled with the fact that the death penalty is used disproportionately against the poor and minorities, and with evidence that a number of innocent people have been falsely given the death sentence for crimes they did not commit, all give further prudential arguments against the use of the death penalty. *For further reading*, see Cardinal Avery Dulles, "Catholic Teaching on the Death Penalty: Has It Changed?" ch. 1 in *Religion and the Death Penalty: A Call for Reckoning*, edited by Erik C. Owens, John D. Carlson, and Eric P. Elshtain, 23–30 (Grand Rapids, MI: Eerdmans, 2004).

Capital sins, also called capital **vices** or seven deadly sins, are considered to be the "head" (*caput* in Latin) and especially injurious or deadly to the life of **virtue** as presented in the Bible. SALIGIA is an acronym derived from the first letters in Latin to enumerate the seven sins: *superbia* (pride or vainglory), *avaritia* (greed, avarice, or covetousness), *luxuria* (lust), *invidia* (envy), *gula* (gluttony), *ira* (**anger**), and *acedia* (sloth). These were given special emphasis in the preaching of the Church fathers and in medieval Christian art, though never systematically treated in great length by the **moral manual**s, or by **Thomas Aquinas**, who focused his structural presentation of the moral life around the virtues instead of sins.

Capitalism, often tied with Western democratic governments, is a contemporary economic system that places a high value on private property, especially in the ownership of the means of production. Capitalism stresses the **creation** of wealth through exchange of goods and services for profit organized in competitive free-market systems and is contrasted with **communism** and **socialism**. Along with these other economic and political systems, its extremes and abuses have been consistently critiqued by the **magisterium** in its **social encyclicals and social teaching** and in its emphasis on the **common good** along with more recent theological analysis such as **liberation theology.**

Cardinal virtues, initially derived from Plato's *Protagoras* and *Republic*, are listed in the Western **virtue ethics** tradition as **justice**, **temperance** (or moderation), fortitude (or courage), and **prudence**, the principal acquired virtues on which the structure of the moral life interrelates and "hangs" (*cardinalis*, Latin for "hinging"). As virtues, these can be contrasted with the opposing **vices** that lead to the **capital sins**. Prudence directs the proper actions of all the virtues.

Caritas in veritate (*Charity in Truth*) is the 2009 **social encyclical** of **Benedict XVI**.

Casti connubii (*Chaste Wedlock*) is the 1930 **encyclical** of **Pius XI** written as a negative response to the 1930 Anglican **Lambeth Conference** Resolution 15, which had given guarded approval to **artificial contraception** in certain **circumstances**. **Arthur Vermeersch, SJ**, assisted by **Francis Hürth, SJ**, reputedly did most of the drafting of the encyclical, which condemned as a "**grave sin**" any form of artificial **birth control**, likening such practices to **onanism**, stating "the Divine Majesty regards with greatest detestation this horrible crime and at times has punished it with death" (*CC* #55–56). The encyclical also stressed adherence to the divinely ordained natural order, which "includes both the primacy of the husband with regard to the wife and children, the ready subjection of the wife and her willing obedience, which the Apostle commends in these words: 'Let women be subject to their husbands as to the Lord, because the husband is the head of the wife, and Christ is the head of the Church' (Eph. 5:22–23)" (*CC* #26), and condemned as serious error any position that claims "such a subjection of one party to the other is unworthy of **human dignity**, that the rights of husband and wife are equal; wherefore, they boldly proclaim the emancipation of women has been or ought to be effected" (*CC* #74). **NFP** seemed to be given tacit approval in the encyclical, although **Pius XII**'s 1951 **Address to the Italian Midwives** gave explicit permission for "serious motives." *Casti connubii* was the most authoritative document of the papal **magisterium** on the subject of birth control and **marriage** prior to **Vatican II** and played an important role in both the discussions of the **Pontifical Commission on Births** (1959–65) as well as influencing **Paul VI**'s 1968 *Humanae vitae*, which repeated the condemnation of artificial birth control but which omitted vocabulary of "grave sin" or "onanism," nor did *HV* call for the subjugation of wives to their husbands.

Castrati **and castration** (e.g., for the Sistine Choir). See **sterilization**

Casuistry is the practice of moral analysis traditionally based on the *casus conscientiae* ("case of conscience"), which comprised a significant part of the **manualist tradition** up to the first part of the twentieth century. Both casuistry and the **moral manuals** aimed to guide seminarians and priests for their pastoral work in the confessional tribunal of the **sacrament of reconciliation** (called **penance**) before **Vatican II**. The method of casuistry begins with outlining a hypothetical moral case as it might come up in the confessional or a counseling session. Next, the morally relevant features are distinguished from the information that would be less important in determining the moral species of the case. A popular twosome used by many manualists were "Titius" and "Bertha," who come to confession and list any number of venial sins before raising an issue more perplexing that would furnish the pedagogical point of the particular case. From the confessional narrative the casuist then identifies the morally relevant features of the case to uncover. Working from a realistic narrative of how a situation might actually surface employs the **inductive approach** to arrive at a proper application of the various **moral principles**. While casuistry and the case method approach have been used for millennia, and while many of Jesus's own teaching parables, as well as the contemporary **WWJD?** ("What would Jesus do?") questions posed in **biblical ethics** could all be termed casuistry, over the course of the sixteen and seventeenth centuries casuistry became increasingly divorced from real-life situations and associated, justly or not, with a legalistic hairsplitting mental gymnastics caricatured by Blaise Pascal in his 1656 *Provincial Letters* critique of Jesuits, such that "Jesuitical" and "casuistical" became pejorative synonyms associated with the same condemnations Jesus made of the sophistry of the Pharisees. While the older manualist tradition of casuistry no longer appears in contemporary moral textbooks, a number of contemporary ethicians have come to rediscover a legitimate role for case analysis not only in the traditional areas of **canon law**, confession, social and **sexual ethics**, but also especially in **bioethics**. *For further reading*, see James T. Bretzke, "Navigating in a Morally Complex World: Casuistry with a Human Face," ch. 6 in *A Morally Complex World: Engaging Contemporary Moral Theology* (Collegeville, MN: Liturgical Press, 2004); John Dedek, *Titius and Bertha Ride Again: Contemporary Moral Cases* (New York: Sheed and Ward, 1974); Albert R. Jonsen and Stephen Toulmin, *The Abuse of Casuistry: A History of Moral Reasoning* (Berkeley: University of California Press, 1988); and James F. Keenan and Thomas A. Shannon, eds., *The Context of Casuistry* (Washington, DC: Georgetown University Press, 1995).

The *Catechism of the Catholic Church* was drafted by a special papal international commission in response to the request coming from the 1985 Extraordinary **Synod of Bishops** and promulgated by **John Paul II** in his

Apostolic Constitution *Fidei depositum*, "The Deposit of Faith," in October 1992. The stated primary purpose of the *Catechism* is to provide an aid for bishops and bishops' conferences (which are the *Catechism*'s designated primary intended audience) in the preparation of catechetical materials better adapted to the needs of their individual dioceses. The 1997 Latin official *Editio typica* corrected some inaccuracies and clarified other entries but also changed some of the previous teaching, for example, on **capital punishment** (compare the old and new versions of *CCC* #2267). Since the *Catechism* is promulgated by the Holy See, it is a document of the **magisterium**, but it is not explicitly a papal document, nor is it a collegial document of all the bishops of the Church in the sense of a conciliar document. Often brief excerpts from other Church documents are used to make its points, and assessing the extrinsic authority of each of its component parts therefore requires a careful **exegesis** and **hermeneutics**, using *Lumen gentium* #25's triple criteria of **character, manner, and frequency**. Special attention must be given to the footnotes referenced in many of the paragraphs, as each of these will have its own extrinsic authority giving the fuller text and context of the passage the *Catechism* is referencing. For example, Matthew's Gospel in reference to a certain point would have greater weight than the **CDF**'s 1975 *Persona humana*, and a papal **occasional allocution** would rank below an **encyclical**, a conciliar definition given as *de fide definita*, and so on. The *Catechism* is not meant to be the universal, exhaustive, and ultimate highest authority of Church teaching for each and every person, place, or situation. It certainly would be an error to accord the *Catechism* as a whole an authority higher than any other document of the magisterium such as conciliar decrees or papal encyclicals. The *Compendium of the Catechism of the Catholic Church* was published in 2005, and many vernacular translations of this as well as the *Catechism* itself are available on the Vatican website, www.vatican.va.

Categorial freedom and acts refers to acts that can be "thematized" or categorized as morally right or wrong in **fundamental option theory**. These acts by themselves, though, do not necessarily involve an individual's total stance toward (or away from) God as the absolute value of one's life.

Categorical imperative. See **Kant, Immanuel**

Causality in moral theology builds on **Aristotle**'s *Metaphysics* as employed by **Thomas Aquinas** and differs considerably from the physical sciences' treatment of cause and effect. Aristotle and Thomas spoke of four types of causes that are closely interrelated: material, formal, final, and efficient. For example, the material cause of a chair would be that out of which the piece of furniture is made (e.g., wood, wicker). The formal cause would be that which gives the chair its "intelligibility" seen by its particular shape or form (e.g., straight-back, recliner, rocker). The final cause is not chronologically "last" in the construction sequence but rather its overall aims or purposes that led to the chair's construction in the first place (e.g., to provide sedentary rest, as a means for gaining income through manufacture and sale, as a thing of beauty pleasing to the eye). Efficient cause is the skill and activity brought to the material and guided by the formal and final causes (e.g., the furniture-making skill of the artisan combined with his or her own physical ability and efforts to complete the chair-making project). While all of these four modes of causality figure prominently in Christian philosophy and systematic theology, in moral theology the distinctions of formal, material, and final are of paramount importance. Formal cause is what gives the form to the material aspect. Just as a cup of water is "formed" into a cylinder, square, rectangle, depending on the "form" of its container, so the shape of our moral actions (*finis operis*) depends most on the relation to the final cause (*finis operantis*) for its true moral meaning. Taking a candy bar that is not one's property may be materially sinful, but unless this action is both formed and guided by an evil **intention**, the "material sin" would not rise to the level of "formal sin." While the action is morally wrong, it is possible that the individual has not actually sinned (e.g., in the case of a young child who still has not mastered impulse control or acquired the notion of **private property**). Similarly, in situations in which evil is caused or permitted (e.g., **compromise with evil**, **lesser evil**, *minus malum*, **double effect**) we cannot come to a sure judgment about the moral significance of what has transpired by merely looking at the material or efficient cause aspects. In other words, from a moral perspective, the answer to the ethical question "what happened?" can only be answered by looking not just at the "what" but also the "why" and the "who" (i.e., the **intention** and **circumstances**) that helped form the agent's actions (efficient cause) in light of the ultimate final cause.

CDF. See **Congregation for the Doctrine of the Faith**

Celibacy is living in sexual **continence**, the expected sexual norm of **chastity** for all those who are not in the state of **marriage**. Celibacy is also a voluntary renunciation of the possibility of marriage required of vowed religious and, increasingly since the fourth century, for priests in the Latin rite. Since clerical celibacy is a discipline of the Church and not a defined dogma, some discussion continues around the possibility of allowing for a married clergy, although the traditional requirement remains in force. *For further reading*, see Donald Goergen, *The Sexual Celibate* (New York: Seabury

Press, 1974); and William C. Spohn, "St. Paul on Apostolic Celibacy and the Body of Christ," *Studies in the Spirituality of the Jesuits* 17 (January 1985).

Centesimus annus ("Hundredth Year") is **John Paul II**'s 1991 **encyclical** commemorating the hundredth anniversary of **Leo XIII**'s *Rerum novarum*, which is considered the first **social encyclical**. *Centesimus annus* condemned both **communism** and many aspects of **capitalism** that lead to oppression of the poor and insufficient attention to the **common good** in the state's role to guarantee **human rights** such as a just living wage, good working conditions, and so on. This was John Paul II's last social encyclical, although the themes of **war** and **capital punishment** were taken up in his 1995 *Evangelium vitae*.

Certitude (moral). See **conscience (certain and doubtful)**

Character, manner, and frequency criteria are given in *Lumen gentium* #25 for properly interpreting the papal **magisterium**, especially the **ordinary magisterium**. Character refers to what is being taught, and here there is a **hierarchy of truths** or importance. Teachings on the Resurrection would obviously rank higher than pronouncements on clerical attire. Manner refers to the extrinsic **authority** used in the teaching. An **encyclical** would be at the top of the ordinary papal magisterium, whereas an **occasional allocution** or remarks at an audience would rank much lower. Frequency indicates how often the teaching or topic has been proposed and how long since it was last reiterated. Careful consideration of all three of these criteria helps in discerning the proper mode of religious respect or *obsequium religiosum* called for in such teachings.

Character (moral) accents the moral identity and process of growth as being central aspects of the moral life and with an enduring importance that goes beyond individual **moral acts**. **Virtue** and **virtue ethics** help foster moral character and proper **conscience** formation. **Teleology**, with its stress on the end-as-goal of moral activity, also complements the understanding of moral character. The character of an individual certainly can be taken into account in **prudential judgments** made in assessing someone's credibility and suitability for various positions, including political office.

Charism of office, also called the *charisma veritatis* (charism of truth or **authority**), refers to the "special assistance of the Holy Spirit" given as part of the grace (*charism* in Greek) of episcopal ordination, which helps the pope and bishops exercise their triple *munera* (functions) of teaching, governing, and sanctifying. This gift, however, is given in a human way and does not mystically protect members of the **magisterium** from the possibility of error or incompleteness in the *munus docendi* or administrative mistakes (e.g., in the **scandal** of **sexual abuse** in the Church) in the *munus gubernandi*. In other words, this grace aids in finding the truth, governing wisely, and preaching well but does not guarantee that these things will happen in an *ex opere operato* mode; it depends very much on the learning, reflection, consultation, discussion, and **discernment** of the individual (*ex opere operantis*). As **Cardinal Avery Dulles, SJ,** notes, "the power of an individual office-holder to express the faith of the Church in a correct and effective manner will depend on a number of imponderables" (*A Church to Believe In* [New York: Crossroad, 1982]. 121). The faithful, though, are still called to reflect on the exercise of the magisterium with *obsequium religiosum* (see *LG* #25). **See also** *infallibilism* and *infallibility*.

Charity has two basic meanings in moral theology (see *ST II-II* Q. 23–46). The primary meaning, also called **love**, denotes the chief of the three theological virtues (the other two being faith and hope) because it is most expressive of the very nature of **God** (see 1 John) and is the only one of the three destined to last for all eternity (see Paul 1 and Cor 13). Charity also refers to an act of **supererogation** of aiding those in need, although helping the poor is not optional since **distributive justice** demands they be given what is necessary to live in **human dignity. See also** *liberation theology*.

Chastity is the **virtue** that helps govern the sexual **appetite**, opposing the **vice** of **lust** and leading to "the successful integration of **sexuality** within the person and thus the inner unity of man in his bodily and spiritual being" expressed in "the relationship of one person to another, in the complete and lifelong mutual gift of a man and a woman" (*CCC* #2337). Chastity also connotes sexual behavior in accordance with the **mores** of the community or as a committed relationship in which one is faithful either to one's spouse or to a **state of life** (e.g., as a vowed religious). **See also** *concupiscence, continence,* and *marriage*.

Christian ethics as a distinctive term is often used in **Protestant ethics** for what Roman Catholics term **moral theology.**

Christian ethics (distinctiveness of) is also called the *Proprium* of Christian ethics and refers to those aspects of Christian ethics that depend in some sense on revelation and are not immediately knowable to non-Christians through the natural law.

Circumstances are an indispensable consideration of every moral act, including those labeled **intrinsic evils**, since every deliberate human moral choice (*actus humanus*) necessarily occurs in a specific time and place. This is why circumstances are included in the three **fonts of morality**, along with the **action** *in se* (*finis operis*) and the corresponding **intention** (*finis operantis*). **Thomas Aquinas** treats circumstances not as "accidents" (i.e., nonessential aspects) of human acts but rather as helps to determine the "species" (moral meaning or nature) of an individual human act (see *ST I-II*, q. 18, a. 10). **Reason** also plays a key role in reflecting on the meaning and the appropriate moral response one is to make in light of these circumstances: "since the reason can direct as to place, time, and the like, it may happen that the condition as to place, in relation to the object, is considered as being in disaccord with reason" (*ST I-II*, q. 18, a. 10). To be sure, circumstances by themselves alone do not determine the moral species of an act, but reason's interpretation of the proper response to a given situation will necessarily differ according to individual circumstances, and so in the "objective" sense we have differing acts depending on their circumstances: "a circumstance gives the species of good or evil to a moral action, in so far as it regards a special order of reason" (*ST I-II*, q. 18, a. 11). This is neither moral **relativism** nor **situation ethics** but simply the objective recognition that different concrete circumstances necessarily produce different situations to which our practical moral reason must respond.

Classicist and historical worldviews were originally developed by Bernard Lonergan, SJ, in his seminal essay "The Transition from a Classicist World-View to Historical-Mindedness," in *Law for Liberty: The Role of Law in the Church Today*, edited by James E. Biechler, 126–33 (Baltimore: Helicon Press, 1967). He sets out two worldviews of understanding change in the world: in the classicist view the universe is largely fixed and static, and change can be seen as either something quite temporary and ephemeral or as a real threat to the God-given established order. Meanwhile, the historical worldview posits that both human nature and the universe are subject to ongoing change and development; therefore such change is often seen as a mark of growth and progress. The classicist view is associated with **physicalism** while the historical worldview has influenced **personalism**. These differences also condition the use and interpretation of the **fonts of moral theology**, especially scripture, **Tradition**, and the **magisterium**. See also *culture and inculturation, deductive and inductive, history and development of moral theology and doctrine,* and *postmodernism.*

Cloning. See **reproductive technologies**, **bioethics**, and *Dignitas personae*

Code of Canon Law. See **canon law**

Collective bargaining. See *Rerum novarum*, and **social encyclicals and social teaching**

Coma. See **states of consciousness: brain death, coma, PVS, MCS, and locked-in syndrome**

Commandments. See **Decalogue**

Commensurability/incommensurability. See **Basic Goods theory**

Commission and omission (sins of). See **sin** and **euthanasia**

The **common good** is a foundational concept in Catholic **social encyclicals and social teaching** that expresses the proper relationship between the individual and society and can be traced back to St. Paul's notion of the Mystical Body of Christ in which the **gifts of the Holy Spirit** likewise are ordered to the common good (see 1 Cor. 12: 7–11). **Thomas Aquinas** notes that the common good is grounded in **God** since God is the height and sum of all that is good (see *SCG* III.17.6); therefore, he ranks care for the common good above **private property**. All economic and political systems such as **capitalism**, **communism**, and **socialism** ought to privilege and promote the common good in their structures and policies. Just laws likewise must be oriented to and serve the common good (see *ST I-II*, Q. 90, art. 2). The common good should not be equated or confused with the notions of either majority rule in democracy or **utilitarianism**, which holds that "morality" is simply measured by that which produces the greatest good for the greatest number. Many times attention to the common good requires policies of a **preferential option for the poor** to ensure that they have the necessary means to live and flourish. The *Catechism of the Catholic Church*, quoting *GS* #26, defines the common good as "the sum total of social conditions which allow people, either as groups or as individuals, to reach their fulfillment more fully and more easily," which highlights three essential elements: first, respect for the person and his or her **human rights**; second, the social well-being and development of the community itself; and third, peace and stability that comes from a just social order (see *CCC* #1905–12). *For further reading*, see Vincent J. Miller, "The Disappearing Common Good as a Challenge to Catholic Participation in Public Life: The Need for Catholicity and Prudence," ch. 11 in *Voting and Holiness: Catholic Perspectives on Political Participation*, edited by Nicholas P. Cafardi, 178–96 (Mahwah, NJ: Paulist Press, 2012).

Common Ground Initiative. See **Consistent Ethic of Life**

Communion (admission to), as **canon law** states, is open to all Catholics except those barred by a **canonical penalty** such as **excommunication** or **interdict** or "others obstinately persevering in manifest **grave sin**" (*CIC* #915). The application of those under a canonical penalty is objective and straightforward, but the interpretation of those "obstinately persevering in manifest grave sin" has occasioned great debate and polarization. Some hold that *CIC* #915 forbids homosexuals from Communion unless they were explicitly to affirm that their condition were a grave disorder or **intrinsic evil** that inclined them to serious **sin**. Others, including some priests and bishops, hold that *CIC* #915 likewise bars all Catholic politicians and voters who do not actively support the recriminalization of elective **abortion** or who support the reproductive choice of a woman to make the personal decision about her pregnancy. Because many of these politicians belong to the Democratic Party, this position has been critiqued for being a covert ecclesiastical support of the other principal party, the Republicans. To date, neither the Holy See nor the USCCB has taken the position that interprets "obstinately persevering in manifest grave sin" in this manner, and the long-standing principle of *odia restringi* (*CIC* #18) states that burdens and penalties are to be interpreted and applied narrowly and strictly; thus, from both a canonical and pastoral perspective, it is advisable to proceed with great caution before denying the sacraments to any individual who seems worthy to request them, *coram Deo*. *For further reading*, see F. Joseph Gossman, "The State of the Soul of Those Presenting Themselves for Communion"; and John Kinney, "Judging Someone Else's Relationship with God," both in *Origins* 34, no. 12 (September 2, 2004): 189–90, and 192–93.

Communism, as distinguished from **socialism**, is the political and economic system identified with Karl Marx and a range of political figures primarily in the former Soviet Union and Eastern Europe as well as mainland China and North Korea (figures such as Lenin, Engels, Stalin, Mao Tse-Tung, and Kim Il Sung). This political form of **communism** holds that all the means of production are to be owned and controlled by the state and that individuals have limited rights granted to them by the state. Atheism is often identified with this version of communism since it is claimed by Marx and others that religion acts as the "opiate of the people," manipulated by **capitalism** to maintain social and economic control over the proletariat working class. The totalitarian and atheistic aspects of communism have been consistently denounced by the Church since the time of **Leo XIII**'s 1891 **encyclical *Rerum novarum***, though the more recent pontificates of **John Paul II** (1978–2005) and **Benedict XVI** (2005–13) have aimed at a more diplomatic engagement of Communist regimes—with some limited success. Sometimes **liberation theology** is criticized as espousing communism, although most liberation theologians would deny the charge's accuracy, stressing instead the aim to redress the real and serious abuses that have grown up in certain poorer societies, for example, in Latin American cultures where a feudalist system combined with elements of capitalism conspired to produce many oppressive social structures.

Communitarianism in philosophy stresses the rights and responsibilities individuals have due to their membership and roles within the community, and harmonizes with the Christian social ethics concepts of **commutative justice** and the **common good**. Communitarianism has been critical of classical liberalism with works such as John Rawls's 1971 classic, *A Theory of Justice*, critiquing a misshapen view of the **human person** as primarily an atomistic individual. Within the Christian tradition, communitarianism is associated with monasticism, especially in the context of the shared life in common. More contemporary communitarian movements within the Church would include the Catholic Worker movement founded by Dorothy Day and Peter Maurin. Communitarianism, like **communism**, in turn is critiqued for its own lack of stress on the rights of the individual and a perception that the individual's own needs and desires are subject to the community as a whole and that the community can demand the individual to sacrifice his or her own legitimate needs and desires to the good of the community.

Commutative justice is differentiated from **distributive justice** and legal justice because it is primarily relational in the one-to-one justice individuals have with each other, although always in the context of human society as a whole. **Compensation**, including **occult compensation** and the obligations of **restitution** for theft or injury, are examples of commutative justice in practice. **See also** *common good*, *communitarianism*, and *contract justice*.

Comparative religious ethics is the subdiscipline of comparative religious studies that analyzes both similarities and differences among world religions in terms of the belief systems, **cultures**, scriptures, rituals, practices, and so forth. **Human rights** discourse is aided by comparative religious ethics in helping to establish and clarify important ethical beliefs that are held, or could be held, by all or most of the world's major religions. However, as a discipline, comparative religious ethics does suffer from its inability to establish a truly neutral stance from which to evaluate all other belief systems, so many ethicians today argue instead for a cross-cultural ethics that would acknowledge this inherent limitation and try to develop dialogue and better analyses that move beyond the cultural worldviews that condition ethical perspectives. *For further reading*, see James T. Bretzke, "Cultural Particularity and the Globalization of Ethics in the Light of Inculturation," *Pacifica* 9 (1996): 69–86; and David Little and Sumner B. Twiss, *Comparative Religious Ethics* (New York: Harper & Row, 1978).

Compensation and occult compensation are two concepts grounded in **contract justice**. Regular compensation holds that wages, payments, or other benefits are paid for goods or services rendered. The need and legitimacy for occult compensation arises when one of the parties in the contract (whether there is an actual contract or merely an implied contract) fails to render to the other party the compensation that is justly due. The Catholic moral tradition drawing on **Thomas Aquinas** has long held that the aggrieved party can take the equivalent of the missing compensation even through occult or unlawful means since such action would restore the imbalance to **commutative justice** caused by the failure of one of the parties to honor the obligations of the contract (see *ST II-II* Q. 66, arts. 3 and 5). However, overly facile recourse to occult compensation is open to abuses and may also subject the aggrieved party to legal or other penalties if the fact of the occult compensation were to be discovered. Further principles offer guidance on occult compensation, including that the right of the creditor is morally certain, that recourse to the law in the **external forum** is impossible or unfeasible, and that reasonable efforts are undertaken to avoid **scandal**. Furthermore, if the original compensation were ultimately paid, then **restitution** would be morally obliged. The main pastoral use of this principle was traditionally found in the tribunal of **confession**, though it is clearly grounded in basic **justice**.

Compromise and compromise/cooperation with evil (*cooperatio in malum*) is a widely used, although often poorly understood, **moral principle** closely allied with **tolerance, double effect**, and **lesser evil**. Compromise recognizes that in many **circumstances** one lacks sufficient power to rectify the evil or ignorant **intention** of the person(s) or institutions engaged in the violations of the moral order. Strictly speaking, one never intends to cooperate in doing evil but rather the *finis operantis* is to lessen the evil done by another, to tolerate an evil in order to avoid a greater harm, or to cooperate in the furtherance of some good that cannot be accomplished without the occurrence of some evil as well. Formal cooperation means sharing in the sinful intent of the principal agent of the evil, which is ipso facto immoral. Material cooperation is the objective aid given or tolerated to the evil caused. All formal cooperation presumes material cooperation, but not all material cooperation is necessarily formal and sinful. If one votes for a political candidate because of the candidate's prowar, proabortion, or racist anti-immigration positions, then the vote constitutes sinful formal cooperation even if the elector would not be directly voting on the actual legislation (see *CCC* #2272). On the other hand, if "a Catholic does not share a candidate's stand in favor of abortion and/or **euthanasia**, but votes for that candidate for other reasons, it is considered remote material cooperation, which can be permitted in the presence of **proportionate reasons**" (July 21, 2004, letter on Catholic voting of **CDF** Prefect **Cardinal Joseph Ratzinger**, to Washington, DC, archbishop Theodore Cardinal McCarrick; see also *EV* #73). **Casuistry** in the **manualist tradition** focused on assessing the levels of participation and responsibility involved in material cooperation acts of **omission** or **commission**. Generally speaking, the closer or more essential the cooperation rendered is to the evil act, the greater the responsibility. For example, a gun made of steel used in a homicide requires the remote cooperation of the steelworker. But since steel is also used for many legitimate purposes, the worker's material cooperation is justified. A gun dealer's cooperation is mediate, being both closer and more essential to the commission of the crime, but selling guns is legal and moral as long as reasonable care is undertaken to keep weapons out of criminals' hands. Immediate cooperation might be the acquaintance who surrenders a gun to a criminal, but even here does not ipso facto constitute formal cooperation because there are several scenarios, such as **ignorance** or duress, that would keep the act as material cooperation alone. *For further reading*, see Gerard Magill, "A Moral Compass for Cooperation with Wrongdoing," ch. 9 in *Voting and Holiness*, edited by Nicholas P. Cafardi, 135–57 (New York: Paulist Press, 2012).

Compromise with evil. See **compromise and compromise/cooperation with evil**

Concrete material norms deal with **circumstances** of a moral act. Due to **contingency and fallibility** that necessarily occur in matters of concrete detail, **Thomas Aquinas** notes that the judgment of **practical reason** cannot have the same universality as norms derived from **speculative reason**. Concrete **moral norms** will likely not be applicable in all cases but rather will furnish a *lex valet ut in pluribus* (a law valid in most [but not all] cases; see *ST I-II*, q. 94, art. 4). Speed limits are examples of concrete material norms. While "drive safely" may be a **universal moral norm** discernible through speculative reason, exactly what constitutes a proper speed limit for any given stretch of road is more difficult to nail down with precision. **Circumstances** (i.e., contingency) will require different posted limits, and even these need to be adjusted under further conditions (e.g., slippery when wet). One universal norm of a single speed limit could not possibly fit the variety of these different cases as even the best-devised traffic laws cannot foresee every possible set of circumstances that might confront us at one time or another. This is where practical reason needs to be helped by the **virtue** of *epikeia* so we can apply the relevant moral norm to our concrete situation in a **prudent** manner.

However, some moral theologians use the term "concrete material norm" in a quite different way, to specify certain material actions that would always be **intrinsic evils**, such as a **direct abortion**. By definition, a "direct" abortion is always morally wrong, so in this abstract sense we have a universal concrete material norm. However, what constitutes a "direct abortion" cannot be spelled out in advance to cover every set of circumstances, foreseeable and unforeseeable. Treatment of an **ectopic pregnancy**, for example, results in the foreseen termination of fetal life, but the moral tradition has long accepted that such treatment is morally licit. It is humanly impossible to formulate a detailed concrete material norm that covers all medical procedures that would give an absolutely clear and unequivocal guide of how to proceed in each and every case. Nevertheless, concrete material norms remain helpful as long as the limitations of **contingency and fallibility** are not forgotten. **See also** *direct and indirect*.

Concupiscence refers to the strong longings or desires that subjugate humans "to the pleasures of the senses, covetousness for earthly goods, and self-assertion, contrary to the dictates of reason" (*CCC* #377). **Thomas Aquinas** divided sense **appetites** into either concupiscible (such as instincts leading to either pursuit or avoidance) or the irascible (such as instincts evidenced in competition, aggression, or defense). While any inordinate desire could be termed concupiscence, most often the term carried a strong connotation of suspect sexual desires, as with the traditional concept of *parvitas materiae in Sexto*, which held that any sexual "matter" would be objectively "grave" and thus always at least a potential **mortal sin**. This theology is coupled with **Augustine**'s notion of **original sin**, which held that Adam and Eve were free of concupiscence in the Garden of Eden but lost their innocence by their first rebellion against **God**. While baptism forgives original sin, the consequences of sin remain, including concupiscence, which **Tradition** describes as an "**inclination** to sin" (see *CCC* #1264, 1426 and 2515). Augustine also postulated that the sin of our first parents led to not only their own concu-piscence but through the sexual act of **procreation** was passed along to the rest of their offspring. This view in turn rendered even proper marital uses of the sexual faculty as somehow suspect, although the traditional theology of **marriage** did list as a legitimate secondary end of marriage the exercise of the "marital debt" (*debitum*) as a "remedy for concupiscence" (*remedium concupiscientiae*). **Pius XI**'s 1930 **encyclical** *Casti connubii* #59 states that "in the use of the matrimonial rights there are also secondary ends, such as mutual aid, the cultivating of mutual **love**, and the quieting of concupiscence which husband and wife are not forbidden to consider so long as they are subordinated to the primary end [of procreation] and so long as the intrinsic nature of the act is preserved [i.e., no **artificial contraception**]." The 1992 *Catechism of the Catholic Church* gives a more positive view of **sexuality**, stating that it embraces "all aspects of the **human person** in the unity of his **body** and soul. It especially concerns affectivity, the **capacity** to love and to procreate, and in a more general way the aptitude for forming bonds of com-munion with others" (*CCC* #2332).

Condom use continues to be hotly debated and in moral theology involves two principal issues: first, as a means of **birth control** (consistently con-demned by the Church's official teaching as in **Pius XI**'s 1930 *Casti con-nubii* and **Paul VI**'s 1968 *Humanae vitae*) and, second, as a **prophylaxis**, that is, in preventing or at least lessening the transmission of **STDs** (sexually transmitted diseases), especially **AIDS**. Since condom usage in the latter case is not to prevent conception but rather to prevent the spread of disease, many moralists contend that the *finis operis* of such usage is prophylaxis (disease prevention) and therefore could be counseled as a means of follow-ing **safe-sex** practices allowable under the principles of the **double effect** and **lesser evil**. Others contend that such practices encourage illicit sexual behavior, would cause **scandal**, or represent morally unacceptable **coopera-tion with evil**. A very small minority further contend that any and every use of a condom is **intrinsically evil** and therefore never permitted, although this particular position has not been embraced by either the **magisterium** or by a significant portion of those engaged in this ongoing *status quaestionis*. **See also** *ABC* (**abstinence**, be faithful, condom use). *For further reading*, see James F. Drane, "Condoms, AIDS & Catholic Ethics: Open to the Transmis-sion of Death?" *Commonweal* 118 (March 22, 1991): 188–92; and several articles in *The Tablet* (April 29, 2006).

Cone, James Hal (b. August 5, 1938), is an influential African American theologian and the Charles Augustus Briggs Distinguished Professor of Systematic Theology at Union Theological Seminary. His 1970 *Black Theology of Liberation* first used the term **"liberation theology"** to counter systemic **racism** in America. His work has been critiqued by some in **womanist theology** as being too male-centered and failing to include sufficiently experiences of black women.

Confession. See **sacrament of reconciliation**

Confidentiality and secrecy in professional ethics require that certain communications be treated as "privileged," such that their content cannot be divulged to another, except under very clear and limited **circumstances**, often called a legitimate "need to know" basis. For example, a therapist must not reveal what has been discussed with a patient *except* under rare situations when the patient might be a threat to his or her own safety or the safety of another. Confidentiality especially binds the medical, legal, counseling, and teaching professions, although everyone has a general obligation to protect confidentiality in even everyday exchanges. Often, civil legislation recognizes and protects confidentiality in professional situations, such as the 1974 Federal Educational Records Privacy Act, which prevents transmission of educational records of legal adults to third parties without their consent (including to parents of college students) or the 1996 Health Insurance Portability and Accountability Act, which governs the disclosure of medical records. **Canon law** also recognizes confidentiality and secrecy in a number of professional venues (see *CIC* #983, #1548 §2, and #1580). The **seal of the confessional** is another form of professional confidentiality, although in this case it is absolute—a confessor may never compromise the secrecy of the confessional forum for any reason whatsoever. **See also** *mental reservation.*

Conflict of duties / conflict of interests occur in situations in which two or more legitimate values, goals, or duties compete with each other. The latter term, widely used in business and professional ethics, calls upon the individual to act in the best interests of the person or entity that she is serving in a particular situation. Thus, a trustee of a school who also owns a business that occasionally is used by the school should not "use" the position of trustee to the advantage of the business and to the detriment of the school (e.g., by charging an inflated price for goods knowing that the school might likely pay the inflated price). Conflict of duties refers to those situations in which two or more legitimate duties cannot be simultaneously met or fulfilled to the same degree as if the duties were not to conflict. In these cases, the conflict must be resolved in favor of the higher duty in that particular context. A parent who also has a job may experience these conflicts, for example, when a business trip makes attendance at a child's school play impossible. The "higher" duty in a particular case is best discerned by the person closest to the situation, who then makes a **prudential judgment** as to which duty to fulfill. Conflict of duties often occurs in exercising **responsible parenthood** including decisions about forms of **birth control**. See also *duties (negative and positive)*.

Congregation for the Doctrine of the Faith (CDF) is the Vatican **dicastery** whose mission is "to promote and safeguard the doctrine on the **faith and morals** throughout the Catholic world: for this reason, everything which in any way touches such matter falls within its competence" (**John Paul II**'s 1988 apostolic constitution *Pastor bonus* #48). Its institutional roots date back to the 1542 Supreme Sacred Congregation of the Roman and Universal Inquisition established to combat Protestant heresy, more commonly the **Holy Office** until shortly after **Vatican II**. The CDF is composed of around two dozen members who are cardinals or bishops and headed by a cardinal prefect with an archbishop secretary. **Benedict XVI (Joseph Ratzinger)** was the cardinal prefect of the CDF from 1981 until the 2005 death of **John Paul II**. The CDF is divided into four functional sections: doctrinal, disciplinary, matrimonial, and priests (which includes adjudication of serious crimes such as clerical **sexual abuse**). Daily tasks are carried out by a clerical staff assisted by a number of consulters who are usually priests with some special competence in one or another area of theology. Bishops making their *ad limina* visits every five years to the Holy See also visit the CDF "for an exchange of information and reciprocal concerns." The CDF provides the *nihil obstat* ("nothing stands in the way") for deans and professors of ecclesiastical faculties and often also provides a theological assessment of certain publications or authors that have occasioned some concern in the Catholic community.

Conjugal love. See **marriage** and **inseparability principle**

Conscience is our fundamental modality of being human morally and the privileged locus of our authentic identity (**autonomy**) and relationship to **God** and God's providential care for us such that the core of the moral life could be summed up in the command "Always follow your formed and informed conscience." Although not primarily a scriptural term, two certain aspects of "conscience" are derived from New Testament variant spellings of the Greek word(s) συνείδησις and rendered as *synderesis* and *syneidesis*, translated (and combined) in Latin as *conscientia* (literally "knowing with"). These terms were interpreted by Scholastic theologians and **Thomas Aqui-**

nas to refer to the aspects of conscience as **habit** and as an "act" of moral judgment. Conscience has a rich and complex **history and development of moral theology**. See the following entries for some of the more important aspects of conscience. *For further reading*, see James T. Bretzke, "The Sanctuary of Conscience: Where the Axes Intersect," ch. 4 in *A Morally Complex World: Engaging Contemporary Moral Theology* (Collegeville, MN: Liturgical Press, 2004); Charles E. Curran, ed., *Conscience: Readings in Moral Theology*, vol. 14 (New York: Paulist Press, 2004); and Linda Hogan, *Confronting the Truth: Conscience in the Catholic Tradition* (New York: Paulist Press, 2001).

Conscience (certain and doubtful) refers to the level of subjective understanding the individual believes he has in relation to a moral issue or decision. A "certain" conscience is not necessarily correct, but the individual sincerely believes that his understanding in this area is true and that he is acting in **good faith**. A correct or "right" conscience is one in which the **conscience faculty** makes a correct judgment about a moral action. Ideally, a conscience should be both certain and correct. A "doubtful" conscience by contrast is experienced when an individual realizes that he lacks moral clarity on a particular issue or decision and thus is genuinely perplexed as to the right or best course of action. The traditional counsel for dealing with a doubtful conscience is to resolve the doubt if at all possible before acting, ideally by consulting trustworthy and well-informed moral teachers, especially the **magisterium**. Every individual must make all reasonable efforts to form and inform their consciences, but in line with the Church's teaching on **primacy of conscience**, a genuinely "certain" conscience must be followed. "A human being must always obey the certain judgment of his conscience. If he were deliberately to act against it, he would condemn himself" (*CCC* #1790). Of course, as the *Catechism* continues, even a "certain" conscience can be "in **ignorance** and makes erroneous judgments about acts to be performed or already committed" and there is a considerable moral tradition regarding **erroneous conscience** that needs to be referenced in conjunction here as well.

Conscience (erroneous), as *GS* #16 notes, "frequently errs from invincible ignorance without losing its dignity," which underscores the **primacy and sanctuary of conscience**. **Thomas Aquinas** makes it clear that if a person believes in conscience that "X" is a commandment of **God**, then to disobey "X" is equivalent to disobeying God, even if, in fact, that which is perceived as "X" is an error and thus not truly from God, who is the fullness of **truth**. Thomas goes on to say that if someone were to forsake what is believed to be the will of God in order to obey any human authority, then that person would further compromise the duty to follow one's conscience by substituting a lower authority for the (mis-)perceived command of the higher authority (see *ST I-II* Q. 19, arts. 5–6). One is always obliged to follow one's **certain conscience** even if it should prove later to be erroneous (see *CCC* #1790). Error comes from ignorance and is either vincible or invincible. Vincible ignorance could be corrected by the individual if reasonable effort were taken, therefore **culpability** for evil actions done under vincible ignorance remains (see *CCC* #1791). Invincible ignorance is more deep-seated and highly resistant even to earnest efforts to uncover this type of error. While a person acting erroneously due to invincible ignorance still commits an objective moral wrong, the action in itself remains an evil, but the person lacks **culpability** for the **moral evil** (see *CCC* #1793). For example, today we hold that **torture** is **intrinsically evil** and so could never be legitimately done even to root out heresy. However, in the Middle Ages, acting out of invincible ignorance, many individuals and institutions that employed torture did so in **good faith**—but erroneous conscience. Ignorance might be better viewed as existing along a spectrum with "vincible" and "invincible" being markers at the opposite ends of this spectrum. Exactly where one passes from vincible to invincible is quite difficult to discern in the concrete, so this is another reason to attend carefully both to **forming and informing conscience**. *For further reading*, see Brian V. Johnstone, "Erroneous Conscience in Veritatis Splendor and the Theological Tradition," in *The Splendor of Accuracy: An Examination of the Assertions Made by Veritatis Splendor*, edited by Joseph A. Selling and Jan Jans (Grand Rapids, MI: Eerdmans, 1994), 114–35, also published as "Conscience and Error," ch. 13 in *Conscience: Readings in Moral Theology, 14*, edited by Charles E. Curran (New York: Paulist Press, 2004), 163–74.

Conscience (faculty of) in the **manualist tradition** refers to the capacity of *recta ratio* (**right reason**) to make two basic kinds of judgment moving from general **moral principles** to concrete applications. The first judgment, the *iudicium de actu ponendo* (judgment concerning the act to be undertaken) refers primarily to the objective nature of the act in itself, for example, whether cheating is objectively right or wrong. The second type of judgment, called *iudicium de positione actus* (judgment about the position of the act) involves more the subjective assessment of the act in question; for example, is helping a friend with a homework assignment an act of friendship (and therefore "right" and "good"), or would this be aiding an act of cheating (and therefore "wrong" and "bad")? Thus, one could err about the objective moral nature of an act and yet still be acting in **good faith** (or good conscience) if the person lacked **culpability** for the **ignorance** that caused the erroneous judgment. However, even in good faith one could not err in the second sort of judgment (*de positione actus*); for example, in this case one would not consider "cheating" to be morally right or "friendship" to be morally wrong. For someone to act in good faith, the person must always try to do what she judges to be right. This is key not only to the Church's teaching on right and **erroneous conscience**, and on **vincible and invincible ignorance**, but more fundamentally to grasping the **goodness and rightness distinction**. Some post–**Vatican II** theologians have stressed less the faculty of conscience understanding in favor of a more **personalist** approach that emphasizes the development of moral **character** and **discernment**. Others, for example, Bernard Lonergan, SJ, hold that it is more proper to speak of conscience as a core human modality; thus the moral consciousness that is expressed in coming to ethical judgments is actually what constitutes the **human person** as truly human. In other words, rather than "having" a faculty of conscience, a person *is* a conscience. *For further reading*, see Josef Fuchs, "The Phenomenon of Conscience: Subject-Orientation and Object-Orientation," ch. 8 in *Christian Morality: The Word Becomes Flesh* (Washington, DC: Georgetown University Press), 118–33.

Conscience (forming and informing; development of) has always been a key aspect of the moral theology of conscience, although in the **manualist** tradition the vocabulary dealt primarily with the judgment made by the **conscience faculty** and proper reception to the teachings of the **magisterium** in what *Lumen gentium* #25 would later term *obsequium religiosum*. In this view, lack of proper formation or information of conscience would lead to an **erroneous conscience** due to either **vincible** or **invincible ignorance**. We also realize better how **character** is affected not only by personal **habits** of **virtue** and **vice** but also by **culture**, media, and myriad other factors that can influence our **capacity** to make good conscience-based moral judgments. Since often these "information" voices are in tension with one another, the practice of moral **discernment** plays an important part in both forming and informing one's conscience.

Conscience (primacy and sanctuary) provides the ground for the dignity of conscience and its absolute binding character on the individual. As **Vatican II**'s *GS* #16 puts it:

> In the depths of his conscience, man detects a law which he does not impose upon himself, but which holds him to obedience. Always summoning him to love **good** and avoid **evil**, the voice of conscience when

necessary speaks to his heart: do this, shun that. For man has in his heart a law written by God [i.e., the *lex indita non scripta*]; to obey it is the very dignity of man; according to it he will be judged. Conscience is the most secret core and sanctuary of a man. There he is alone with God, Whose voice echoes in his depths.

The privileged place where one meets God is termed the sanctuary since it is both holy and sacred, and it should be a "safe" place in which no outside authority—even a legitimate authority—can lawfully enter. The medieval "right of sanctuary" made churches a refuge for one pursued by legal authorities since by claiming sanctuary the refugee was in effect putting his case before **God**. Blessed John Henry Cardinal Newman called conscience the "aboriginal vicar of Christ," which expresses the primacy of conscience, namely that in the process of forming, informing, and then obeying the voice of conscience we seek to follow what we honestly believe is God's voice for us.

This does not mean that conscience is always the infallible voice of God; we can still have a **certain conscience** that is nevertheless objectively mistaken (e.g., **erroneous conscience**). But from **Thomas Aquinas** onward, the Church has consistently upheld that we are obliged to follow our certain conscience if it has been properly formed and informed (see *ST I-II* Q. 19, arts. 5–6). Aquinas held that this obligation binds, even in the face of **excommunication** (see Thomas Aquinas's 4 *Sent.* 27.1.2.q.4. ad 3; 27.3.3.expos. textus; and 38.2.4.q.3).

As **Vatican II**'s "Declaration on Religious Freedom," *Dignitatis humanae* #3 states: "In all his activity a man is bound to follow his conscience in order that he may come to God, the end and purpose of life. It follows that he is not to be forced to act in manner contrary to his conscience. Nor, on the other hand, is he to be restrained from acting in accordance with his conscience, especially in matters religious." **Joseph Ratzinger**'s (later **Benedict XVI**) commentary on *Gaudium et spes* asserted: "Over the pope as the expression of the binding claim of ecclesiastical authority, there still stands one's own conscience, which must be obeyed before all else, necessary even against the requirements of ecclesiastical authority. This emphasis on the individual, whose conscience confronts him with a supreme and ultimate tribunal, and one which in the last resort is beyond the claim of external social groups, even of the official Church, also establishes a principle in opposition to increasing totalitarianism" (*Gaudium et spes*, pt. 1, ch. 1 in *Commentary on the Documents of Vatican II*, edited by H. Vorgrimler [New York: Herder & Herder, 1968]). The 1992 *Catechism of the Catholic Church* reminds us: "A human being must always obey the certain judgment of his conscience.

If he were deliberately to act against it, he would condemn himself" (*CCC* #1790). Not following one's conscience then would condemn someone because that person would then be acting against what one genuinely believed to be the voice of God—erroneously or not. The primacy of conscience notion is echoed in the proper understanding of **moral autonomy** as opposed to **heteronomy**.

Consequentialism is an ethical theory that denies the premise of an objective moral order knowable through the **natural law** and instead posits that ethical **rightness** or wrongness of an action is determined by a consideration of the consequences of the action. Thus, any "good" **end justifies the means** and is incompatible with notions of **intrinsic evil**, **deontology**, or **virtue ethics**. **Utilitarianism**, which holds that the morality of an action is determined by what produces the "greatest good for the greatest number," is a form of consequentialism. In addition to moral **relativism**, there are many problems with both of these theories. It is exceedingly difficult to determine just what count as "good consequences," or how these consequences can be accurately predicted, or how the rights and dignity of the minority are protected if it would seem that their sacrifice would produce "better" consequences or a "greater good" for the majority. **John Paul II**'s 1993 *Veritatis splendor* (*VS* #75) sharply condemned both consequentialism and utilitarianism as incompatible with Roman Catholic moral theology, although he identified **proportionalism** as also being a form of consequentialism—which many theologians dispute. The pope also called consequentialism a form of **teleologism**, meaning that morality was determined from the end (τέλος [telos]) of an action. Some also call this teleological ethics, but this term should not be confused with **teleology** as employed by **Thomas Aquinas** or with a good deal of the Catholic moral tradition, which looks first to the **good** related to the true nature of a being and then considers those actions that would correspond to that nature and help realize its proper end or goal as well as condemning those actions that would run counter to the end of that nature (*contra naturam*).

Consistent Ethic of Life, also termed the Seamless Garment Ethic, is an approach to Catholic **social teaching** advanced in 1983 by Chicago's Cardinal Joseph Bernardin (April 2, 1928–November 14, 1996) that links all human life issues together—**abortion, assisted suicide, capital punishment**, and **war**—building on the premise that all human life is sacred and should be protected by law and the **common good** be supported by human institutions. To garner support for public policy initiatives, Bernardin began a Common Ground Initiative that hoped to break through some of the political and ideological impasse over issues such as the legal status of abortion. This movement was opposed by some American hierarchs such as Cardinals O'Connor (New York), Law (Boston), Hickey (Washington, DC), and Baum (Vatican), who viewed cooperation with individuals who did not fully accept all of the Church's moral teachings to be problematic. The movement also lost momentum due to Bernardin's own advancing cancer and subsequent death in 1996. Nevertheless, the basic themes of the Consistent Ethic of Life certainly were echoed in **John Paul II**'s 1995 *Evangelium vitae* as well as in a number of social teaching documents of the **magisterium** since that time. *For further reading*, see Cardinal Joseph Bernardin, *A Moral Vision for America*, edited by John P. Langan (Washington, DC: Georgetown University Press, 1998).

Constancy of Tradition argument. See **Tradition**

Constantianism is a pejorative term used to denounce accommodation of Christianity to political and secular values, stemming from the fourth century when the Emperor Constantine legalized Christianity and made it the state religion. **See also** *biblical ethics*; *Bonhoeffer, Dietrich*; *Hauerwas, Stanley*; and *Yoder, John Howard*.

Continence is usually defined as **abstinence** from conjugal relations within **marriage** practiced as part of the **virtues** of **temperance** and **chastity** and as a legitimate form of **birth control**. In the Catholic tradition all men and women who are not in a legitimate marital relationship would be called to a life of continence, even if this **celibacy** would not be lifelong for those who might eventually marry. **See also** *concupiscence* and *marriage*.

Contingency and fallibility are used by **Thomas Aquinas** in his discussion on the exercise of **practical reason** in the **natural law**: "The practical reason, on the other hand, is busied with contingent matters [i.e., "change"], about which human actions are concerned: and consequently, although there is necessity in the general principles, the more we descend to matters of detail, the more frequently we encounter defects [i.e., "fallibility"] (*ST I-II* Q. 94, art. 4). Proper understanding of these terms is crucial in the interpretation and application of various levels of **moral norms**, especially **concrete material norms**. In Aquinas's vocabulary "contingency" does not mean "plan B" if plan A should prove unworkable; it means, rather, the quality of impermanence and change that is necessarily a part of all human **circumstances**. Similarly, "fallibility" does not mean "false" but rather an expression of **finitude and facticity** in our knowledge of how best to proceed in a given situation. One can use good **prudential judgment** and still be liable to fallibility. **See also** *deductive and inductive.*

Contra naturam (Latin, "against nature") refers primarily to the moral **character** and end of the **human person** rather than the "laws of nature" in the sense of the physical sciences. *Contra naturam* is used primarily with **teleology** to denote any action that goes against the perceived "natural order," understood as related to the human being's true moral nature. Such an action, since it counters or obstructs true human moral nature, is ipso facto against the **natural law** and **intrinsically evil**. Problems arise with this term when interpreted too narrowly in a **physicalist** perspective because it is notoriously difficult to determine which "is" in what part of "nature" should furnish the moral "ought" of norms (see **naturalistic fallacy**). The **manualist tradition** stressed the proper end of an individual **faculty**, such as speech or sex, holding that any activity that violated or hindered the proper use of the respective faculty, such as *locutio contra mentem*, violated at the same time its nature (*contra naturam*) and was ipso facto immoral. Today the **magisterium** prefers "**disordered**" for behaviors formerly labeled *contra naturam*.

Contraception is a form of **birth control** using intentional measures to prevent conception from occurring by preventing either fertilization of the ovum by the sperm or the successful implantation of the fertilized ovum in the uterine wall. The official position of the **magisterium**, however, focuses mostly on contraception as the artificial blocking of fertilization, viewing such obstacles as being *contra naturam* and therefore **intrinsically evil**. Both the more recent Catholic moral tradition and the magisterium recognize that there are some instances in which contraception is morally legitimate, such as through the practice of **NFP** and also in emergency contraception after rape. This issue of postrape contraception was debated in the 1960s when the **Holy Office** (now the **CDF**) allowed nuns in the Belgian Congo to take contraceptive measures to prevent pregnancy since they were in chronic danger of being raped. This position was reconfirmed in the 1990s in the wake of rapes during the war in Bosnia-Herzogovina. The judgment that contraceptive measures were allowed in this situation is based on the principle of legitimate self-defense and was articulated by Giacomo Perico, SJ, in the July 3, 1993, issue of the semiofficial *Civilta Cattolica*. Perico, writing about a woman forced to have sex, said "it is morally licit that she take recourse in the only means available, contraceptives, to avoid a possible pregnancy." The 2009 5th edition of *ERD* #36 states, "A female who has been raped should be able to defend herself against a potential conception from the sexual assault.

If, after appropriate testing, there is no evidence that conception has occurred already, she may be treated with medications that would prevent ovulation, sperm capacitation, or fertilization." The bishops of England and Wales have adopted a similar principle in allowing for the use of the so-called morning-after pill in cases of rape and nonconsensual sex. While termination of a pregnancy is still seen as **abortion** and intrinsically evil, there is no corresponding absolute "right" of just anyone's sperm to reach the ovum of a woman who is not a marital partner or who has been forced against her will to have sex. For the fuller treatment of the question of a married couple seeking to limit or prevent pregnancies, see **birth control**, **marriage**, and **responsible parenthood**. *For further reading*, see John T. Noonan Jr., *Contraception: A History of Its Treatment by the Catholic Theologians and Canonists*, enlarged ed. (Cambridge, MA: Harvard University Press, 1965, 1986); Leslie Woodcock Tentler, *Catholics and Contraception: An American History* (Ithaca, NY: Cornell University Press, 2004). **See also** *Address to Italian Midwives, Casti connubii, debitum, Humanae vitae, Pontifical Commission on Births, safe sex*, and *sterilization*.

Contract justice involves agreements or promises offered and then accepted after due consideration of the terms by the relevant parties with the intention to create a legally binding contract. Once the contract has been duly constituted, then the presumption is that the resulting pact will be kept, as expressed in the Latin axiom *pacta sunt servanda* (pacts are serviced [or kept]). **See also** *common good, communitarianism, commutative justice*, and *compensation*.

Contract view of marriage. See *debitum* and **marriage**

Contrition (perfect and imperfect) designate the sorrow a penitent has for the sins she has committed. Perfect contrition is the full remorse for **sin** because it has offended **God** and others, whereas imperfect contrition (sometimes also called attrition) is remorse for sins due to shame, disgrace, or the fear of punishment that the sins committed bring upon the sinner. Since the **Council of Trent**, the Church has held that at least imperfect contrition is necessary for the valid reception of the **sacrament of reconciliation** (see *DS* 1451–65, 1678, 1704; and *ND* 1614–15, 1624, 1644), whereas perfect contrition would be sufficient for the **forgiveness** of even **mortal sin** without recourse to the sacrament of reconciliation. Of course, perfect contrition is difficult both to achieve and to know with certainty that one has realized it. For this reason the Church teaches that the ordinary manner in which one is assured of the forgiveness of serious sins is through the celebration of the sacrament of reconciliation. Contrition should be accompanied by the desire not to sin again and to amend one's life in a process of **conversion** to avoid the **occasions of sin** in the future.

Conversion in the New Testament is expressed primarily by the Greek words *"metanoia"* (μετάνοια) and *"epistrophe"* (ἐπιστροφή), whose noun and verb forms' full range of nuance is difficult to translate exactly and completely into English. The terms involve reflection, regret, repentance, and a positive turning around toward a new relationship and direction in one's life. In the **sacrament of reconciliation, contrition** for one's **sins**, coupled with a firm purpose of **amendment**, commitment to avoid where possible **occasions of sin** in the future, and willingness to do **penance** for one's transgressions all express the various aspects of conversion. Expressions of *metanoia* (μετάνοια) and *epistrophe* (ἐπιστροφή) in the New Testament are given in the second-person plural imperative and connected to an announcement of the Gospel message, thus underscoring the communal dimension of the life of conversion and discipleship (see Mt. 4:17; Mk. 1:15 and Acts 3:19).

Cooperation with evil (*cooperatio in malum*). See **compromise and compromise/cooperation with evil, lesser evil, material cooperation,** *minus malum*, **proportionate reason**, and **tolerance**.

Coram Deo and *coram homnibus*, "before God" and "before humanity," refer to the distinction often associated with matters of **conscience**. Only God knows us completely and there may be things that humanity will judge differently than God does, or that humanity would not know either fully or at all. How we stand *coram Deo* is clearly more crucial than how we appear *coram homnibus*. **See also** *forum, internal and external*.

Core (basic) freedom. See **fundamental option theory**

The **Council of Trent** met in three sessions from 1545 to 1563 to deal with the challenges posed by the Protestant Reformation, defining doctrines on a range of issues such as the seven **sacraments** and the Eucharist, and instituting many reforms. Implementation of the conciliar decrees was entrusted to the pope, which helped foster greater centralization of Church power in a growing Vatican bureaucracy of **dicasteries**. It is the most important ecumenical council up to **Vatican II**.

Counsels. See **evangelical counsels**

Courage, an organization founded in 1980 by Rev. John Harvey, OSFS, lists as its first goal "To live chaste lives in accordance with the Roman Catholic Church's teaching on **homosexuality**." Viewing homosexuality primarily as a disease, Courage employs a twelve-step program similar to Alcoholics Anonymous and endorses **reparative therapy**. Although the movement has been endorsed by several Church leaders such as Cardinal Lopez Trujillo of Colombia, its approach remains controversial because of the implied claims of being able to cure or at least contain what it describes as destructive homosexual tendencies.

Courage (virtue). See **cardinal virtues** and **prudence and prudential judgment**

A **covenant** is the foundational metaphor for **marriage** in the 1983 *Code of Canon Law* (*CIC* # 1055), instead of the contract paradigm used in the 1917 *Code*. The theological notion of covenant is quite important in **biblical ethics** and comes originally from the Old Testament, which provides the core relationship between **God** and God's Chosen People: "I will take you as my people and I will be your God" (Ex. 6:7; see also Ex. 12:14–17, 31:16–17; Dt. 4:2, 13:1; Mal. 3:6–7). This also provides the context for liberation from slavery in Egypt, the giving of the **Decalogue**, and the gift of the Promised Land. While Jesus abolished some Mosaic laws (see Heb. 8:13, 10:15–18; Gal. 3:23–25; 2 Cor. 3:7–17; Eph. 2:15; Rom. 7:6), he makes it clear that the covenant remains although its deeper meaning now is revealed in his Gospel preaching (see the six antitheses in the **Sermon on the Mount**, Mt. 5:17–48). The notion of covenant is also quite important for grounding the **communitarian** dimension of the moral life, especially valuable in notions such as the **common good** and as a partial antidote to **social sin and structural evil**.

Crass or supine ignorance. See **ignorance**

Creation, from our human perspective, can be a starting point for all theology since the Judeo-Christian faith holds that **God** is not only the author and sovereign ruler of all life, the founder of **law**, but also the source and summit of everything God has made. This is the principle of *exitus et reditus* (going out and returning), which holds God to be both the source and ultimate returning point of all creation and for humans our *Summum Bonum*. In contemporary ethics, creation plays an especially important role in **ecology and environmental ethics** and is a special concern of **feminist ethics** as well as both **ecumenism** and interreligious dialogue.

Creative fidelity. See **Häring, Bernard, CSsR**

Credenda and tenenda (singular, *credendum* and *tenendum*) are Latin terms for "things to be believed" and "things to be held." *Credenda* requires an **assent** of faith, that is, to a doctrine that has been solemnly defined (*de fide definita*), such as the dual nature of Jesus Christ as both true **God** and true man. If one were unable to believe a key article of faith, then such a person could not claim to be a Christian. Denial or teaching something contrary to an article of faith constitutes heresy subject to appropriate **canonical penalties**. Articles of faith that must be believed are distinguished from other teachings or disciplines duly proposed in an authoritative manner by the **magisterium** that are required to be "held" as *tenenda/tenendum*. For example, *tenendum* (and not *credendum*) was the term employed in **Vatican I's** 1870 formal definition of papal **infallibility** (see *DS* #3074). The 2005 **CDF** "Note on the Minister of the Sacrament of the Anointing of the Sick," recalling *CIC* 1003 § 1 "that only priests (Bishops and presbyters) are ministers of the Sacrament of the Anointing of the Sick," lists this doctrine as "definitive *tenenda*. Thus, neither deacons nor laypeople can exercise this ministry, and any such action would constitute simulation of the sacrament." Here the kind of assent asked for would be compliance, that is, that neither deacons nor the laity attempt to celebrate this sacrament, and not the faith assent for the doctrines contained in the Nicene Creed. **John Paul II's** 1994 apostolic letter *Ordinatio sacerdotalis* on the impossibility of ever ordaining women to the priesthood was later declared in the **CDF's** 1995 *Responsum ad dubium* "to be held [*tenendum est*] always, everywhere, and by all, as belonging to the **deposit of the faith**."

Crimes and delicts in **canon law** are punished by an appropriate **canonical penalty** because they go beyond misdeeds such as minor liturgical infractions or other less serious irregularities. Examples of a *delicta graviora* (grave delict) would be **sexual abuse** of a minor or the *crimen sollicitationis* (crime of solicitation) in which a confessor uses the confessional forum to arrange a sexual liaison. Clerical sexual abuse cases are subject to the **zero tolerance** policy outlined in the **Dallas Charter** and are adjudicated by the **CDF**.

Culpability (Latin, *culpa*, for fault) refers to moral responsibility for one's decisions and actions. Culpability can only be predicated for a moral act (*actus humanus*) that in turn implies **freedom** and **intention**. Acts over which an individual has no control, or in which there was no true intention, could not be culpable acts. Both the **manualist tradition** and **canon law** recognize factors that can diminish culpability, including lack of **advertence**, development of a bad **habit** that lessened freedom, diminished capacity due to chemical impairment (e.g., drugs or alcohol), heightened emotions (e.g., "crimes of passion"), mental defect, and so on. Criminal law has developed an extensive tradition on levels and factors of culpability ranging from purposeful at the high end down to knowingly, recklessly, and negligently at the low end of responsibility.

Cultural anthropology. See **culture and inculturation**

Culture and inculturation provide the ground and process by which the Gospel takes authentic, effective root in the life of both individuals and whole societies. "Culture" has many meanings ranging from a cultivated taste for the arts, music, and cuisine to the social science discipline of **anthropology** and to popular expressions such as "**culture of life** versus **culture of death**." While there is no one established definition of culture in moral theology, most would agree that every truly human being must have a culture in the sense of a given society's integrated collection of beliefs, patterns of behavior, institutions, symbol systems, and language as well as those aspects expressive of culture described as a cultivated taste for the arts, and so on. Culture is one of our basic modalities of being human; in other words, one can only be human as a cultural being, and attempts to strip away culture to find "true human nature" will arrive only at an abstraction that has at best limited value for moral analysis. Inculturation, a neologism dating back the 1970s, is one aspect of the theological and ecclesial response to Jesus's valedictory mandate to go and teach "all nations" (Mt. 28:19, παντα τα εθνη, literally "all ethnicities"). Demanding of non-Western indigenous Christian converts a de facto attempt at reenculturation into some variety of Western cultural Christianity is clearly erroneous. Both **Vatican II**'s "Decree on Missionary Activity," *Ad gentes*, and **Paul VI**'s 1975 postsynodal apostolic exhortation, *Evangelii nuntiandi*, stress the necessity for adaptation as an intrinsic part of evangelization: "with due regard for the philosophy and wisdom of these peoples; it will be seen in what ways their customs, views on life, and social order, can be reconciled with the manner of living taught by divine revelation. From here the way will be opened to a more profound adaptation in the whole area of Christian life" (*AG* #22). *For further reading*, see James T. Bretzke, "Cultural Particularity and the Globalization of Ethics in the Light of Inculturation," *Pacifica* 9 (1996): 69–86; James T. Bretzke, "A New Pentecost for Moral Theology: The Challenge of Inculturation of Ethics," *Josephinum* 10, no. 2 (Summer/Fall 2003): 250–60; Gerald A. Arbuckle, *Culture, Inculturation, and Theologians: A Postmodern Cri-*

tique (Collegeville, MN: Liturgical Press, 2010); and Ary A. Roest Crollius, ed., *Inculturation: Working Papers on Living Faith and Cultures*, 18 vols. (Rome: Centre Cultures and Religions, Pontifical Gregorian University, 1982–96).

Culture of life and **culture of death** is an expression popularized by **John Paul II** in his 1995 encyclical *Evangelium vitae* to denote the struggle between values that are ultimately promotive of life or not (see *EV* #21, 28, 50, 77, 82, 86–87, 92, 95, 98, 100). Unfortunately, this expression has been abused by many to vilify *ad hominem* or caricature opponents on a range of issues such as **birth control, abortion, ANH** for **PVS** patients, and **euthanasia** as well as the political process (e.g., labeling certain candidates "prodeath"). Strictly speaking, there can be no "culture" that exists independent of individuals and communities, and dividing people into one of two classes that are either totally "culture of life" (e.g., those that practice **NFP**) or totally "culture of death" (e.g., those who oppose recriminalization of abortion) does a real disservice to the tradition of careful moral analysis and may well be guilty of self-righteousness, **calumny**, or **slander. See also** *culture and inculturation* and *simul iustus et peccator*.

Curran, Charles E. (b. March 30, 1934), is a priest in good standing of the diocese of Rochester, New York, and an internationally renowned moral theologian who served as president of the CTSA, SCE, and the American Theological Society. He earned his S.T.D. in moral theology in 1961 at the Pontifical Gregorian University in Rome (under Francis Furlong, SJ) and then studied at the newly opened Alphonsianum under **Bernard Häring, CSsR**. In 1968, after the release of *Humanae vitae*, while teaching at the Catholic University of America (CUA), Curran, along with some six hundred theologians, submitted a critical response to **Paul VI's encyclical**, ultimately published in two volumes as *Dissent In and For the Church* and *The Responsibility of Dissent: The Church and Academic Freedom* (both New York: Sheed and Ward, 1969). In the area of **sexual ethics**, especially in **homosexuality**, Curran acknowledged that some of his views did **dissent** from the **ordinary magisterium**, such as the possible lack of sinful matter in the Sixth and Ninth Commandments of the **Decalogue** *(parvitas materiae in Sexto)*. In a seminal article "Catholic Social and Sexual Teaching: A Methodological Comparison" published as chapter 5 in his *Tensions in Moral Theology* (Notre Dame, IN: University of Notre Dame Press, 1988), 87–109, Curran contrasted the marked differences in the development of the **magisterium**'s social and sexual teaching in three methodological shifts: from a **classicist to historical worldview**; from an abstract **physicalist** to a **personalist** view of human nature; and from a **legalism** to a relationality-responsibility model in which "gray areas" would militate against absolute **moral certitude** for each and every position. His theology of compromise incorporates elements of the principles of **gradualism** and the **lesser evil** and concludes certain unions; for example, a monogamous same-sex couple could represent a compromise with an **ideal** that for them would be unrealizable, therefore this compromise may be necessary so these individuals can find greater peace and satisfaction in their lives. In 1986, the **CDF**, after a long investigation, concluded "that one who dissents from the Magisterium as you [Curran] do is not suitable nor eligible to teach Catholic theology." Subsequent civil litigation after his dismissal from CUA found that Curran had no right to academic freedom, and he ultimately accepted the Elizabeth Scurlock University Professor of Human Values Chair at Southern Methodist University. The bibliography by and about Curran is vast, but on the issue of his difficulties with the CDF, *for further reading*, see especially his *Faithful Dissent* (Kansas City, MO: Sheed and Ward, 1986); and *Readings in Moral Theology, No. 6: Dissent in the Church*, eds. Charles E. Curran and Richard A. McCormick (New York: Paulist Press, 1988), which contains articles representative of both ends of the theological spectrum; and his *Loyal Dissent: Memoir of a Catholic Theologian* (Washington, DC: Georgetown University Press, 2006).

D

Dallas Charter was adopted in 2002 by the **USCCB** "for addressing allegations of **sexual abuse** of minors by Catholic clergy. The charter also includes guidelines for reconciliation, healing, accountability, and prevention of future acts of abuse," and the charter, along with accompanying information, is available on the USCCB website. The charter also set up essential norms of particular **canon law** to govern its implementation in the United States, although initially the dioceses of Baker, Oregon (Bishop Robert Vasa), and Lincoln, Nebraska (Bishop Fabian Bruskewitz), along with six of the thirty-two eparchies (dioceses) of the Eastern Church, indicated they would not cooperate with all aspects of the charter's mandated audits, judging them to be ill-conceived in certain key aspects. Review boards on sexual misconduct allegations have been established and the charter established a **zero tolerance** policy for any substantiated claim of sexual misconduct with a minor. **See also** *crimes and delicts*.

Death penalty. See **capital punishment**

Death with dignity is a basic tenet of the Christian understanding of earthly life, which **John Paul II** termed a "penultimate reality" that counters an unacceptable **vitalism**. Earthly life remains always a "sacred reality entrusted to us, to be preserved with a sense of responsibility" (*EV* #2). Christian faith, especially belief in the Resurrection, signifies biological death not as a final end but rather as a passage to the fullness of life. Catholics are empowered to make appropriate decisions (e.g., **AHCD**) regarding the end of life, including the cessation of medical means that are no longer proportionate to their legitimate end of either healing or sustaining life. However, "death with dignity" can be a code phrase used by some, such as the Hemlock Society, for ethically unacceptable **euthanasia** or forms of **physician-assisted suicide** (**PAS**). Modern health care research, in discussion with the pioneering work of Dr. Elisabeth Kübler-Ross, contends that there are discernible stages in the acceptance of death, especially in the face of a diagnosed terminal illness: (1) initial denial of the terminal diagnosis, (2) anger at the disease,

(3) bargaining with **God** or others to avoid death, (4) depression when the bargaining proves unsuccessful in reversing the disease, and (5) ultimate acceptance in greater peace with the terminal illness. Hospice care, which has grown dramatically, is perfectly acceptable with Catholic teaching so long as reasonable care is undertaken to respect the bioethical principle of **autonomy** of the patient and the moral distinctions between **ordinary and extraordinary means**. *For further reading*, see Elisabeth Kübler-Ross, *On Grief and Grieving: Finding the Meaning of Grief through the Five Stages of Loss* (New York: Simon & Schuster, 2005); Thomas R. Kopfensteiner, "Death with Dignity: A Roman Catholic Perspective," *Linacre Quarterly* 63 (November 1996): 64–75; and Thomas R. Kopfensteiner, "Protecting a Dignified Death: A Contemporary Challenge for Moral Reasoning," *New Theology Review* 6 (November 1993): 6–27.

Debitum (Latin) can mean any "debt," but in moral theology usually refers to the rights and obligations each married partner has to the other's **body**, especially in rendering sexual relations upon reasonable request and in a manner *per se* apt for **procreation**. The term comes from the Latin Vulgate translation of the Greek word *"opheilen"* (ὀφειλὴν) in 1 Corinthians 7:3 as *debitum*: "The husband should give to his wife her conjugal rights (ὀφειλὴν), and likewise the wife to her husband" (NRSV). The paying of the *debitum* was also seen as serving one of the secondary **ends of marriage**, namely as a "remedy" for **concupiscence**. **Thomas Aquinas** speaks of marriage as involving "a contract whereby one is bound to pay the other the marital debt: wherefore just as in other contracts, the bond is unfitting if a person bind himself to what he cannot give or do, so the marriage contract is unfitting, if it be made by one who cannot pay the marital debt" (*ST III-Supplement* Q. 58, art. 1, *Rispondeo*). This teaching furnishes a good deal of the theological grounding for the **canon law** diriment **impediment** to marriage based on the inability to physically complete the marital act, e.g., due to impotence (see *CIC* #1084 §3).

Decalogue (δέκα λόγοι, *déka lógoi*, "ten words" in the Greek Septuagint translation of the Hebrew מירבדה תרשע (*aseret ha-dvarîm*, "the ten items") is the preferred translation over "Ten Commandments" as it stresses better how the Israelites viewed this divine revelation (see Ex. 20:1–17 and Dt. 5:6–21), that is, as a positive gift given them by **God** that indicated how they could be God's chosen people of the **covenant** living holy as God is holy. Of course, the Decalogue also is a set of commandments that must be observed to follow God's divine plan and thereby flourish (see Dt. 30:15–20). Various divisions of the ten words are used though **Augustine**'s division of the two tablets received by Moses and are still customary in the Latin rite, namely those that deal with right relation with God (commandments 1–3) and those that deal with human society (commandments 4–10). For the *Catechism of the Catholic Church*'s teaching on the nature of the Decalogue, see *CCC* #2052–73.

Deductive and inductive are two basic but different approaches to reasoning that have important bearing on the interpretation of **moral norms** and their concrete applications. Deductive reasoning begins by articulating a **moral principle** in the abstract and then seeks to apply it to a concrete situation, whereas inductive reasoning moves in the opposite direction, starting with looking at all of the morally relevant features in a concrete situation and then looking to **discern** the relevant moral principle to apply to the situation at hand. The deductive approach is often linked with **physicalism** as well as the **classicist view** of a static world in which the norms likewise would be both absolute and unchanging, somewhat like the Pythagorean theorem in Euclidian geometry, which postulates that in any right triangle the square of the hypotenuse is equal to the sum of the square of the other two shorter legs. Deductive reasoning works best in formulating abstract propositions that by definition would be considered eternal, universal, immutable, and unchanging. Inductive reasoning is more in line with **personalism** and the **historical worldview**, which focuses on the particularity of individuals and their **circumstances** that to some extent will necessarily be unique and subject to what **Thomas Aquinas** termed **contingency and fallibility** (see *ST I-II* Q. 94, art. 4). The **inductive approach** emphasizes discovery of norms and values by the individual, recognizing that these will also be culturally or historically conditioned and, therefore, except in rather general abstract formulations, difficult to set out as detailed moral norms, binding for all times and in all times, places, and circumstances. Many of the debates and disagreements of concrete moral issues can be traced to a tension between these two reasoning paradigms because often one side reasons deductively while the other side proceeds inductively, and neither comes to the same conclusion.

Defamation. See **calumny and defamation**

Defense. See **just war theory**

De fide definita ("concerning a defined article of the faith") is the technical designation for a doctrine that has been formally defined by the Church's **magisterium** and that must be believed or held (see *credenda and tenenda*) by the faithful. Such a doctrine is therefore not open to denial, further speculation, or revision. The articles of the Nicene Creed, the two Marian dogmas on the immaculate conception and the assumption, and the doctrine of papal **infallibility** defined by **Vatican I**'s 1870 *Pastor aeternus* would all be examples of *de fide definita* doctrines given in the extraordinary magisterium. To date, no concrete moral teaching has been so defined, although **John Paul II**'s 1995 *Evangelium vitae* did employ a new formula that resembles *de fide definita*, though without using the precise terminology (see *EV* #57: "Therefore, by the authority which Christ conferred upon Peter and his Successors, and in communion with the Bishops of the Catholic Church, *I confirm that the direct and voluntary killing of an innocent human being is always gravely immoral.*" See also *EV* #62 for a similar pronouncement on **abortion**).

De fide vel moribus (concerning faith or mores/morals). See **mores versus morals distinction**

Dei Verbum (*Word of God*) is **Vatican II**'s 1965 "Dogmatic Constitution on Divine Revelation." Although never solemnly defined before the Council, **Tradition** as articulated by the **magisterium** was commonly held to constitute a separate source of revelation distinct from sacred scripture but still part of the **deposit of faith**. While the canon of the Bible was closed at the end of the apostolic age, if Tradition were accepted as an independent source of ongoing revelation transmitted and interpreted by the magisterium, this would add considerable **authority** to magisterial teaching and pronouncements. Vatican II, however, declared that while Scripture and Tradition were both to be venerated (see *DV* #9), Scripture alone ultimately functioned as the *norma normans non normata* (the norming norm not itself normed by something else) and stood over even the magisterium, whose "teaching office is not above the word of God, but serves it, teaching only what has been handed on, listening to it devoutly, guarding it scrupulously and explaining it faithfully in accord with a divine commission and with the help of the Holy Spirit" (*DV* #10). While clearly not adopting a Protestant *sola scriptura* (scripture alone) approach, this constitution and the other documents of Vatican II, such as the "Decree on Seminary Training," *Optatam totius*, put great emphasis on scripture, proclaiming it to be the soul of all theology, and calling upon moral theology explicitly to be more nourished by scripture (*OT* #16). This in turn demands a proper **exegesis** and **hermeneutics** of the Bible not only for **biblical ethics** but indeed for the whole of the discipline of moral theology.

Delectatio morosa (morbid delight) refers to entertaining bad or impure thoughts—often of a sexual nature. The **manualist tradition** held that a prolonged dwelling on such thoughts could lead one to commit the sins that were being imagined, as well as these thoughts being sinful in themselves. The expression also is used when someone takes a perverse delight in the misfortunes of an enemy, which is a **sin** against **charity** that could lead to **detraction**. See also *parvitas materiae in Sexto*.

Delict. See **crimes and delicts**, **canon law**, and **canonical penalties**

Denzinger. See *Enchiridion symbolorum definitionum et declarationum de rebus fidei et morum* (*Handbook of Creeds and Definitions*)

Deontology (Greek δεον, [deon] "duty") is the moral theory contrasted with **teleology** by C. D. Broad in his *Five Types of Ethical Theory* (New York: Harcourt Brace, 1930). Deontological **moral norms**, sometimes termed an "ethics of duty," call us to fulfill those moral tasks, responsibilities, and obligations that are proper to our particular nature. These moral norms also establish parameters of what must not be done (prohibitions and proscriptions) as well as **prescriptions** of what must be done. The latter are given as moral duties or responsibilities and often indicate at least a certain basic minimum set of expectations of what we must achieve in our moral life. The ethical approach of **Immanuel Kant** is largely deontological.

Deposit of faith (Latin, *depositum fidei*) refers to the corpus of divine revelation of sacred scripture and **Tradition** given through Christ and entrusted to the Church, which is to safeguard it from error (e.g., heresy) and to interpret and proclaim it faithfully to all peoples for their salvation (see *DV* #10). While this deposit of faith is given to all believers, and here the theologians have a particular role to play (see *GS* #62), it is the special *munus* of the **magisterium** to preserve and proclaim authoritatively this revelation and especially in reference to the discipline of moral theology to exercise this ministry in matters of **faith and morals** (*de fide vel moribus*). See also *de fide definita* and *Denzinger*.

Desuetude, meaning "disuse," is used primarily in **canon law** to denote laws and customs that have fallen in broad and sustained lack of observance and so lose their binding force. The expression can also be used in the development of doctrine to denote theological propositions that may once have been held but that are no longer so regarded, such as the teaching on limbo, **interest-taking (usury)**, or the condemnation of **religious liberty**. See also *Dignitatis humanae, Mirari vos, Quanta cura*, and *Syllabus of Errors*.

Determinism is a moral theory that either denies the existence of **free will** or holds it to be severely limited such that humans really do not possess true **freedom** in their moral choices and actions, which instead are largely dependent upon preexisting **circumstances**. While there is a range of views among proponents of this theory, the theory itself is incompatible with the Catholic understanding of the **natural law** and **moral acts and agency**.

Detraction is a violation of **charity** that harms the reputation of another person by disclosing harmful information without a valid reason—even if that information may be true (see *CCC* #2477–79). The *Code of Canon Law* (*CIC* #220) underscores that "no one is permitted to harm illegitimately the good reputation which a person possesses nor to injure the right of any person to protect his or her own privacy." This would also include demonizing someone's political views unless it was clear that the political party or organization would be absolutely inimical to the Christian faith (such as the Nazis or Ku Klux Klan). Often detraction can be caused by **rash judgment** and is also coupled with taking sinful delight in the misfortunes of another, a form of *delectatio morosa*. Since the information communicated through detraction may objectively be true, it is distinguished from **calumny** and **slander** although the terms and the corresponding moral offenses are closely related.

Deus impossibilia non iubet (**God** does not command things that are impossible) in the moral tradition refers primarily not to things that are a **physical impossibility** (like flying unaided) but to those things that are termed a moral impossibility. The commands of the **Decalogue**, the *lex aeterna*, and the **natural law**, while certainly difficult at times, are considered to be always both morally and physically possible since God's grace is always available to fulfill these dictates. This axiom has been used often, especially in **sexual ethics**, to counter the charge that the teaching of the Church's **magisterium** might be impossible to fulfill, for example in **Pius XI**'s 1930 *Casti connubii* #61 condemning artificial **birth control**:

> There is no possible circumstance in which husband and wife cannot, strengthened by the grace of God, fulfill faithfully their duties and preserve in wedlock their **chastity** unspotted. This truth of Christian Faith is expressed by the teaching of the **Council of Trent**. "Let no one be so rash as to assert that which the Fathers of the Council have placed under anathema, namely, that there are **precepts** of God impossible for the just to observe." God does not ask the impossible, but by His commands, instructs you to do what you are able, to pray for what you are not able that He may help you.

Irenaeus's axiom *gloria Dei vivens homo* (the glory of God is the **human person** fully alive, *Adversus Haereses*, Bk IV, ch. 20, sec. 7) may be helpful in discerning what genuinely is a command of God since that which most gives God praise and glory will be genuine human flourishing, whereas anything that claims to be a **divine command** but that also seems counterproductive to truly human flourishing should be suspect.

Development of moral doctrine. See **history and development of moral theology**

Dicastery is the technical term for a Vatican office, such as the **CDF**. Other important dicasteries whose functions deal with moral matters include the Apostolic Penitentiary for matters dealing with the **sacrament of reconciliation**, the Pontifical Councils for the Family; Economic Justice and Peace; Pastoral Care of Migrants and Refugees; and the *Cor unum* (Latin, "One heart") for Christian and Human Development. **See also** *Apostolic Signatura* and *Roman Rota*.

Dignitas personae (*Dignity of the Person*), the 2008 **CDF** "Instruction on Certain Bioethical Questions" released in *in forma communi*, confirmed and updated its earlier 1987 Instruction *Donum vitae* in light of new developments in **reproductive technologies** and embryonic ethical issues. The Instruction's basic principle holds that the "dignity of a person must be recognized in every human being from conception to natural death" and goes on to condemn or sharply critique a large variety of technologies such as newer forms of **contraception**, **in vitro fertilization**, selective embryo reduction, **PGD** (preimplantation genetic diagnosis), embryo transfers, and a range of other genetic engineering practices.

Dignitatis humanae (*Human Dignity*), **Vatican II**'s 1965 "Declaration on Religious Freedom," marked a real development of doctrine in the Church's understanding of the inviolable rights of all people to worship as their own **conscience** dictated. This "right to religious freedom has its foundation in the very dignity of the **human person** as this dignity is known through the revealed word of God and by reason itself. This right of the human person to religious freedom is to be recognized in the constitutional law whereby society is governed and thus it is to become a civil right" (*DH* #2). For centuries the Church had taught that "error has no rights," and since Catholicism was the only "true" religion, this would mean that it should be the only religion allowed in any rightly constituted state, although Catholics could practice **tolerance** if they lacked the political power necessary to outlaw other religions.

Gregory XVI's 1832 **encyclical** *Mirari vos* denounced the idea of legally protected religious liberty as "insanity," and this condemnation was reiterated by
Pius IX in his 1864 *Quanta cura* and the accompanying *Syllabus of Errors*.
Because of this long-standing and highly authoritative teaching of the **magisterium**, the proposed conciliar revision of this teaching was hotly debated.
John Courtney Murray, SJ, helped draft the final document, which eventually passed by a substantial margin of 2,308 to 70. *Dignitatis humanae*, along
with Vatican II's *Gaudium et spes* #16, provide the key texts on the sacred
inviolability of conscience, even an **erroneous conscience**, and this teaching
is repeated in the *Catechism of the Catholic Church* (see #1776, 1790).

Dignity (human). See **Human person, dignity, and rights**

Direct and indirect as used in moral theology primarily concern the relationship of the **intention** (*finis operantis*) to the choice and execution of the
action *in se* or **moral object** (*finis operis*) of the action. While this distinction can be employed in a range of moral concepts, such as "direct" versus
"indirect" **scandal**, the principle is most widely used in medical ethics. For
example, Catholic moral teaching holds that a **direct abortion** is an **intrinsic
evil** that may never be legitimately performed even in light of **circumstances**
and further intentions (e.g., to reduce the psychological or financial burden of
the mother). However, an indirect abortion would be allowed, as in the case of
an **ectopic pregnancy**, removal of a cancerous uterus, and so on. Employing
the principle of the **double effect**, what makes such a medical intervention
morally licit is not that the fetus inadvertently got in the way of an otherwise
licit surgery, but that the reason for the surgery itself is to resolve some medical issue and thus is not directed to terminate otherwise viable fetal life. Even
though it is clearly foreseen that the fetus will die as a result of this procedure,
this is an indirect abortion that is allowable due to **proportionate reason**.
While the ectopic pregnancy and cancerous uterus examples are settled cases
in moral **casuistry**, other more complex cases have arisen around which there
is significant disagreement, as in the situation when it is medically impossible
to save both the mother and fetus but is possible to save the mother if the pregnancy is terminated. Some argue that this is morally impermissible and that
both the mother and fetus must be left to die since the intervention constitutes
a direct abortion, whereas others argue that in this sort of case the procedure to
save the life of the mother would be an indirect abortion that was undertaken
to save the only life that could be saved.

Discernment in theology searches for the Holy Spirit as a guide to **wisdom** and **prudence** in the judgments made in our concrete lives. St. Ignatius

of Loyola formulated two sets of "Rules for the Discernment of Spirits" in his *Spiritual Exercises* (*SpirEx.* #313–27) to help in distinguishing the promptings of the Evil Spirit from those of **God**, since often the Evil Spirit can masquerade as an angel of light. Following the entire path of the suggested thought or course of action helps discern whether the end is truly good or not. Contemporary ethicians such as **James Gustafson** and William Spohn hold that before moving to the question of what we ought to do, it is important to consider how we discern, and how we develop Christian **character** that can better support the ongoing practice of discernment. *For further reading*, see Richard Gula, *Moral Discernment* (New York: Paulist Press, 1997); James Gustafson, "Moral Discernment in the Christian Life," in *Norm and Context in Christian Ethics*, edited by Gene H. Outka and Paul Ramsey (London: SCM Press, 1968), 17–36; also published as ch. 5 in Gustafson's *Theology and Christian Ethics* (Philadelphia: Pilgrim Press, 1974); William C. Spohn, "The Reasoning Heart: An American Approach to Christian Discernment," *Theological Studies* 44 (1983): 30–52; also published in *The Reasoning Heart*, edited by Frank M. Oppenheim (Washington, DC: Georgetown University Press, 1986), 51–72.

"**Disordered**" expresses an action, desire, or **inclination** to something or someone that is contrary to a proper orientation of the will. This term, used with increasing frequency by the **magisterium**, denotes something intrinsically contrary to human flourishing (i.e., *contra naturam*) or something that is disproportionate to a choice founded in **right reason**. For example, bestiality would always be *contra naturam* to a proper human sexual expression, whereas excessive **mortification** could be disordered to the legitimate spiritual practices of **penance** and **asceticism** even though penitential acts of themselves can be quite legitimate under the proper circumstances.

A **dispensation** is an exemption given by a legitimate authority to a law or rule that still remains both valid and in force. **Canon law** makes provision for a wide number of dispensations (e.g., from fast and **abstinence** regulations, certain rules governing the celebration of **marriage**, the obligation to recite the Divine Office, and the like). *Epikeia* also makes provision for a self-granting of dispensation based on either interpreting the mind of the legislator or the imperfection or impossibility of the law in a particular instance.

Dissent is a relatively recent, somewhat ambiguous term that before 1972 did not appear in theological dictionaries and encyclopedias in moral theology, so there is no real **manualist tradition** here. Many debates over the term are closely linked to contested issues such as **birth control** (especially **Paul VI's**

1968 *Humanae vitae*), **sexual ethics** (especially issues connected with **homosexuality**), **intrinsic evil**, **primacy of conscience**, and so on, in relation to the teaching **authority** of the **magisterium** and *Lumen gentium* #25's call for *obsequium religiosum*. Other issues revolve around professional roles of theologians and academic freedom for research that at times results in disciplining by the **CDF**, the **USCCB** doctrine committee, or individual bishops. **Charles Curran**'s 1986 censure by the CDF and his subsequent dismissal from his teaching position at CUA occasioned a considerable amount of publication on the possibility or impossibility of a legitimate dissent from noninfallibly defined teachings of the **ordinary magisterium**. Long-time collaborator **Richard McCormick, SJ**, summed up one commonly held view of the ecclesial ramifications of the Curran censure by the CDF:

> The first is that, to be regarded as a Catholic theologian, one may not dissent from *any* authoritatively proposed teaching. The second is that "authentic theological instruction" means presenting church teaching and never disagreeing with it, even with respect and reverence. Third, and correlatively, sound theological education means accepting, uncritically if necessary, official Catholic teaching. The impact of such assertions on the notion of a university, of Catholic higher education, of theology and of good teaching is mind-boggling. All too easily, answers replace questions and conformism replaces teaching as "theology" is reduced to [Lawrence] Kohlberg's preconventional level of reasoning (obey or be punished) (Richard A. McCormick, "L'Affaire Curran," *America* 154 [1987]: 266).

At the other end of the theological spectrum, **Germain Grisez** calls dissent "a cancer growing in the Church's organs and interfering with her vital functions which is an inevitable sickness of faith when the firm anchor of the magisterium is discarded and the faithful are cast adrift on the heaving sea of dissent" (Grisez, "How to Deal with Theological Dissent," *Homiletic and Pastoral Review* 87, no. 2 [November 1986]: 23, 29). Still others argue that the "faithful have a right to that 'other information' [i.e., 'serious dissent by competent theologians from the authentic teaching of the Roman magisterium on moral issues'] for the formation of their consciences. To deny that right is objectively immoral" (Philip S. Kaufmann, "Probabilism and the Right to Know of Moral Options," *Commonweal* [September 12, 1980]: 497).

Some fear that public dissent creates such **scandal** that it should never be allowed, whereas others support the position of Msgr. William B. Smith, the long-time moral columnist for *Homiletic and Pastoral Review*, who states, "If, in a given but rare instance, it happens in time that some aspect of that

authentic teaching [of the magisterium] is not completely true, it still remains here and now a true guide for action, that this is what the Holy Spirit
wants by directing, that is assisting, as a norm for action at this time," adding
that the "only way for genuine dissent in theory and practice to be legitimate
is to accept and adopt an illegitimate ecclesiology which not only changes
but also contradicts the teachings of Vatican II about the nature of sacred
and certain Catholic teaching and the very nature of the Church (*LG* 25;
DV 7–10)" (Smith, "The Question of Dissent in Moral Theology," in *Persona Verità e Morale: Atti del Congresso Internazionale di Teologia Morale
[Roma, 7–12 aprile 1986]* [Rome: Città Nuova Editrice, 1987]: 252–53).

Some hierarchs take a more nuanced view, such as former **NCCB** president Archbishop Daniel Pilarczyk, who noted that the specific role of the
theologians "calls them to explore the implications of Church teaching, to
investigate it, to refine it, to probe it, to push back its horizons. If not all
Church teaching is guaranteed to be infallible, then some of it could be fal-
lible, reformable, conceivably even incorrect. It is part of the theologian's
responsibility to speak to Church teaching which he or she conscientiously
believes to be inexact or erroneous" ("Cincinnati Archdiocese Pastoral Letter
on Dissent," *Origins* 16, no. 9 [July 31, 1986]: 177). Others such as **Cardinal Avery Dulles** give as an example of legitimate dissent the current teaching on **capital punishment**, saying that while personally he supported this
position, Catholics were not bound in conscience to agree with it, but they
should be "attentive to the guidance of the pope and the bishops" (Dulles,
"Authority and Conscience," in *Readings in Moral Theology, No. 6: Dissent in the Church*, edited by Charles E. Curran and Richard A. McCormick
[New York: Paulist Press, 1988], 97–111). Another issue raised by Archbishop (later Cardinal) Roger Mahoney is that "theologians in university
situations are likely to be overinfluenced by the reigning ethos of academic
freedom. It therefore becomes more necessary than ever for the Church to
have firm authority structures so as to preserve its rich and ancient heritage
and to address new problems in the light of Christ" ("The Magisterium and
Theological Dissent," *Origins* 16, no. 21 [November 6, 1986]: 375). This
concern has been taken up by the CDF in its 1990 "Instruction on the Ecclesial Vocation of the Theologian," ***Donum veritatis***.

Finally, the word "dissent" itself has a range of meanings that could extend from "lack of understanding" to "outright rebellion." As one commentator suggests, the term itself is the wrong concept to use in referring to
contemporary, well-educated, adult Catholics in their attempts to dialogue
and agree or disagree with magisterial teaching: "Adults don't 'dissent'; they
discuss and deliberate and converse and dialogue. Yes, and argue. Sometimes
they come to agreement and arrive at a common position; sometimes they

are unable to." The commentator cites the New Testament example of Paul and Barnabas in this regard. On the other hand, the term "dissent" seems to hold a *Roma locuta causa finita*, case-closed position, which "may be the very point the adult participant finds unconvincing. In church usage the concept of dissent brings with it a note of moral failure. Those who dissent are viewed, not simply as disagreeing with the orthodox position, not even as being objectively wrong. They are viewed as being morally deficient, having a sort of virus that must be either controlled or perhaps even eradicated lest it contaminate others" (George B. Wilson, "'Dissent' or Conversation among Adults?" *America* 180 [March 13, 1999]: 9).

Dissolution. See **annulment and dissolution**

Distributive justice holds that the material goods of the world are held in trust for all members of society and thus should be distributed to each primarily according to need as far as possible (see *ST II-II*, Q 61, art. 2). Distributive justice can also be extended to political participation, **human rights**, and a sharing of burdens and risks associated with living in society, including military **defense**, health care therapies, drug experimentation, and the like. In Catholic **social teaching**, distributive justice is expressive of the **common good**, and its claims would normally trump other **justice** claims (e.g., **private property rights** would have to be ceded to care of the genuinely needy) even if these would contravene **contract justice**.

Divine command ethics views that because **God** is the author of all morality, a proper theological ethics should stress obedience to God's commands as the truest formulation of the human ethical duty. Protestant theologian **Karl Barth** (d. 1968) was a strong proponent of this theory. Critiques of this theory note its inherent **subjectivism**, tendencies toward **Voluntarism** and **heteronomy**, and antipathy to the **natural law** and **Thomas Aquinas**'s notion of the moral law as primarily a *lex indita non scripta* expressed in the legitimate role of **conscience**'s **moral autonomy**.

Divine law is found in the **deposit of faith**, especially in the **Decalogue**. It is sometimes also termed the *lex aeterna* (eternal law), although this term distinguishes God's revelation or special mandates that are not part of the **natural law** accessible to all men and women through **reason**. **Thomas Aquinas** in his "Treatise on Law" (*ST I-II* Q. 90–97) further distinguishes divine law from the *lex aeterna*, delineating four types of law (eternal, natural, human, and divine). Thomas understands divine law as coming from biblical revelation, divided into the old law of the Old Testament **covenant** and the Gospel's new law. Understanding and acceptance of the divine law is connected with the infused theological virtues, especially faith. Some theologians such as **Karl Barth** speak of a **divine command ethics** that would likewise be grounded in divine law, although their use of this term differs from the schema of Aquinas. **See also** *biblical ethics*, *infused knowledge and infused virtues*, *faith and morals*, and *law and gospel*.

Divine sovereignty is rooted in the Judeo-Christian understanding of monotheism and expressed in the first tablet of the **Decalogue** (commandments 1–3). God's **divine law**, or *lex aeterna*, is the ground of the **natural law** and the source of the objective moral order and all that is good (see *bonum* and *Summum Bonum*). Reference to divine sovereignty has been used to condemn a range of actions from **suicide** (see *CCC* #2280–81) to **contraception** (see *HV* #13). It has also been employed more problematically in the past to condemn any number of innovations such as vaccines and trains (as was done in the pontificate of **Leo XIII**) as well as to raise serious doubts about the morality of **NFP**, all **reproductive technologies**, and a number of scientific and medical advances in **bioethics**. Since *Deus impossibilia non iubet* (God does not command the impossible), a careful theology and **discernment** must be undertaken when calling upon "Divine Sovereignty" or "God's will" for either support or condemnation of anything. **See also** *Karl Barth, heteronomy and theonomy* and *Voluntarism*.

Divino afflante Spiritu, the 1943 **encyclical** of **Pius XII**, opened the way for Catholic biblical scholars to employ the historical-critical method **exegesis** and **hermeneutics** in **biblical interpretation** that had been adopted by Protestant scholars, and thus also helped pave the way for both a Catholic and **ecumenical** approach to **biblical ethics**. **See also** *Providentissimus Deus*.

Divorce in the Catholic tradition is the juridical **dissolution** of a legitimate **marriage bond**, called either *divortium plenum* or *divortium perfectum* (meaning "complete" divorce). A sacramental marriage validly constituted (*ratum et consummatum*) can never be dissolved, although under **canon law** from the time of the twelfth century jurist Gratian a *divortium a thoro* (separation from the marriage bed, sometimes also termed *divortium imperfectum*) could be obtained when an ecclesiastical court recognizes that the couple has separated (see *CCC* #2383 and *CIC* #1151–55). This does not give them an **annulment**, nor does it leave them free to marry again so long as both parties are alive. The only divorce that the Catholic Church would recognize as allowing one or both of the parties to marry again is the dissolution of a non-Christian marriage in which one of the parties now wishes to become a Catholic and marry a Catholic—the so-called dissolution in favor of the faith (*privilege [Pauline and Petrine]*).

Doctor Angelicus, Doctor Communis, and Doctor Universalis are three common titles used for **Thomas Aquinas** (1225–74) with Doctor Angelicus (**Angelic Doctor**) employed most widely.

Domestic partners is a term that has a broad range of meanings, including legal specifications. It can refer to two adults with a special care relationship, such as a disabled sibling or an elderly parent who is "partnered" for health care or other benefits with the other adult who has financial responsibility for their maintenance. The most common usage, though, refers to adults who are not related to one another but who live in a nonmarital or **premarital sex** relationship. Depending on the law or specific contracts (such as health care coverage), these "domestic partner benefits" can apply to both types of arrangements. In the former case there would be no difficulty under Catholic moral teaching, though in the latter instance it would come under the strictures against **fornication** or **same-sex unions**.

Donum veritatis (*Gift of Truth*), the 1990 **CDF** "Instruction on the Ecclesial Vocation of the Theologian" released in *in forma communi*, gives directives to theologians on their professional *obsequium religiosum* of loyalty to the **magisterium**. In cases of genuine **doubts** about the truth or aptness of a magisterial document, the Instruction directs that theologians should report these concerns privately to the proper magisterial office, adding that **freedom** of **conscience** never condones public **dissent** (#38). Instead, theologians are exhorted to answer the "call to suffer for the truth, in silence and prayer" (#31). **See also** *charism of office* and *Roma locuta causa finita.*

Donum vitae (*Gift of Life*), the 1987 **CDF** "Instruction on Respect for Human Life in Its Origin and on the Dignity of Procreation" released in *in forma communi*, articulates the Church's opposition to a range of **reproductive technologies** such as **IVF** and even **AIH** since these practices violate the **inseparability principle**, which holds that the **procreative and unitive dimensions** of the marital act may never be physically separated even if the larger aim is to aid successful **procreation**.

Double effect principle (commonly termed "PDE") is well established in the **casuistry** from the **manualist tradition** to the present (see *CCC* #2263, *ST II-II*, Q. 74, art. 7). It is used in quandary situations in which a single composite action has at least two foreseen effects that cannot be separated:

one that is good and desired and others that are bad and are tolerated. Amputation to remove a gangrenous limb, treatment of an **ectopic pregnancy**, and **just war theory** all use the PDE. While PDE has been the subject of much debate and **development of moral doctrine** over the centuries, the opinions of most moralists hold that for such an act to be morally licit, the **action** *in se* (*finis operis*) must be good (e.g., saving a life) or indifferent; the **intention** (*finis operantis*) of the agent must be good; no **moral evil** means must be used, though **ontic evil** may be tolerated (e.g., the loss of a limb); and there must be **proportionate reason** to cause the evil effect (e.g., if nothing is done, a life will be lost). The principles of **totality, cooperation with evil, tolerance**, and the *minus malum* all share much of the moral grounding of the PDE. While **proportionalism** also employs the PDE, the two are not equivalent in all respects. *For further reading*, see Charles E. Curran and Richard A. McCormick, eds., *Readings in Moral Theology, No. 1: Moral Norms and Catholic Tradition* (New York: Paulist Press, 1979); and Richard A. McCormick, *Doing Evil to Achieve Good: Moral Choice in Conflict Situations*, edited by Richard A. McCormick and Paul Ramsey (Chicago: Loyola University Press, 1978).

Doubt. See *dubium*, **conscience (certain and doubtful)**, *lex dubia non obligat*, and **probabilism and probabiliorism**

Doubtful law. See *lex dubia non obligat*, and **probabilism and probabiliorism**

Dubium (Latin, "**doubt**" or "question for clarification"). Doubts, especially those involving a **doubtful conscience**, should be resolved if possible before acting. **See also** *lex dubia non obligat* and *Responsum ad dubium* (Response to a Question/Doubt).

Dulles, Cardinal Avery, SJ (August 24, 1918–December 12, 2008), came from a politically and socially prominent Presbyterian New York family. Dulles journeyed from agnosticism to Catholicism at the end of his undergraduate time at Harvard and entered the Jesuits in 1946. Dulles received his S.T.D. from the Pontifical Gregorian University in 1960 and embarked upon a distinguished career as a professor at Woodstock, Catholic University of America, and Fordham and as a prolific author publishing more than seven hundred articles and twenty-two books. He was elected president of both the CTSA and the American Theological Society and served on the International Theological Commission as well as several other ecclesiastical committees. Created cardinal at age eighty-two by **John Paul II** in 2001, Dulles was ineligible to participate in the 2005 papal conclave but continued writing and lecturing until the effects of the polio contracted as a youth progressively paralyzed him and rendered him mute until his death. Many of his earlier works, such as his 1971 *Survival of Dogma* and his 1974 *Models of the Church*, cast him as a progressive, whereas some of his later writing took on a more conservative stance, for example, his 2007 *Magisterium: Teacher and Guardian of the Faith*. Other works, such as his 1982 *A Church to Believe In: Discipleship and the Dynamics of Freedom*, mark a middle position. Even in his later years he continued to write about the legitimate roles of theologians as distinct from the **magisterium**, the possibility of **dissent** from noninfallibly defined teachings of the **ordinary magisterium**, and the dangers of **infallibilism**. *For further reading* in addition to Dulles's works, see Patrick W. Carey, *Avery Cardinal Dulles, SJ: A Model Theologian, 1918–2008* (New York: Paulist Press, 2010).

Duties (conflict of). See **conflict of duties/conflict of interests**

Duties (negative and positive) may be certain duties (either **proscriptions** or **prescriptions**) that bind always and in every instance (*semper et pro semper*) or those that are generally binding but that have legitimate exceptions (*semper sed non pro semper*). Negative duties are prohibitions that always must be respected, such as "thou shalt not murder," whereas positive duties are prescriptions, such as "pray always," that need not be fulfilled in each and every instance if another legitimate duty would take precedence, such as attending to one's employment (**conflict of duties** principle). This concept is key in understanding *Humanae vitae* #16's allowance for **NFP**, which interprets the prescription of "be fruitful and multiply" as a positive duty allowing for legitimate exceptions, whereas other artificial means of **birth control** are seen as violations of a negative duty that could never be legitimately tolerated (see *HV* #14).

Dystopia (Greek for "hard place"), the opposite of **utopia**, denotes a political state that is repressive and totalitarian, such as depicted in George Orwell's *1984*, that does not respect individual **human rights**, or that pays insufficient attention to the **common good**.

E

Easter duty, mandated by the Fourth Lateran Council in 1215, is one of the 6 precepts of the Church enjoining all Catholics who had made their First Communion to receive Communion at least once during the Easter season. Ideally, the sacrament of reconciliation should precede the reception of Communion, although this would only be required if an individual was in the state of mortal sin. Fulfillment of the Easter duty can be done any time in Lent through Trinity Sunday, the first Sunday after Pentecost.

Ecclesia discens and *ecclesia docens* are the Latin terms for the "learning" (*discens*) and the "teaching" (*docens*) aspects of the Church (*ecclesia*). After the Council of Trent it was customary to identify the *ecclesia docens* solely with the magisterium and to a lesser extent with the clergy, and the *ecclesia discens* with the laity, whose principal role was to accept and apply the teaching handed down by the hierarchy with a reverential *obsequium religiosum*. Cardinal Avery Dulles observes that this sharp division led to the notion of *sensus fidelium* ceasing "to function as a distinct theological source" (Dulles, *A Church to Believe In: Discipleship and the Dynamics of Freedom* [New York: Crossroad, 1982], 112). Since Vatican II there has been greater awareness of the epistemological reality that in order to teach, one must first learn (even if gifted with the special assistance of the Holy Spirit through the charism of office). Building on Paul's understanding of the many gifts given by the Spirit for the good of the whole community (see 1 Cor. 12:3–31; Rm. 12:6–8), there is a greater awareness today that all Christians share in both functions of teaching and learning, and many laypeople assist the teaching office through consultations, membership on ecclesial commissions (including in the Vatican), and so on, although it remains the magisterium's special *munus* to teach authoritatively, especially in matters of faith and morals. See also *ultramontanism*.

Ecclesia semper reformanda (the Church is always being reformed) is a traditional theological maxim also employed by Luther that underscores the reality of the need for continual reform and conversion of the whole

Church (visible head and members), acknowledging that throughout history the Church has never fully satisfied the mission entrusted to it by Christ. Since the Church is sinful due to all of its human members, institutional weaknesses also inevitably arise, so this maxim can be a helpful corrective to the tendency to overlook or minimize the institutional faults or to overexaggerate the wisdom and holiness of the Church, especially its leaders. **See also** *history and development of moral doctrine, infallibilism,* and *ultramontanism.*

Ecology and environmental ethics is a discipline and moral issue that has mushroomed in importance in the last several decades, and is raised as a special concern in **feminist ethics, liberation theology,** and increasingly in the **social encyclicals and social teaching** of the **magisterium,** for example, as highlighted by **Benedict XVI** in his 2009 **encyclical** *Caritas in veritate*: "The environment is God's gift to everyone, and in our use of it we have a responsibility towards the poor, towards future generations and towards humanity as a whole" (*CV* #48, see especially 48–52, and #27, 67, 69). The theology of **creation,** globalism, climate change, sustainability, population growth, ethical treatment of animals, protection of species and natural resources, public policy, and developing technologies are just a few of the interconnected ethical issues in this broad field.

Economic Justice for All is the 1986 **pastoral letter** of the **NCCB** drafted under the chairmanship of Milwaukee archbishop Rembert Weakland, OSB, on the United States economy. The letter gives biblical and theological foundations as well as an outline of concrete policy positions in light of Catholic **social teaching,** which was seen by some as an implied critique of unrestrained laissez-faire free-market **capitalism** and the policies of the Reagan administration (1981–89). John Donahue, SJ, was the primary biblical consultant, and David Hollenbach, SJ, was the leading social ethician who collaborated in the drafting of the document.

Ectopic pregnancy, or tubal pregnancy, is a life-threatening medical condition in which the embryo implants not in the uterus but in the fallopian tube. This case has been the locus of considerable **casuistry** and **development of moral doctrine** over the years. Concern that the removal of the ectopic fetus not constitute an **intrinsically evil** act of **direct abortion** led to a **rigorist** opinion of "better two deaths than one murder," so nothing should be done that risked the fetus's death. Others argued that the lodging of the fetus in the fallopian tube rather than the uterine cavity constituted a form of unlawful entry that allowed removal under the self-defense principle of the **double**

effect. Still others suggested that the pathological condition should be left to deteriorate into cancer, and then under the **totality principle** the entire fallopian tubes could then be removed to treat this pathology, with the resulting fetal death an **indirect abortion**. The moral debate has subsided since for many years a full or partial salpingectomy (removal of the fallopian tube) was the only available medical procedure. At present there is no treatment option that can save the life of both the mother and the fetus, and regardless of which option is chosen, the fetus has no statistical chance of surviving. Thus choosing a treatment option does not weigh the life of mother over that of the fetus, but more simply saves the only life that can be saved.

Recent biomedical advances now make a less-invasive procedure possible to resolve this life-threatening danger and include the possibility of saving the fallopian tubes for possible future pregnancies. One of these is a form of laparoscopic surgery (salpingostomy or laparotomy), which, from a physical (and not moral) perspective, "directly" removes the ectopic fetus through an incision in the wall of the fallopian tube, which is then cauterized, maintaining the future functional integrity of the tube. This is considered minor surgery, and the recovery time is much less than with the total removal of the fallopian tube (salpingectomy). Another approach that avoids surgery altogether is pharmaceutical, using a drug such as methotrexate, which stops the embryonic cell growth, though like any drug there are some negative side effects that must be considered. These newer treatment options have reopened the moral debate on whether these constitute a direct or an indirect abortion. The majority of moral theologians accept these new treatment options, including some who initially rejected one or the other therapy. Others vehemently oppose this view as a form of **proportionalism** condemned by *Veritatis splendor* (although the **encyclical** does not address this issue), and to date there is no intervention from the **magisterium**. Thus, this is a *quaestio disputata* in which the principle of **probabilism** applies and the less-invasive methods may be advised and chosen in **good faith**. *For further reading*, see Benedict M. Ashley, Jean K. deBlois, and Kevin D. O'Rourke, *Health Care Ethics: A Catholic Theological Analysis*, 5th ed. (Washington, DC: Georgetown University Press, 2006); see p. 82 in which the authors explicitly hold that new treatments are morally licit in accord with *ERD* #48, (the book also has an imprimatur from the Archdiocese of Chicago); and Martin Rhonheimer, *Vital Conflicts in Medical Ethics: A Virtue Approach to Craniotomy and Tubal Pregnancies* (Washington, DC: Catholic University Press of America, 2009).

Ecumenism and ecumenical ethics coming from the legacy of **Vatican II** marks a significant **development of moral theology and doctrine** moving away from the Reformation/counter-Reformation mutual polemical antagonism, distrust, and misunderstanding. *Gaudium et spes* evidences greater awareness of the presence of the Holy Spirit beyond the Catholic Church, *Dignitatis humanae* pronounced religious freedom as a fundamental **human right** of **conscience**, *Optatam totius* called for privileging Scripture in theology, and the "Decree on Ecumenism," *Unitatis redintegratio*, explicitly mandated ecumenical dialogue and collaboration that is seen in relations between the Vatican and the **World Council of Churches**. Professional organizations once largely Protestant or Catholic, such as the SCE and the CTSA, now welcome each other as members, and individual theologians likewise have done much to build bridges, such as Protestant **James Gustafson**, who mentored key Catholic moralists such as **Lisa Sowle Cahill** and William Spohn and collaborated with **Richard McCormick, SJ**, and Catholic institutions such as Notre Dame, which welcomed as faculty **Stanley Hauerwas** and **John Howard Yoder**. *For further reading*, see James T. Bretzke, "Ecumenical Ethics in the Historical Context of Vatican II Moral Theology," *Josephinum Journal of Theology* 6 (Summer/Fall 1999): 18–38; and James M. Gustafson, *Protestant and Roman Catholic Ethics: Prospects for Rapprochement* (Chicago: University of Chicago Press, 1978).

Eisegesis means reading into a text preconceived ideas or positions that the text itself would not support. It is the opposite of **exegesis** that is the legitimate approach to discover a text's true meaning, and that is important in any **hermeneutics**, especially in **biblical ethics**.

Emergency contraception. See **contraception**

Emotivism maintains that the moral judgments about "**rightness**" and "wrongness" are not based on an objective moral order but simply express the holder's own personal attitudes toward an ethical proposition. Thus, to say "genocide is morally wrong" is really just another way of stating "I find genocide to be repugnant and I want you to abhor it as well." Emotivism is incompatible with the foundational premises of a **natural law** theory, which holds there is an objective moral order that can be known and applied to all human beings, and thus is quite at odds with the Roman Catholic moral tradition. **See also** *positivism*.

Enchiridion symbolorum definitionum et declarationum de rebus fidei et morum is a compendium or handbook (*enchiridion* in Greek) of the major doctrinal and moral texts of the Catholic Church, originally commissioned by **Pius IX** in 1854 and updated frequently since. Sometimes also termed *Denzinger-Schönmetzer* for its popular German–Latin edition (abbreviated *DS*), an English version is the *Neuner-Dupuis* (abbreviated *ND*), named after its translators Josef Neuner, SJ, and Jacques Dupuis, SJ. **See also** *de fide definita*, *de fide vel moribus*, and *orthodoxy*.

Enculturation (or **socialization**) is the process by which an individual as a young child becomes an integrated member of a particular culture, integrating its belief systems, customs, mores, and ethos. In theological usage enculturation is sometimes mistakenly used to refer to **inculturation**, which properly refers to the process by which the Gospel takes authentic root in a particular culture. **See also** *acculturation and enculturation*, and *culture and inculturation*.

Encyclical (Latin, *encyclicus*, from Greek ἐν κύκλῳ, en kykloi, "encircling") denotes a circular letter sent by bishops in the early Church, but since the early nineteenth century the term refers to one of the highest forms of (usually noninfallible) papal **ordinary magisterium** for teachings addressed either to all bishops, all Catholics, or in some instances (such as **John XXIII**'s *Pacem in terris*), to all peoples.

The **end (never) justifies the means** is used variously in moral reasoning, and depending on this usage the principle is either morally licit or illicit. **Consequentialism** and **utilitarianism** hold that the end of an action alone justifies virtually any means used to reach that end. If surrendering an innocent man would effectively stem a violent mob bent on large-scale mayhem and save scores of lives, then these two theories would seem to allow the man's sacrifice as a regrettable "means" to the larger positive "end." However, the Catholic position views sacrificing an innocent person as the **intrinsic evil** of murder. Treating a **human person** merely and only as a "means" violates that individual's basic **human dignity** as a creature of **God** made in God's own image (*imago Dei*). While a person who is a teacher is certainly employed as a means toward education, she still retains a basic dignity and worth that would not be ascribed to another means to education such as a library book. In **Thomas Aquinas**'s **teleology**, the distinction and interrelation between what counts as an "end" and what constitutes a "means" is paramount. In this **teleological** view the choice of means is discerned in terms of the act itself (*finis operis*), the **intention** (*finis operantis*), and the fittingness and **proportionate reason** in view of the **circumstances**. Following the principle of the **double effect**, major surgery involving a large incision is morally acceptable if it is part of the means to remove a cancerous tumor, but the exact same incision would be immoral self-mutilation if it were used as a means for a different end, such as performance art (lack of proportionate reason) or **torture** (intrinsic evil). In this set of cases, therefore, it is very clearly the proper end that justifies (or does not justify) the means chosen. If the "end" does not justify the "means" here, then what else possibly could?

End of the act. See *finis operis and finis operantis*

Ends of marriage (*bonum prolix, bonum fidei, bonum sacramenti*). See **marriage**

Ensoulment is the moment in the conception and gestation process when **God** infuses an immortal soul into the new human being. This soul is absolutely precious and unique and is the core feature in the theological **anthropology** of humans as the *imago Dei* (image of God) and the primary reason Catholic moral teaching states that **abortion** is morally wrong, since all fetal life should be treated as being sacred even from the "moment of conception" (see *GS* #51). It is the soul that gives humans their primary dignity and worth rather than simply being a higher order sentient being. It cannot be determined with physical certainty exactly when ensoulment occurs. **Aristotle** and **Thomas Aquinas** believed it occurred at the so-called quickening in the uterus, that is, at about forty days for male embryos or ninety days for female embryos. **John Paul II** acknowledges "the presence of a spiritual soul cannot be ascertained by empirical data" (*EV* #60). Contemporary **bioethics** suggests that while the "earliest" moment might be once the conceptus has been formed from the union of the sperm and the egg (several hours after coitus), since the developing embryo can still split and recombine (twinning) until the development of the primitive streak around fourteen days, many theologians surmise this might be a more realistic earliest moment for potential ensoulment. Still others point to the fact that between 25 percent and 75 percent of fertilized ova and developing embryos are never successfully implanted in the uterine wall and therefore conclude that perhaps successful implantation might be a better marker. Because there is absolutely no way of proving or deciding this issue medically, the position of the **magisterium** continues to be to proceed as if the embryo were already ensouled at the moment of conception. *For further reading*, see Richard A. McCormick, "Who or What Is the Preembryo?" ch. 14 in *Corrective Vision: Explorations in Moral Theology* (Kansas City, MO: Sheed and Ward, 1994), 176–88; Josef Fuchs, "'Soul' and 'Ensoulment' in the Individual Coming into Being of the Human Person," ch. 5 in *Moral Demands and Personal Obligations* (Washington, DC: Georgetown University Press, 1993), 74–87. See also the *quaes-*

tio disputata series of articles by Mark Johnson, Jean Porter, and Thomas Shannon on "delayed hominization" in *Theological Studies* 56 (December 1995): 743–70; 57 (1996): 731–34; and 58 (1997): 708–17.

Envy. See **capital sins**

Epikeia comes from the Greek (επικεια) for "fitting or fair interpretation" of a law referenced in **Aristotle**'s *Nicomachean Ethics* (5.10) to correct a defective law in terms of universal legal justice, such as the **impossibility** or inhumanity of the law, or if the mind of the legislator could reasonably be interpreted such that the **dispensation** or modification in question would likely be granted. Exceeding the posted speed limit on a deserted highway in order to bring a medical emergency more quickly to the hospital would be a judgment of *epikeia*. **Francisco Suárez** interpreted the use of *epikeia* narrowly, seeing it as a dispensation from law under limited conditions. **Thomas Aquinas** considered *epikeia* a **virtue** exercised by **practical reason** that aimed at the perfection of law and thus, like all good virtues, should be practiced so that a proper **habit** would result (see *ST II-II*, Q. 120). While *epikeia* was usually limited to human **positive law**, there also is a debate dating back to the Middle Ages whether *epikeia* could also be applied to the **natural law**, given that historicity and change are foundational aspects of human **nature**. See also *impossibility (physical versus moral), laxism, legalism, positive law, probabilism and probabiliorism, rigorism, tutiorism,* and *Voluntarism. For further reading,* see Josef Fuchs, "Epikeia Applied to Natural Law?" ch. 10 in *Personal Responsibility and Christian Morality* (Washington, DC: Georgetown University Press, 1983), 185–99.

Equiprobabilism. See **probabilism and probabiliorism**

Eros. See **agape, eros, and** *philia*, and **love**

Erroneous conscience. See **conscience (erroneous)**

Error. See **ignorance**

Eternal law. See *lex aeterna*

Ethical and Religious Directives for Catholic Health Care Institutions (*ERD*), promulgated by the **USCCB**, gives the **moral norms** and principles that should govern Catholic hospitals and other health care institutions. The 2009 fifth edition is available on the USCCB website, www.usccb.org.

Ethical naturalism. See **naturalistic fallacy**

Euthanasia, whether active or passive, is always a morally illicit means to deal with pain and **suffering**. Active euthanasia is doing something (commission) whose **direct** object is the termination of life (e.g., by administering a lethal dose of a pain killer). Passive euthanasia is the omission or withholding of some drug or therapy with a view toward ending life. Care should be taken, though, not to confuse legitimate termination of **extraordinary means** with passive euthanasia. As the **CDF** in its 1980 *Iura et bona*, the *Catechism of the Catholic Church* (see #2277–78), and **John Paul II** have all noted, when "medical procedures which no longer correspond to the real situation of the patient, either because they are by now disproportionate to any expected results or because they impose an excessive **burden** on the patient and his family" and "when death is clearly imminent and inevitable, one can in conscience 'refuse forms of treatment that would only secure a precarious and burdensome prolongation of life, so long as the normal care due to the sick person in similar cases is not interrupted.'" In such cases, forgoing or terminating "extraordinary or disproportionate means is not the equivalent of **suicide** or euthanasia; it rather expresses acceptance of the human condition in the face of death" (*EV* #65). See also *ANH*, *death with dignity*, and *vitalism*. *For further reading*, see Richard M. Gula, *Euthanasia: Moral and Pastoral Perspectives* (New York: Paulist Press, 1995).

Evangelical counsels are poverty, **chastity**, and obedience, which form the vows common to religious life. See also *supererogation* and *vocation*.

Evangelii nuntiandi, **Paul VI**'s 1975 postsynodal apostolic exhortation on evangelization, called for inculturation by evangelizing **culture** "not in a purely decorative way, as it were, by applying a thin veneer, but in a vital way, in depth and right to their very roots" (*EN* #20). This in turn presents a "task of assimilating the essence of the Gospel message and of transposing it, without the slightest betrayal of its essential truth, into the language that these particular people understand, then of proclaiming it in this language" (*EN* #63). In moral theology this calls for deep **discernment** to distinguish what are truly **universal moral norms** of the **natural law** from culturally grounded mores or customs that are subject to **contingency and fallibility** (see *ST I-II*, Q. 94, art. 4). **See also** *acculturation and enculturation*, and *culture and inculturation*.

Evangelium vitae, **John Paul II**'s 1995 **encyclical** "The Gospel of Life," uses the dichotomy of "**culture of life**" versus "**culture of death**" to address as major threats to human life **abortion**, **euthanasia**, and **capital punishment**. In this last area, capital punishment, *EV* modifies traditional Catholic teaching that, rather than an exercise of **retributive justice**, the only legitimate use of the **death penalty** would be to protect society, and concludes that since other means to defend society short of imposing capital punishment now exist, then the morally legitimate contemporary usage of capital punishment would be virtually nonexistent (see *EV* #56). Following this encyclical, the ***Catechism of the Catholic Church*** revised its relevant section to reflect this more stringent position (see *CCC* #2267). **See also** *history and development of moral theology and doctrine.*

Evil (*malum/mala*, in Latin) is classed in the **manualist tradition** either as a *malum morale* or as a *malum physicum* ("moral evil" or "physical evil"). Moral evil violates God's ***lex aeterna*** and the **natural law** which is our human participation in God's eternal law. When done with **sufficient knowledge and consent**, moral evil constitutes **sin** for which the individual has **culpability**. While sin "offends" God, it is moral evil's harmful effects on us and others that "offend" God, just as children who hurt themselves or others can be said to "offend" the parents who love their children and always want what is best for them. **Intrinsic evil** is considered a ***malum in se***, that is, something whose evil did not depend primarily on mitigating **circumstances** or **intention**. *Malum physicum* in contemporary moral theology is usually referred to as **ontic evil** or "premoral evil" to avoid misinterpreting "physical" as somehow excluding emotional, spiritual, or psychological pain and **suffering**. Ontic evil is a genuine evil but without the moral valence (e.g., sinful **intention** or culpability) and is not considered a violation of God's law. Ontic evils can include sickness, death, and natural disasters as well as unavoidable evils caused or tolerated in the process of trying to accomplish a good end (such as in cases of legitimate **cooperation with evil** and the exercise of the **double effect principle**).

Evil (intrinsic). See **intrinsic evil**

Evil (lesser). See **lesser evil** and ***minus malum***

Evil (ontic). See **ontic evil**

Ex cathedra (from the chair [of Peter]). See **charism of office**, **infallibility**, and **magisterium**

Excommunication. See **canonical penalties**

Exegesis comes from the Greek word that means to "bring out the sense" and refers to the method of textual interpretation of texts, especially the Bible, by first seeking to discover what the original text meant in its own form and context and for its intended audience, and then to bring that meaning to a contemporary interpretation of the text and application to a current audience that is part of **hermeneutics**. The opposite of exegesis is **eisegesis**, in which one reads into the text preconceived ideas in order to find supposed validation for these views. This approach is often found in **proof-texting** and taking texts out of their particular context. **See also** *biblical ethics.*

Existentialism gained popularity in the nineteenth and twentieth centuries by stressing that any adequate philosophical reflection on human nature must begin with the human subject considered in her personal fullness. In other words, not merely the rational "thinking" dimension but also the feelings, emotions, life **circumstances**, and so on. This "turn toward the subject" is picked up especially in moral theology in the **inductive approach** of **personalism** as contrasted with **deductive** reasoning based on **physicalism**, as well as in the emphasis on individual **autonomy**. Many existentialist thinkers, especially those who espouse **postmodernism**, critique more traditional systematic or academic philosophy, including **Scholasticism**, as being overly abstract and too removed from concrete **human experience** to make any normative judgments.

Exitus et reditus refers to the principle that **Thomas Aquinas**, following Pseudo-Dionysius, used to describe as an organizing principle God's gift to us of all of the created world and being our ***Summum Bonum*** and final resting place (see *ST I-I*, Q. 1, art. 7).

Experience. See **human experience** and **fonts of moral theology**

"Expert in humanity" is a relatively recent expression used to substantiate the **magisterium**'s claim to teach with **authority** in moral matters, especially in the areas of **sexual ethics** and **social teaching**. **John Paul II** used this in his 1987 **encyclical** *Sollicitudo rei socialis* (#41), referencing **Paul VI**'s 1967 *Populorum progressio* (#42). The theological warrants for this claim of expertise are the **charism of office** and authority coming from the **special assistance of the Holy Spirit** to the magisterium in its exercise of the ***munus*** (ministry, office) to teach authoritatively in interpreting revelation and the **natural law**. As with any claim of expertise, supporting credentials would generally need to be validated before the expertise would be accepted by others.

Ex opere operato (effect comes from [*ex*] the work [*opus* or *opere*] performed by itself [*operato*]) and *ex opere operantis* (effectiveness depends on the person doing the work [*operantis*]) are terms usually found in the theology of sacraments, which were major points debated at the time of the Protestant Reformation. In addition to works of piety, whose efficacy function s*ex opere operantis* in the process of sanctification, these terms also have an important application in how one understands the function and authority of the **magisterium** because the effectiveness of the **charism of office** depends at least in part on just how well the bishop or pope teaches, governs, and sanctifies (*ex opere operantis*) and does not happen automatically (*ex opere operato*). **See also** *infallibilism* and *infallibility*.

External forum. See **forum, internal and external**

Ex toto genere suo (*grave* or *leve*) (from the totality of its nature [grave or light]) is an expression used in the **manualist tradition** to designate certain types of **sins** that could be judged by their very nature to be always seriously wrong and therefore potential **mortal sins**. While the term "*leve*" (light) could replace "*grave*" in the axiom (e.g., in telling white lies), the usual understanding of the principle was that from an objective point of view there would be no realistic possibility of reducing the sinful matter from grave to light. All sexual sins belonged to this category since in matters of the Sixth Commandment there was presumed no paucity of matter (*parvitas materiae in Sexto*). Likewise, those actions were termed **intrinsic evils** by reason of their **moral objects** or *finis operis*, regardless of further consideration of the other two **fonts of morality**, namely **intention** (*finis operantis*) and **circumstances**. The concept of *ex toto genere suo* was strongly reaffirmed by **John Paul II** in *Veritatis splendor*, in which he condemned the opinion "as erroneous which maintains that it is impossible to qualify as morally evil according to its species [*malum ex genere suo*] the deliberate choice of certain kinds of behaviour or specific acts, without taking into account the intention for which the choice was made or the totality of the foreseeable consequences of that act for all persons concerned" (*VS* #82). Denial of this fundamental principle on intrinsic evil would, in the pope's view, make it "impossible to affirm the existence of an 'objective moral order' and to establish any particular norm the content of which would be binding without exception."

Extraordinary magisterium. See **magisterium, infallibility,** *credenda* and *tenenda*, *de fide definita*, and **ultramontanism**

Extraordinary means. See **ordinary and extraordinary means**

F

Facticity. See **finitude and facticity**

Faculty in moral theology refers to the inherent **capacity** or practical ability to do something with **intention** to realize a goal or end. For example, humans have the faculty of speech, which has a goal of the communication of truth. Anything that would obstruct or frustrate that legitimate end, such as speech contrary to what one believed (*locutio contra mentem*), would be *contra naturam* to the proper end of speech and therefore immoral. Another important faculty regards the use of **sexuality** as ultimately ordered to **procreation**. Anything that prevented the realization of this end, such as artificial **birth control**, could be considered at least "intrinsically dishonest" (*intrinsece inhonestum* in the vocabulary of *Humanae vitae* #14) and therefore forbidden by the **natural law**. The **faculty of conscience** was also traditionally viewed at least in part as the power of *recta ratio* or "**right reason**" to make a morally correct choice of action. Just what constitutes a genuine faculty and its possibilities and limits remains debated in concrete situations and often involves a consideration of the notion of **physical versus moral impossibility** as well as the **physicalist and personalist** paradigms.

Faculty of conscience. See **conscience (faculty of)**

Faith and morals (*de fide vel moribus*). See **mores versus morals distinction**

Faith Ethics school (*Glaubensethik*). See **Moral Autonomy school and Faith Ethics school**, **biblical ethics**, *Proprium*, and **scripture and ethics**.

Fall, the. See **original sin**

Fallibility. See **contingency and fallibility**; see also *charism of office*, *infallibility*, *magisterium*, and *obsequium religiosum*.

Familiaris consortio, **John Paul II**'s 1981 postsynodal apostolic exhortation on Christian marriage and the family, outlines in considerable detail the pontiff's views on **marriage**, **birth control**, especially the **inseparability principle** of the unitive and procreative aspects of the conjugal act, and the family, as well as his understanding of **gender**, especially the proper primary role of women as wives and mothers. He states that "true advancement of women requires that clear recognition be given to the value of their maternal and family role, by comparison with all other public roles and all other professions. . . . And society must be structured in such a way that wives and mothers are not in practice compelled to work outside the home, and that their families can live and prosper in a dignified way even when they themselves devote their full time to their own family." The document also references **inculturation** (*FC* #10) and **gradualism** (*FC* #9, 34).

Family. See *Familiaris consortio*, **marriage**, and **responsible parenthood**

Farley, Margaret, RSM, taught Christian ethics at Yale Divinity School from 1971 until her retirement in 2007. Past president of both the SCE and the CTSA, Farley's work on **feminist** and **sexual ethics** is widely respected, although her *Just Love: A Framework for Christian Sexual Ethics* (New York: Continuum, 2006) was critiqued in a 2011 notification by the **CDF** for various positions on issues such as **masturbation** and **same-sex unions** that contradicted those of the **magisterium**.

Feeding tube (e.g., **PEG tube**). See **advance health care directive; ANH; autonomy (bioethical principle); euthanasia; ordinary and extraordinary means; states of consciousness: brain death, coma, PVS, MCS, and locked-in syndrome**; and **vitalism**.

Feminism and feminist ethics are extremely important in their impact on the history and **development of moral theology**, especially with the large number of Roman Catholic women doing theological ethics such as **Lisa Sowle Cahill, Sr. Margaret Farley, RSM**, and many others, including Protestants such as **Beverly Wildung Harrison**. Feminism especially rejects oppression and discrimination that are rooted in **sexism**, gender bias, patriarchy, and so on. While there is no unified or single theory of "feminist ethics," in general this approach seeks to unmask social, cultural, political, and religious forces that negatively affect any oppressed group, especially women, and to identify and promote programs, institutions, courses of action, and analyses, including **affirmative action**, that promote the flourishing and voice of members of these oppressed categories. More controversial issues in feminist ethics revolve around **abortion** as an exercise of reproductive choice; the legitimate role of **anger** as a positive value; proper **hermeneutics**, especially in **scripture and ethics**; **sexuality** and gender; leadership in the Church (e.g., **women's ordination**); interpretations of the **natural law**, **postmodernism**, and so on. **Mujerista** and **womanist theology** are exemplars of a feminist **liberation theology**. *For further reading*, see Charles E. Curran, Margaret A. Farley, Richard A. McCormick, eds., *Readings in Moral Theology No. 9: Feminist Ethics and the Catholic Moral Tradition* (New York: Paulist Press, 1996); and Cristina L. H. Traina, *Feminist Ethics and Natural Law: The End of the Anathemas* (Washington, DC: Georgetown University Press, 1999). **See also** *abortion, anger, hermeneutics, liberation theology, mujerista theology, Ordinatio sacerdotalis, womanist theology,* and *women's ordination.*

Feminist ethics. See **feminism and feminist ethics**

Ferendae sententiae are imposed or declared **canonical penalties**, contrasted with *latae sententiae* or so-called automatic penalties.

Fertility treatments. See **reproductive technologies**

Fides et ratio (*Faith and Reason*) is **John Paul II**'s 1998 **encyclical** on the essential relationship between faith and **reason** to combat modern errors of superstition (faith without reason), **relativism**, agnosticism, **secularism**, and **nihilism** (philosophy without faith). While stating that the Church has no one philosophy of its own, the many contemporary errors compel the **magisterium** in its service to truth to contradict philosophical opinions that run counter to Christian doctrine (see *FR* #49–50). **See also** *Syllabus of Errors.*

Finis operis and finis operantis ("end of the action/agent") are the interrelated terms that describe, in light of the **circumstances**, the **action** *in se* and the corresponding **intention** that directs the moral object chosen in the action. For example, a physical action described as "knife cutting open a chest" does not adequately describe the "action *in se*" since we need to determine the circumstances governing the action and the corresponding intention of the knife-wielder. If the knife is being used in an attack, then the *finis operis* determined by the intention (*finis operantis*) of the knife-wielder is to cause bodily harm. But if the knife were wielded by a doctor as the first step in an emergency operation to open the chest cavity to perform cardiac massage, then both the *finis operis* and the corresponding *finis operantis* are quite different and morally sound. As with any moral action, a complete evaluation can only be accomplished by looking at a composite of all three **fonts of morality** (*fontes moralitatis*). **See also** *actus hominis* and *actus humanus*, and *intrinsic evil*.

Finitude and facticity refer to the inescapable limitations that condition all human **freedom** and play an important role in assessing the moral relevance of the **circumstances** and **intention** in moral acts.

Finnis, John (b. 1940). See **Basic Goods theory**

Fletcher, Joseph (1905–91). See **situation ethics**

Fonts of moral theology are the principal sources used in the discipline and include scripture, **Tradition, reason**, and **human experience**. The **natural law** is the reason-based reflection on human experience that gives us a normative understanding of the moral life both in terms of **prescriptions and proscriptions** of **deontology** and in the **teleology** of the ultimate direction and goal of human moral flourishing. The Catholic Church also ascribes a special role to the **magisterium** in the authoritative articulation of the **deposit of faith** and the natural law. **See also** *authority*.

Fonts of morality (*fontes moralitatis*) are the **action** *in se* (*finis operis*), the **circumstances** in which the action occurs, and the **intention** (*finis operantis*) of the moral agent in choosing and performing the action *in se*. A moral action is an ***actus humanus*** as contrasted with an ***actus hominis*** and requires both **sufficient knowledge** and **sufficient consent** to the act, which in turn presumes **freedom**. If any of these requisite elements is missing, then the action would not be a true moral action even if it were still performed by a **human person**. **Intrinsically evil** actions presume consideration of intention and circumstances, and indicate that no additional motives or other mitigating circumstances could turn a morally evil object into a morally good one. Thus, murder is **intrinsically evil**—even if the victim is a sexual abuser or had done some other heinous acts that may have provoked the homicidal rage on the part of the murderer.

Ford, John Cuthbert, SJ (1902–89), did his doctoral dissertation on the validity of virginal **marriage** (e.g., spirituality of Josephite marriage), at the Pontifical Gregorian University (1937) under **Arthur Vermeersch, SJ**, and **Francis Hürth, SJ,** and he went on to become one of the most important American Catholic moral theologians in the era immediately prior to **Vatican II**. He taught for many years at the Jesuit School of Theology in Weston, Massachusets and, with his Jesuit colleague **Gerald Kelly, SJ**, who taught at the Jesuit theologate in St. Marys, Kansas, wrote a number of books and articles, including the annual "Notes on Moral Theology" in *Theological Studies* that were considered to be an authoritatively sound exposition and interpretation of official Catholic moral teaching, especially in the areas of sexual and medical ethics. Ford wrote against carpet bombing in World War II because it violated the traditional **just war** principle of noncombatant immunity. Having battled alcoholism himself, he wrote extensively on that topic and in support of Alcoholics Anonymous, arguing that for many individuals alcoholism was both an addiction and a disease, and therefore this would reduce, and possibly even eliminate, the moral **culpability** of the alcoholic for drinking. A member of the **Pontifical Commission on Births**, Ford is most remembered for his staunch defense of the traditional condemnation of any form of artificial **birth control**. Along with **Germain Grisez** and others, Ford helped write the so-called four-person minority report (Ford, **Marcelino Zalba, SJ**, Jan Visser, CSsR, and Stanislas de Lestapis, SJ) of that commission, which went on to furnish the foundation for **Paul VI**'s 1968 **encyclical *Humanae vitae***. After this, Ford effectively retired from teaching but continued to write, mostly in defense of *Humanae vitae*, until shortly before his death. *For further reading*, see John C. Ford and Gerald Kelly, *Contemporary Moral Theology* (Westminster, MD: Newman Press, 1958–63); and Eric Marcelo O. Genilo, *John Cuthbert Ford, SJ: Moral Theologian at the End of the Manualist Era* (Washington, DC: Georgetown University Press, 2007).

Forgiveness as modeled by **God** as a response to **sin** and offense is extended in the **sacrament of reconciliation**, as well as commended by Jesus in many of his healing stories, parables, the Lord's Prayer, and his post-Resurrection mission to his disciples (see Jn. 20:23).

Forma communi and forma specifica. See *in forma communi and in forma specifica*

Formal and material distinction. See **causality**

Formal cooperation. See **compromise and compromise/cooperation with evil**, and **causality**

Formal sin. See **sin** and **causality**

Fornication and adultery traditionally are both considered sins against **chastity**. Fornication is sex between two unmarried persons and today is usually termed **premarital sex** or possibly **domestic partnerships**. Adultery is sex when one or both of the partners is married to another and so would additionally be seen as countering the legitimate **ends of marriage**.

Fortitude. See **courage, cardinal virtues**, and **gifts of the Holy Spirit**

Forum, internal and external, in **canon law** (see *CIC* #130) distinguishes the customary external forum of governance from legitimate situations in which the acts of governance are kept secret for serious reasons. Forum also protects the conscience rights of individuals, safeguarding the **seal of the confessional**, and so on. However, the most common instance in pastoral theology is the so-called internal forum solution, which deals with certain second marriage **annulment** cases. If evidence that for some reason was not presented in the external forum of the marriage tribunal were to be presented in the internal forum of the **sacrament of reconciliation** and were to lead to moral certainty that if such evidence had been presented in the tribunal the annulment would likely have been granted, then the person would be in the eyes of God (*coram Deo*) free to marry, even if in the human tribunal (*coram homnibus*) the marriage **bond** still seems to hold. In this sort of limited case the priest may counsel the individual that he is free to return to the sacraments as long as sufficient care is taken to avoid **scandal**. However, the priest is unable to solemnize the second marriage unless a formal decree of nullity is eventually obtained. Sometimes in pastoral counseling and in the sacrament of reconciliation priests have invoked the "internal forum solution" to address marriages that have definitively broken down and have counseled such individuals to return to the sacraments without attempting the annulment process, but this practice has repeatedly been condemned by the Holy See.

The **four last things** expressed in Christian eschatology are death, judgment, heaven, and hell. Christians are exhorted to meditate on these realities to help them lead better lives to prepare for their own death as well as to pray for the souls in purgatory.

Francis—Pope (elected March 13, 2013), succeeded **Benedict XVI** who was the first pope in more than six centuries to resign. Born Jorge Mario Bergoglio (December 17, 1936) in Argentina to Italian immigrants, he later entered the Society of Jesus and served a term as Provincial (1973–79), and ultimately was named by **John Paul II** as bishop of Buenos Aires and was created a cardinal in 2001. Pope Francis established a number of "firsts" in the opening weeks of his pontificate: the first Latin American and Jesuit to become pope and the first to take the name of Francis—honoring the beloved saint of Assisi; the first pope to ask the people gathered in St. Peter's Square to bless him before he bestowed his *urbi et orbi* benediction; the first to choose to remain living in the Vatican hotel rather than move immediately into the Apostolic Palace; the first to celebrate the Holy Thursday evening liturgy in a prison; and the first to wash the feet of women (including a Muslim) rather than adhering to the liturgical rubrics that demand that only males may have their feet washed in this service. He retained his episcopal motto *Miserando atque eligendo*, derived from the Venerable Bede's homily on Matthew 9:9–13: "because he saw him through the eyes of mercy and chose him." A chemist by training, Bergoglio had the reputation of being theologically conservative and a sharp critic of **liberation theology**, yet as archbishop of Buenos Aires he lived in a simple apartment, did much of his own cooking, and rode the bus—preferring always to stay as close to the poor as possible, and as pope he has eschewed a number of the traditional trappings of office. As archbishop he was also noted for his open-ness to **ecumenism** and interreligious dialogue. Negatively, Bergoglio, while Jesuit Provincial, had been accused by some of complicity with the Argentine military in the period of the state terrorism called the Dirty War (Guerra Su-cia) of the 1970s, including unsubstantiated charges that he was involved in helping the government kidnap two Jesuits who were working with the poor. The surviving Jesuit, though, has denied this charge. Pope Francis's easy and outgoing style made him an instant celebrity and provided a marked contrast with the more reserved and formal approach of his predecessor Benedict XVI.

Freedom. See **free will and freedom**

Free will and freedom counter the philosophical theory of **determinism** and have also been the locus of many theological debates both within Ca-tholicism (e.g., between Jesuits and Dominicans on the relationship to God's grace) as well as with various strands of Protestant thought (such as Calvin's doctrine of predestination). Freedom is our most fundamental **human right** that we have from God, who has inscribed the **natural law** in our human **conscience** (*lex indita non scripta*). Without the corresponding capacity to formulate a desire (e.g., **intention**) and then translate it into action (*finis operantis*) and at least **sufficient consent**, an agent would lack **moral au-tonomy** (e.g., **culpability**) for bad actions or merit for good ones. Christian spirituality, moral **discernment**, and **virtue ethics** all highlight that freedom can be strengthened the more we develop our moral **character** through prac-ticing the **habits** of the **virtues** and ridding ourselves as far as possible from inordinate attachments or **vices**.

Fuchs, Josef, SJ (1912–2005), like his contemporary **Bernard Häring, CSsR,** was German and one of the most important twentieth-century moral theologians teaching in Rome (at the Pontifical Gregorian University). Serving on the **Pontifical Commission on Births,** Fuchs played a major role in drafting the majority Final Report, and this experience deeply influenced his subsequent understanding not only of **birth control** and **marriage** but also of the **natural law, moral norms,** and related concepts such as **intrinsic evil.** Fuchs himself never self-identified as espousing **proportionalism,** although he acknowledged that others labeled him as such. He is also identified with the **Moral Autonomy school** and with **revisionist moral theology,** and while never adopting a posture of explicit **dissent** from any teachings of the **ordinary magisterium,** Fuchs did raise issues that he believed showed internal inconsistencies or led to incoherent or unsustainable conclusions in certain approaches. He remained both a priest and theologian in good standing until his death. *For further reading,* see his own essay collections: *Personal Responsibility and Christian Morality* (1983); *Christian Ethics in a Secular Arena* (1984); *Christian Morality: The Word Became Flesh* (1987); and *Moral Demands and Personal Obligations* (1993); and significant treatments of Fuchs in Mark E. Graham, *Josef Fuchs on Natural Law* (2002); Cristina L. H. Traina, "Josef Fuchs and Individual Integrity," ch. 5 in her *Feminist Ethics and Natural Law: The End of the Anathemas* (1999), 169–202 (all Washington, DC: Georgetown University Press); and James F. Keenan, "Josef Fuchs at Eighty, Defending the Conscience While Writing from Rome," *Irish Theological Quarterly* 59 (1994): 204–10.

Fuga mundi (Latin, "fleeing the world") is a spiritual attitude often associated with strict forms of monasticism that holds that a better form of Christian discipleship (*sequela Christi*) is found in **asceticism** and withdrawal from the secular world.

The **fundamental option theory** builds on the theological **anthropology** of Karl Rahner, which holds that in becoming truly human an individual exercises a transcendental, athematic choice for what the person holds to be truly absolute. **God** as the ***Summum Bonum*** would be the true absolute, although in **freedom** an individual could also choose that which is opposed to God as the orientating absolute of one's life. Individual choices or categorical actions are those that can be thematized and identified by the individual as "good" or "bad" and that will strengthen or weaken one's core choice (i.e., the fundamental option), and that also at a certain point could actually reverse that choice. In brief, this theory is another way of speaking about the state of grace and the state of sin and how one falls into the latter through

mortal sin. Admittedly, Rahner's theory is complex and difficult to easily grasp, so it has been subject to a number of misunderstandings that have been critiqued by the **magisterium** in documents such as the **CDF**'s 1975 *Persona humana* #10 and **John Paul II**'s 1993 *Veritatis splendor* (see *VS* #65–68). *For further reading*, see Thomas R. Kopfensteiner, "The Theory of the Fundamental Option and Moral Action," in *Christian Ethics: An Introduction*, edited by Bernard Hoose (Collegeville, MN: Liturgical Press, 1998), 123–34.

G

Gaudium et spes is **Vatican II**'s 1965 "Pastoral Constitution on the Church in the Modern World." Since the title of Church documents comes from the opening words, there was a sharp debate among the council fathers before deciding the initial word order should be *gaudium et spes* (joy and hope) rather than *luctus et angor* (grief and anguish). While both elements are present in the document, clearly "joy and hope" carry a more positive stance toward **culture**, the world, and other religions. *GS* #16 outlined the teaching on **conscience**, and *GS* #47–52 dealt with **marriage** and **responsible parenthood** in **personalist** language. Traditional Church teaching had long held that **procreation** (***bonum prolix***) was *the* primary end of marriage, but *GS* #50 raised the love or "unitive" dimension to equal dignity. Since **Paul VI** had explicitly removed treatment of **birth control** from the council's agenda due to the ongoing deliberations of his **Pontifical Commission on Births**, no explicit treatment of **contraception** is included in the constitution. In terms of **social teaching**, *GS* dealt with the economic and political orders, and #27 lists a large number social problems that are particularly offensive to the "integrity of the **human person**," such as slavery, genocide, **abortion, euthanasia, torture**, subhuman living conditions, and "disgraceful working conditions, where men are treated as mere tools for profit, rather than as free and responsible persons." The document also provides a strong impetus for **ecumenism and ecumenical ethics**.

Gender. See **sexuality, gender, sexual orientation, and sexual ethics**. See **also** *feminism and feminist ethics*

Genetics. See **bioethics** and *Dignitas personae*

GIFT (gamete intrafallopian transfer) is a reproductive technology in which eggs are removed from a woman's ovaries and then placed with a male's sperm in one of her fallopian tubes, which allows fertilization to take place within the woman's body rather than in vitro, thus avoiding some of the moral issues connected with **IVF**.

Gifts of the Holy Spirit is an expression used by the Patristic authors and in Isaiah 11:2, which lists seven: wisdom, understanding, counsel, fortitude, knowledge, piety, and fear of the Lord. **Thomas Aquinas** treats these in the *ST II-II*, and the sacraments, especially Confirmation, strengthen Christians in living their lives in accordance with these **virtues** (see *CCC* #1285).

Gilleman, Gérard, SJ. See **biblical ethics** and **manualist tradition**

Glaubensethik (German, "belief ethics"). See **Moral Autonomy school and Faith Ethics school**; see also *biblical ethics*, *Proprium*, and *scripture and ethics*.

Gloria Dei vivens homo (the glory of **God** is the **human person** fully alive) is an oft-quoted theological axiom of Irenaeus (*Adversus Haereses*, bk. IV, ch. 20, sec. 7). If humans are made in the image of God (*imago Dei*), then what most supports and promotes genuine human flourishing will likewise most give God praise and glory as well. This axiom can be used to help discern **moral impossibility** since by definition those things considered to be impossible, whether physically or morally, could not be enjoined upon humans to fulfill without considerable frustration and harm. Anything that claims to be a **divine command** but that seems counterproductive to truly human flourishing could not be a genuine command of God. **See also** *Deus impossibilia non iubet* and *Summum Bonum*.

Gluttony. See **capital sins**

God is the most important term in all of moral theology, and while most everyone has a workable definition or description of who "God" is and what God "requires" of us, the theological tradition wisely counsels against coming to conclusions too quickly on this score. *Si comprehendis, non est Deus* (if you comprehend [what you believe to be "God"] it is not God) and *Deus semper maior* (God is always greater [than we can comprehend or imagine]) are two maxims that indicate the complexity of just who God is for limited human beings to grasp. Nevertheless, the Christian moral tradition lays out a number of key premises that help guide us. Humans are made in the image of God (the *imago Dei*), and the **natural law** is our human participation in God's *lex aeterna* (eternal or **divine law**). God is not only the ground of the objective moral order but is the fullness of all that truly is good (*bonum*). The **Decalogue** gives an important outline for moral living, and one task of **biblical ethics** is to help us understand and, along with *paranesis*, motivate us to live better our identity as God's children and disciples of Christ. God never commands what is a **moral impossibility** or what would not promote true human flourishing (*Deus impossibilia non iubet*). Moral **discernment** done in the sanctuary of **conscience** is the privileged place in which humans seek God to discover what God is asking of them. Inauthentic images of God and outright heresies have created no end of real difficulties for both believers and the entire human community. From **torture** and wars to simple hard-hearted **moralism**, all practiced in God's name, we see how important it is to meditate continually on just who God is and what God is giving us the grace to do and become.

Good. See *bonum* and **goodness and rightness distinction**

Good faith and bad faith refer to one's primary moral **intention** (e.g., the *finis operantis*) in a moral act. While in most cases the meaning of these terms is self-evident, there is an important **casuistry** principle related to the **formal and material distinction** in causality, and **St. Alphonsus Liguori** in his *Teologia moralis* (bk. VI, treatise IV, n. 610) enjoined confessors not to give too much instruction to an individual lest the person's **conscience** be disturbed, and not to lay on her obligations she would not likely meet. **Gerald A. Kelly, SJ**, offered the following example:

> Suppose the confessor should discover that the penitent has a serious obligation to pay a debt but is not conscious of this duty. The ordinary rule is to remind him of this obligation. Yet, before imparting the reminder, the confessor ought to ask himself: "Is it likely that he will refuse to fulfill this duty, and thus his present good faith will be converted into bad faith?" If there is good reason to believe that this latter would be the case, then the ordinary rule would be: say nothing about the obligation. (Kelly, *The Good Confessor* [New York: Sentinel Press, 1951], 11)

See also *gradualism, ignorance, sacrament of reconciliation, scrupulosity,* and *tolerance.*

Goodness and rightness distinction notes the interrelation between an action, which objectively may be morally "right" or "wrong," and its corresponding **intention** (*finis operantis*), which may not necessarily be the same, such as giving alms primarily for vainglory rather than aiding the poor. Here the external action is "right," but the motivating intention is wrong (vainglory rather than **charity**). The donor's *finis operis* is corrupted by the evil intention and for him the composite action weakens rather than strengthens the moral **character**'s goodness (see *CCC* #1755). Debate continues over the moral meaning of the opposite scenario, namely doing the objectively "wrong" action in **good faith** with a good intention. While the action remains "wrong," does the effect on the agent's character strengthen its goodness, increase its badness, or somehow remain morally neutral (without any real effect at all)? The **manualist tradition** treated this under the rubric of **vincible and invincible ignorance**. Today we recognize **torture** as **intrinsically evil**, but we also admit that many who practiced torture in dealing with heresy did so out of good motives and therefore did not commit **formal sin**, or at worst had very diminished **culpability**. The question remains whether this sort of act could increase someone's moral goodness if the ignorance were invincible and the person honestly believed himself to not only be doing a "right" act but also an act that increased **virtue**. Another aspect of the goodness and rightness distinction concerns the relation of **God** to moral rightness, that is, is something "good" only because God so wills it and God in **divine sovereignty** could will otherwise, or is something good in itself, which even God could not change without destroying God's own nature? This is the theological issue connected with **Voluntarism** and **nominalism**. *For further reading*, see Josef Fuchs, "Historicity and Moral Norm," ch. 6 in *Moral Demands and Personal Obligations* (Washington, DC: Georgetown University Press, 1993), 91–108; and James Keenan, "The Distinction between Goodness and Rightness," ch. 1 in *Goodness and Rightness in Thomas Aquinas' Summa Theologiae* (Washington, DC: Georgetown University Press, 1992), 3–20. **See also** *bonum ex integra causa, malum ex quocumque defectu.*

Gossip, even if widely practiced, can still harm the reputation of another and weaken the bonds of community. It is a violation of **charity** and can be sinful, especially in more serious forms such as **calumny**, **detraction**, **rash judgment**, and **slander**.

Grace (cheap and costly). See **Bonhoeffer, Dietrich**

Gradualism in political policy refers to incremental change over a period of time, for example, to reduce segregation and its negative effects through steps such as affirmative action and integration. In moral theology the term refers to ongoing **conversion** and growth in moral **virtue**. As **John Paul II**'s postsynodal apostolic exhortation *Familiaris consortio* #9 describes, "a dynamic process develops, one which advances gradually with the progressive integration of the gifts of God and the demands of His definitive and absolute love in the entire personal and social life of man." The pope also distinguishes between the "law of gradualism" as a **moral principle** and "gradualism of the law," the latter rejected as an untenable premise of two or more sets of God's laws for different persons or situations (see *FC* #34). Sometimes gradualism is also identified with a "theology of compromise" put forward by **Charles Curran** and other moralists, which holds that in certain situations an individual might not be able to fulfill completely certain moral obligations and the best that she can do in such situations is to fulfill only partially what the moral obligation would entail (such as for someone with a same-sex orientation who might find it very difficult to live a celibate life but who could "compromise" and at least live a stable monogamous relationship with one partner). **See also** *impossibility (physical versus moral)*.

Grave matter. See **sin** and *parvitas materiae in Sexto*

Grave sin. See **sin**

Greed. See **capital sins**

Grisez, Germain (b. 1929). See **Basic Goods theory** and *Humanae vitae*

Guilt is associated with moral responsibility for which one has genuine **culpability.**

Gustafson, James (b. 1925), is an American Protestant ethician who studied under H. Richard Niebuhr at Yale and had a great influence on both Protestant and Catholic American ethicians such as **Stanley Hauerwas**, William Spohn, and **Lisa Sowle Cahill**. See **discernment, ecumenism and ecumenical ethics**, and **Protestant ethics**

H

Habit and virtue (*habitus* "to have"; *virtus* "excellence, courage") in moral theology draw on **Aristotle**'s metaphysics as developed by **Thomas Aquinas** (see *ST I-II*, Q. 49–54) and must be distinguished from the common use of "habit" as a behavior routine repeated so often that it can become subconscious. While repetition and routine are important aspects of moral habits, at its core a habit is a quality that disposes us to exercise our **free will** and **reason** to choose and act in **conscience** according to **goodness and rightness (virtue)** or badly and wrongly (**vice**). Bad actions that become habitual can lessen our moral **freedom** and **culpability** while habitual good actions strengthen our will and develop our **character** so that difficult moral challenges are met more easily over time. Natural or acquired human virtues such as the **cardinal virtues** help direct our reason and order passions and inclinations so that with repetition we might more readily attain the end of the particular virtue, for example, giving another his due through the practice of **justice** (see *ST I-II*, Q. 55–61). **Sin** or lack of practice weakens all of these virtues, and vices can be acquired, strengthened, weakened, or counteracted in the same manner as with the acquired virtues (see *ST I-II*, Q. 71–81). Supernatural habits include the **theological virtues** (faith, hope, and **charity**) that are given or "infused" by God; they help us with grace to reach our supernatural end or *Summum Bonum* of complete union with God (see *ST I-II*, Q. 62–70). These too can be strengthened or weakened in much the same manner as with the acquired virtues and vices, though there are no "infused vices" since this would be incompatible with a God who is all good.

Hamartia (*'αμαρτια*, "missing the mark") comes from archery to denote when an arrow goes astray from its intended target and is one of the New Testament terms for **sin**. Hamartology denotes the theology of sin and its effects. The other principal New Testament terms that can be translated as "sin" are **hubris** (*ὑβρις*, **pride**) and *adikia* (αδκια, unrighteousness). The Latin term for sin, *peccatum*, connotes more the notion of crime or deliberate wrongdoing than the Greek terms. St. Paul's cry of lament in Romans 7 speaks powerfully of this power of sin that goes more deeply than individual discrete acts of wrongdoing. The Christian response to an awareness of missing the mark by our sins is **conversion** (μετανοια, *metanoia*). **See also** *pecca fortiter.*

Hammurabi, Code of. See *lex talionis*

Häring, Bernard, CSsR (November 10, 1912–July 3, 1998), was born in Böttingen, Germany, the same year as **Josef Fuchs, SJ**, and like him was one of the leading Catholic moral theologians of the last half of the twentieth century, teaching primarily at the Alphonsianum in Rome (1949–87) and lecturing around the world. His 1954 *Das Gesetz Christi: Moraltheologie für Priester und Laien*, published in English as *The Law of Christ* (Westminster, MD: Newman Press, 1963), marked a major turning point from the older **manualist tradition** to a more biblically nourished and **personalist** approach to moral theology. Although carefully scrutinized for **orthodoxy** by the **Holy Office** (today the **CDF**), no action was taken against the book and Häring became an important *peritus* (theological expert) at **Vatican II**, especially in the drafting of *Gaudium et spes* and *Optatam totius*, and he served on the **Pontifical Commission on Births**. A new **moral manual**, *Free and Faithful in Christ: Moral Theology for Priests and Laity* (3 vols.; Middlegreen, Slough: St. Paul Publications, 1978, 1979, 1981), posits the leitmotif of Christian morality a **conscience**-based moral **discernment** of "creative fidelity" to Jesus's Gospel message and places him in the **Faith Ethics school**. Häring's question of *Humanae vitae* and other aspects of **sexual ethics** such as **divorce**, and accusations of **dissent**, led to another investigation by the CDF in which Häring ultimately was exonerated, a process detailed in *Fede, storia, morale: Intervista di Gianni Licheri* (Rome: Edizione Borla, 1989; published in English as *My Witness for the Church* [New York: Paulist Press, 1992]). At his death Häring had published some eighty books and one thousand articles, both scholarly and popular. *For further reading*, see his *Shalom: Peace. The Sacrament of Reconciliation*, rev. ed. (Garden City, NJ: Doubleday Image Book, 1967, 1969); *Medical Ethics*, rev. ed. (Middlegreen, Slough: St. Paul Publications, 1972, 1974); *Timely and Untimely Virtues* (Middlegreen, Slough: St. Paul Publications, 1986); and *No Way Out? Pastoral Care of the Divorced and Remarried* (Middlegreen, Slough: St. Paul Publications, 1990).

Harrison, Beverly Wildung (b. 1932), is a Protestant **feminist ethician** who taught for thirty-four years at Union Theological Seminary in New York City. She argues strongly for **abortion** as a fundamental **human right** of reproductive choice and **freedom**, and she highlights the positive power of **anger** in confronting **patriarchy**, **sexism**, and other forms of oppression.

For further reading, see her *Making the Connections: Essays in Feminist Social Ethics* (Boston: Beacon Press, 1985); and *Our Right to Choose: Toward a New Ethic of Abortion* (Boston: Beacon Press, 1983).

Hauerwas, Stanley (b. 1940), is a past president of the SCE who studied under **James Gustafson** at Yale and taught along with **John Howard Yoder** and Alasdair MacIntyre at Notre Dame before moving to Duke University. He is quite skeptical of **natural law**, a strong opponent of **Constantianism**, and a strong supporter of **pacifism**. See also *biblical ethics, ecumenism and ecumenical ethics, Protestant ethics*, and *virtue ethics*.

Health care power of attorney (HCPoA). See **advance health care directive**

Hermeneutics is the science of the interpretative process of texts, whether written, verbal, or nonverbal (e.g., semiotics). Every text comes with a context; even a simple "Stop" sign must be read, interpreted, and applied with that context in mind. **Exegesis**, especially of biblical and legal texts such as the *Code of Canon Law*, is a necessary prelude to the application of these texts to a particular situation as well as to related disciplines such as **biblical ethics**. A "hermeneutics of suspicion" is a form of ideology critique often associated with **feminist ethics** and **postmodernism**; it demands that material that has seemed to support oppression in the past (such as some biblical texts that present women as inferior to men) must be read in a manner that unmasks and delegitimizes such oppression. In some instances a "hermeneutics of recovery" that aims at uncovering or rediscovering the original meaning of a text can be used to rectify practices of oppression that have grown up over time. More recently, a "hermeneutics of generosity" has been advanced to counterbalance potential excesses arising from the ideology critiques based on a hermeneutics of suspicion. *For further reading*, see Sandra M. Schneiders, *The Revelatory Text: Interpreting the New Testament as Sacred Scripture* (San Francisco: HarperSanFrancisco, 1991).

Heterodoxy (Greek, "other" [i.e., false] "opinion") is the opposite of **orthodoxy**. A genuinely heterodox opinion strains the bonds of communion and works against the authentic belief systems of the Christian faith, but it must also be acknowledged that this term is too easily employed against adversaries in legitimate theological debates. **See also** *Congregation for the Doctrine of the Faith, probabilism, quaestio disputata and status quaestionis*, and *Roma locuta causa finita*.

Heteronomy and theonomy (Greek: *hetero*, "other"; *theo*, "God"; and *nomos*, "law") are forms of the imposition of the moral law from some source outside the **conscience sanctuary** of the individual person and therefore a violation of the authentic **moral autonomy** and **primacy of conscience** held by the Catholic moral tradition and **Thomas Aquinas**, who maintained that even if an individual were to be excommunicated from the Church for holding a position in conscience, then the individual *must* follow his or her conscience (4 *Sent.* 27.1.2.q.4. ad 3; 27.3.3.expos.textus; and 38.2.4.q.3). Totalitarianism is a form of heteronomy, and while theonomy seems initially to be equivalent with **divine law** (*lex aeterna*), theologically the problems associated with **Voluntarism, nominalism,** and, to a lesser extent, **divine command ethics** all remain. **See also** *Moral Autonomy school and Faith Ethics school.*

Heterosexism is a term used to critique the view that heterosexual orientation is necessarily normative for all people. Those who claim that heterosexuality is the only **sexual orientation** in accord with human nature engage in a form of **sexism** that improperly discriminates against **homosexuality** and especially **same-sex unions**. While not widely shared by many moral theologians, still some scholars do subscribe to this position. **See also** *queer theory/theology.* **For further reading**, see Patricia Beattie Jung and Ralph F. Smith, *Heterosexism: An Ethical Challenge* (Albany: State University of New York Press, 1993).

Hierarchy of values or truths in moral theology is related to **conflict of duties**. Because of our human **finitude**, we often find it impossible to do everything that we might like. Thus, at a given moment in time we must discern what is the highest value for us here and now. For example, in general we could say that students should place a high value on coming prepared to class, but if there were to be an illness or death in the family, then on that particular class day the higher value would be to treat the illness or comfort the mourning. Both values remain true and valid, but in this case they collide and one cannot adequately fulfill them both. Similarly, in the truths of the Catholic faith not all tenets are of equal importance, as **Vatican II**'s "Decree on **Ecumenism**," *Unitatis redingratio* #11, reminds us: "in Catholic doctrine there exists a hierarchy of truths [*hierarchiam veritatem*], since they vary in their relation to the fundamental Christian faith." This point is also reiterated in the *Catechism of the Catholic Church* at #90 and #234. **See also** *duties (negative and positive)*, and *semper sed non pro semper.*

Historical worldview. See **classicist and historical worldviews**

History and development of moral theology and doctrine is a factual reality easily verified. The **classicist worldview** may find this threatening to its understanding of "constancy of **Tradition**," **infallibility**, or the **charism of office** by which the **magisterium** exercises its teaching *munus*. The **historical worldview** recognizes that change is often a positive sign that gives concrete evidence of the Holy Spirit's activity in the Church as well as the Church's own openness to the Spirit's role to teach those things we could not bear earlier (see Jn. 14:16–17, 26; Jn. 16: 7–15). Some things forbidden in the past are now permitted (e.g., **interest** on loans); other things once permitted are now forbidden (e.g., slavery). Practices once recommended (executing heretics) are now deplored while the opposite would be true for **organ donations**, **ecumenism** and **religious liberty**, and so on. Other significant developments have occurred in moving from a **physicalist** to a **personalist** paradigm in understanding **marriage** more as a **covenant** rather than just **contract justice** rendering the **debitum**, and recognizing that the *bonum prolix* of **procreation** is not the single "primary" **end of marriage**. **Casuistry** likewise has been refined in approaches to resolving difficult **bioethics** cases such as **ectopic pregnancy**, although many issues continue to be sharply debated (*status quaestionis* and *quaestio disputata*). The context in which moral theology is now taught as well as who is doing the teaching have likewise greatly influenced the discipline's development. Up to the first half of the twentieth century, most moral theology relied on the **manualist tradition** and was taught in Latin by priests to seminarians primarily to prepare them for pastoral work, especially in the tribunal of the **sacrament of reconciliation** (i.e., **penance** or **confession**). Now moral theologians include a large number of laypeople, especially women, and moral theology is taught in the vernacular in both undergraduate and graduate programs of theology. **Vatican II**'s *Optatam totius* #16 has led to greater use of scripture and the flourishing of **biblical ethics**, and moral theology is intimately engaged in bioethics, **ecology and environmental ethics**, ecumenism, **feminist ethics**, **gender**, and **liberation theology**, in addition to the standard topics of **conscience**, **moral norms**, **natural law**, **sexual ethics**, and so on. *For further reading*, see John T. Noonan Jr., *A Church That Can and Cannot Change: The Development of Catholic Moral Teaching* (Notre Dame, IN: University of Notre Dame Press, 2005); Charles E. Curran, ed., *Change in Official Catholic Moral Teachings: Readings in Moral Theology No. 13* (New York: Paulist Press, 2003); and James F. Keenan, *A History of Catholic Moral Theology in the Twentieth Century: From Confessing Sins to Liberating Consciences* (New York: Continuum, 2010).

HIV/AIDS is the acronym for human immunodeficiency virus/acquired immunodeficiency syndrome, an incurable (at this writing) disease of the auto-immune system that can be transmitted via blood (e.g., transfusions, sharing dirty needles), unprotected sex, and from mother to child during birth. **See also** *ABC* and *safe sex*.

Holiness Code refers to the main legal block of the Old Testament found in Leviticus 17–26, which contains a number of **prescriptions** and proscriptions that observant Israelites would be expected to follow in order to fulfill God's command to "be holy as I am holy" (see Lv. 19:2; 20:26). The expression also refers to many other ethical prescriptions contained in the Old Testament Mosaic **covenant**. For contemporary **biblical ethics**, problems arise in how to interpret certain passages that are clearly outmoded (such as buying slaves from neighboring nations in Lv. 25:44, or against the supposed "abomination" of the practice of eating shellfish in Lv. 10:10). While "abomination" normally connotes something gravely offensive to the moral order and God's creative intentionality for humans, many biblical exegetes caution against applying that interpretation in passages such as these. They suggest instead that in these contexts "abomination" refers either to practices at variance with other ancient Near Eastern cultures, or items (such as shellfish) that do not seem to fit into the categories of what would constitute their proper classification (e.g., a fish should have fins and scales and a lobster has neither; see Lv. 11:10–12). Other activities, such as heterosexual and homosexual temple cult prostitution, are condemned principally for being idolatry and for attempting to manipulate the gods and less for being sexual activity outside of **marriage**.

The passages of the Holiness Code that most vex us today are those that call for **capital punishment** for homogenital violations, such as Leviticus 18:22 and 20:23. Some fasten on such passages and interpret them as undeniable evidence that "God hates fags!" but most would reject such **hermeneutics**. While clearly homogenital behavior is strongly condemned, it is less clear just what is the grounding for such condemnation or how we should interpret this in today's context in which we have a more developed understanding of **homosexuality** as well as a more compassionate approach to punishment for all transgressions. While simplistic **proof-texting** must be avoided, it is still difficult simply to dismiss biblical passages that one finds problematic. This tension can be found even in official Church documents such as the ***Catechism of the Catholic Church***, which notes that based "on Sacred Scripture, which presents homosexual acts as acts of grave depravity" on one hand nevertheless does not call for the **death penalty** and instead observes that such individuals "do not choose their homosexual condition; for most of them it is a trial. They must be accepted with respect, compassion, and sensitivity. Every sign of unjust discrimination in their regard should be avoided" (see *CCC* #2357–58). *For further reading*, see Leland J. White, "Does the Bible Speak about Gays or Same-Sex Orientation? A Test Case in Biblical Ethics: Part I," *Biblical Theological Bulletin* 20 (1995): 14–23.

Holy Office is the pre-**Vatican II** name for what today is the **CDF**. The full original name was the Holy Office of the Roman Inquisition.

Homosexuality remains one of the most sharply contested areas of **sexual ethics**, and positions and conclusions taken are heavily dependent on understandings derived from paradigms such as **physicalism** versus **personalism**, **Tradition**, the **natural law**, and the interpretation of **Scripture and ethics**, especially **exegesis** of biblical material such as the Old Testament **Holiness Code** and Paul's use of a **vice list** in 1 Corinthians 6:9–11. The **magisterium** views homogenital activity as a violation of scripture, Tradition, and the natural law. Contemporary magisterial documents such as the **CDF**'s 1975 *Persona humana* #8 and the *Catechism of the Catholic Church* acknowledge that for most individuals with a same-sex orientation this is neither freely chosen nor evidence of serious personal sinfulness that somehow sets these individuals apart from others, and they should not be treated with discrimination (*CCC* #2358). Homosexuality is portrayed as a disease somewhat like diabetes, which is incurable but controllable, and therefore demands that gay men and women accept a special call to a life of **celibacy** and sexual **continence** (*CCC* #2359). Special attention is given to how the Christian community can best minister pastorally to gay men and women, and here the various Church documents frankly do not adopt the same pastoral tone or strategy. The CDF's 1986 *Homosexualitatis problema*, "Letter to Bishops on the Pastoral Care of Homosexual Persons," highlighted serious concerns with overly lenient pastoral approaches. It did not deny *PH* #8 on the constitutional nature of same-sex orientation but asserted that this orientation itself was intrinsically **disordered** and could lead more easily to sexual sins. A contrasting accent is seen in the **NCCB**'s 1997 *Always Our Children: A Pastoral Message to Parents of Homosexual Children and Suggestions for Pastoral Ministers*, which stressed compassion and acceptance of homosexuals by their parents and others. The CDF required a revision, issued in 1998, to address concerns about "clarity" regarding Church teaching on same-sex activity. In 2005, the Congregation for Catholic Education issued its "Instruction Concerning the Criteria for the Discernment of Vocations with Regard to Persons with Homosexual Tendencies in View of Their Admission to the Seminary and to Holy Orders," calling for caution but not outright denial in accepting gay men for priesthood. The contrasting position on homosexuality sees it not as a disease but as a positive good, given by **God**, to be lived out in **chastity** in much the same way as heterosexuals do. *For further reading* from a variety of perspectives, see Robin Scroggs, *The New Testament and Homosexuality* (Philadelphia: Fortress Press, 1983); Jeannine Gramick and Pat Furey, eds., *The Vatican and Homosexuality: Reactions to the Letter to the Bishops of the Catholic Church on the Pastoral Care of Homosexual Persons* (New York: Crossroad, 1988); James P. Hanigan, *Homosexuality: The Test for Christian Sexual Ethics* (New York: Paulist Press, 1988); Jeffrey Siker, ed., *Homosexuality in the Church: Both Sides of the Debate* (Louisville, KY: Westminster John Knox Press, 1994); John Harvey, *The Truth about Homosexuality: The Cry of the Faithful* (San Francisco: Ignatius Press, 1996); and Patricia Beattie Jung with Joseph Andrew Coray, eds., *Sexual Diversity and Catholicism: Toward the Development of Moral Theology* (Collegeville, MN: Liturgical Press, 2001). **See also** *courage* and *reparative therapy.*

Hospice care. See **death with dignity, ordinary and extraordinary means, advance health care directive**, and **vitalism**

Hostis humani generis (enemy of the human race) had been used to justify **torture** and murder of individuals whose crimes were considered so monstrous as to provide an exception against the provisions for humane treatment for prisoners of war, or for the **proscription** against torture, or the *ius in bello* criterion of **just war theory**. While there was considerable academic discussion over the possibility of **tyrannicide** or **regicide** to remove a very evil leader who was causing serious harm to large numbers of people, this position is now much more difficult to maintain in the view of murder and torture being **intrinsic evils**. Nevertheless, this expression has been misused by some public officials to justify inhumane treatment of prisoners in the so-called War on Terror. Every individual is made in the image of God (*imago Dei*) and thus even a mass murderer retains basic intrinsic **human rights**.

Hubris (ὕβρις, **pride**) is one of the Greek terms employed in the New Testament for **sin**, and pride is one of the seven **capital sins**. In the ancient Greek mythology hubris was not primarily seen as boasting or overemphasis on one's accomplishments or possessions but rather failing to acknowledge one's proper station in life as a human, vis-à-vis the pantheon of gods. On the path up to Delphi, the oracle through which humans could consult the deities, was posted the warning "Know thyself," which admonished the visitor to remember that she was on holy ground and approaching the gods, so a proper spirit of reverence was required. In Christian theology, failure to remember that we are God's creatures or to conform our will and actions to God's law could be seen as hubris. The other principal New Testament terms for "sin" are **hamartia** (*'αμαρτια*, missing the mark) and ***adikia*** (αδκια, unrighteousness). The Latin term for sin, *peccatum*, connotes more the notion of crime or wrongdoing than the Greek terms do. **See also** *pecca fortiter*.

Human dignity. See **human person, dignity, and rights**

Human experience, though difficult to quantify or qualify, nevertheless remains one of the indispensable **fonts of moral theology**. A moral system that excluded human experience as a key source would run the risk of becoming merely an abstraction divorced from concrete reality. **See also** *Deus impossibilia non iubet*, *deductive and inductive*, and *physicalism and personalism*.

Human person, **dignity**, and **rights** are three core interrelated concepts in Catholic **social teaching**. The dignity of the human person is grounded in the ***imago Dei***, and rights come not merely from social contracts but from universal **justice** and the **natural law**, applicable to all regardless of time, place, **gender**, race, status, and so on. In the **history and development of moral theology**, we have progressively come to greater consensus and fuller understanding of the scope of human rights, for example, **religious liberty**, freedom of **conscience**, work, health care, and so on, including what constitutes violations of human dignity, such as **sexism**, **structural evil**, and forms of discrimination. *For further reading*, see David Hollenbach, *The Global Face of Public Faith: Politics, Human Rights, and Christian Ethics* (Washington, DC: Georgetown University Press, 2003).

Human rights. See **human person, dignity, and rights**

Humanae vitae, **Paul VI**'s 1968 **encyclical** "On the Regulation of Birth," reaffirmed the Church's traditional teaching on **birth control**, calling directly willed artificial contraception *intrinsece inhonestum* ("intrinsically dishonest," *HV* #14) but allowing for moral recourse to a woman's infertile periods (e.g., **NFP**, *HV* #16). Using the **double effect principle**, an exception allowed for the moral use of drugs (and possibly including **condom use** to prevent disease transmission) that have a foreseen contraceptive effect as long as the primary purpose and **intention** (*finis operis and finis operantis*) was to treat a medical issue (*HV* #15).

Attention to its historical context is crucial to a proper understanding of *Humanae vitae*. The recent development of the progesterone pill offered a method of **contraception** that many, including the Thomistic **natural law** philosopher Jacques Maritain, thought might avoid the moral problems associated with a **physicalist** *contra naturam* interpretation of barrier methods such as diaphragms and condoms. **Pius XII**'s 1951 "**Address to Italian Midwives**" had already accepted the morality of avoiding **procreation** for serious reasons, and **Vatican II**'s *Gaudium et spes* affirmed in **personalist** terms the necessity of "harmonizing **conjugal love** with the responsible transmission of life" (*GS* #51). Sociological studies also linked multigenerational systemic poverty with inability to control family size. **John XXIII** established a **Pontifical Commission on Births** to study this complex question with a possible view of modifying Church teaching. This commission was greatly expanded to seventy-two members under his successor Paul VI, including married laypeople along with clerical theologians, bishops, and Cardinal Ottaviani, the head of the **Holy Office** (today the **CDF**). This commission's final "Majority Report" in 1966 called for allowing married couples to make a **conscience**-based decision in light of **responsible parenthood** about both family size and the means to achieve this. While these factors suggested the possibility of change, other aspects pulled in the opposite direction, such as the long-standing **Tradition** against all forms of **birth control** and the relatively recent condemnation of artificial contraception in **Pius XI**'s 1930 **encyclical** *Casti connubii*, written to counteract the **Anglican Communion**'s **Lambeth Conference** acceptance of artificial contraception. Finally, a group of four theologians (Jesuits American **John Ford**, Spanish **Marcelino Zalba**, and French Stanley de Lestapis along with Dutch Redemptorist Jan Visser) dissented from the Pontifical Commission's "Majority Report" and drafted their own position paper with the help of others, including Germain Grisez, which ultimately furnished the basis for *Humanae vitae*.

The encyclical is organized into three major sections of which the last is the longest: "New Aspects of the Problem and Competency of the Magisterium" (*HV* #1–6); "Doctrinal Principles" (*HV* #7–18); and "Pastoral Directives" (*HV* #19–31). In the first section *HV* # 2 acknowledged the demographic problem but raised concern over human progress in "the domination and rational organization of the forces of nature, such that he [humans] tends to extend this domination to his own total being, [including] laws which regulate the transmission of life." *HV* #3 raises the possibility of a revision of ethical norms in light of the **totality principle** but then rejects this. *HV* #4 affirmed that none "of the faithful could possibly deny that the Church is competent in her magisterium to interpret the natural moral law." *HV* #5 acknowledged the work of the Pontifical Commission on Births, but *HV* #6 noted the proposed solutions of "Majority Report," which "departed from the moral teaching on marriage proposed with constant firmness by the teaching authority of the Church."

The second section on doctrinal principles introduces **marriage** and responsible parenthood, noting that these "must be accurately defined and analyzed" (*HV #7*). *HV #8–9* expound marriage as a relationship of total love and self-giving revealed in the context of God's love. *HV #10* speaks of the possibility of limiting family size for serious reasons, but adds that couples "are not free to act as they choose in the service of transmitting life, as if it were wholly up to them to decide what is the right course to follow. On the contrary, they are bound to ensure that what they do corresponds to the will of God the Creator." *HV #11* notes that God has ordained in nature that not every conjugal act will be fertile, but that the Church calls for "the observance of the **precepts** of the natural law, which it interprets by its constant doctrine, teaches that each and every marital act must of necessity retain its intrinsic relationship to the procreation of human life." *HV #12* then introduces what in effect is a new **moral principle** in magisterial teaching regarding the conjugal act, namely the so-called **inseparability principle**: "established by God, which man on his own initiative may not break, between the unitive significance and the procreative significance which are both inherent to the marriage act," adding that only "if each of these essential qualities, the unitive and the procreative, is preserved, the use of marriage fully retains its sense of true mutual love and its ordination to the supreme responsibility of parenthood to which man is called." Building on the inseparability principle, *HV #13* asserts that "to use this divine gift [of sexual relations] while depriving it, even if only partially, of its meaning and purpose, is equally repugnant to the nature of man and of woman, and is consequently in opposition to the plan of God and His holy will." Respect for **divine sovereignty** in the area of conception also acknowledges "that one is not the master of the sources of life but rather the minister of the design established by the Creator." *HV #14* lists as "unlawful birth control methods," **direct abortion**, permanent or temporary **sterilization**, and artificial contraception. Most of the argumentation implicitly counters the position developed in the **Pontifical Commission on Births**'s "Majority Report," including invocation of the principles of the **lesser evil** and totality: "Neither is it valid to argue, as a justification for sexual intercourse which is deliberately contraceptive, that a lesser evil is to be preferred to a greater one, or that such intercourse would merge with procreative acts of past and future to form a single entity, and so be qualified by exactly the same moral goodness as these." This paragraph then concludes with the judgment that "it is a serious error to think that a whole married life of otherwise normal relations can justify sexual intercourse which is deliberately contraceptive and so intrinsically wrong [*intrinsece inhonestum*]." Lest an overly physicalist interpretation be given to this prescription, the very next paragraph, *HV* #15, allows for the licit use of means that have foreseen contraceptive effects as long as the "impediment is not directly intended."

HV #16 outlines the morality of "recourse to infertile periods." Since the argumentation here is often poorly understood, it merits careful consideration. To begin with some of the more common misunderstandings: first, that NFP is "licit" because it is "natural" or "organic," while artificial contraception is wrong because its "artificiality" makes it "unnatural," as in the subtitle of the tract *Natural Family Planning: Nature's Way—God's Way* (Milwaukee: DeRance, Inc., 1980). This line of argument falters under one version of the so-called **naturalistic fallacy**, which erroneously concludes that anything "artificial" is somehow morally suspect. If this were the case then most of our food, shelter, clothing, and means of production would be illicit because they were "artificial" when "natural" alternatives might exist. A second misunderstanding is a corollary of this mistaken principle, holding that any human intervention in biological processes is "playing God" and therefore an affront to divine sovereignty. If this were correct then most medications and surgeries would be immoral for the same reason, and clearly the Church does not hold this position. The third common misunderstanding involves a highly suspect and convoluted interpretation of the intention of couples practicing NFP and holds that such couples are clearly not "contra-life" since they must realize that NFP has a higher statistical failure rate over other methods of artificial contraception, and therefore their unwillingness to practice **safe sex** shows that they are somehow more pro-life in relation to conception than those who use artificial contraception. Artificial contraception likewise is not absolutely foolproof, as most people know, so it would be impossible to limit this "argument" only to those who practice NFP, not to mention the serious problems this approach raises for the exercise of **prudence**. Instead, the actual argument advanced in *HV* #16 revolves around the distinction between **negative and positive duties**, which bind differently. Practicing artificial contraception is seen as violating the negative duty regarding not physically blocking the possibility of conception. This negative duty binds *semper et pro semper* ("always and in each instance"). Using NFP, though, is not seen as physically blocking the possibility of conception but rather simply using the naturally occurring infertile period to avoid fulfilling the positive duty to "be fruitful and multiply." While this positive duty remains always "true" in marriage, it is equally true that no married couple can fulfill this duty each and every moment. Thus, like all positive duties, it binds *semper sed non pro semper* ("always but not in every instance"). This last-named argument remains a locus of ongoing debate among both theologians and the general population.

HV #17 uses both **consequentialism** and the **slippery slope argument** to add more reasons against the use of artificial contraception, noting that if its use becomes widespread, the consequences "could open wide the way for marital infidelity and a general lowering of moral standards" and for the man to "forget the reverence due to a woman, and, disregarding her physical and emotional equilibrium, reduce her to being a mere instrument for the satisfaction of his own desires." A larger problem looms on the governmental level in giving this practical power to "public authorities who care little for the precepts of the moral law," questioning whether there is anything to prevent them "from favoring those contraceptive methods which they consider more effective? Should they regard this as necessary, they may even impose their use on everyone." *HV* #18 concludes the doctrinal principles section by acknowledging that this teaching likely will be unpopular, but that "it comes as no surprise to the Church that she, no less than her divine Founder, is destined to be a 'sign of contradiction.'"

The third section, "Pastoral Directives" (*HV* #19–31), is the longest and shows the greatest development of thinking regarding birth control as a pastoral issue. *Casti connubii*'s vocabulary of artificial contraception being a "**grave sin**" and "horrible crime" that the "Divine Majesty regards with greatest detestation" and at times "punished it with death" (*CC* #55–56) is not echoed in *Humanae vitae*. Instead, *HV* #19 states that, like Christ, the Church knows human "weaknesses, she has compassion on the multitude, she welcomes sinners." *HV* #20 affirms that the teaching "cannot be observed unless God comes to their help with the grace by which the goodwill of men is sustained and strengthened," and this highlights the role of prayer and sacraments. Instead of suggesting that nonobservance bars individuals from the sacramental life of the Church, it explicitly invites married couples who find difficulty with observing this discipline to avail themselves of the sacraments by which the Church as the "herald of salvation . . . flings wide open the channels of grace through which man is made a new creature responding in **charity** and true freedom to the design of his Creator and Savior, experiencing too the sweetness of the yoke of Christ," including frequent recourse to "that unfailing fount which is the Eucharist" (*HV* #25). Priests in particular are called to mirror the compassion of Christ such that their pastoral stance "always be joined with **tolerance** and charity, as Christ Himself showed in His conversations and dealings with men. For when He came, not to judge, but to save the world, was He not bitterly severe toward **sin**, but patient and abounding in mercy toward sinners," and furthermore that married couples can "find stamped in the heart and voice of their priest the likeness of the voice and the love of our Redeemer" (*HV* #29).

Although Paul VI was to reign for another decade, *Humanae vitae* was his last encyclical, and its reception on virtually every level from practice to theory was conflicted at best, including outright **dissent** on the part of many and noncompliance by even more. After more than four decades, statistics show that there is no discernible difference between Catholic and non-Catholic practice of artificial contraception. At the press conference at the Vatican at the promulgation of the encyclical (dated June 25, 1968), a reporter explicitly asked whether this teaching should be considered **infallible**; the clear answer given was "no," indicating the official position that this encyclical was part of the **ordinary magisterium** and hypothetically open to change or significant revision at some future point in time. Reaction from various bishops' conferences around the world was both muted and mixed, and large numbers of theologians and even some bishops openly and loudly challenged both the reasoning and conclusions of the encyclical. Others strongly defended it as supporting the constant tradition of the Church and as being a prophetic sign to a world increasingly marked by moral **relativism**, **subjectivism**, and **secularism**. Use of artificial contraception is only rarely confessed as "sin," leading some to conclude that the teaching of *Humanae vitae* has not yet truly been "received" as a *sensus fidelium*. The moral debates of this *status quaestionis* remain at an impasse, especially over whether artificial contraception is an **intrinsic evil** and whether couples are free in conscience to come to a different conclusion about the practical aspects of responsible parenthood from the teaching articulated in *Humanae vitae*. Nevertheless, adherence to the doctrine of *Humanae vitae* continues to function as a de facto litmus test of **orthodoxy** in ecclesial circles. *For further reading* on the vast bibliography connected with *Humanae vitae* in magisterial documents as well as a variety of representative positions on the encyclical, see James T. Bretzke, *A Research Bibliography in Christian Ethics and Catholic Moral Theology* (Lewiston, NY: Edwin Mellen Press, 2006).

Humani generis. See **Pius XII**, *Roma locuta causa finita*

Hume's Law or **Hume's Guillotine**. See **naturalistic fallacy**

Humility is the **virtue** that "consists in keeping oneself within one's own bounds, not reaching out to things above one, but submitting to one's superior" (*SCG* #4, ch. 55) and to **God**. Humility is linked in the **cardinal virtues** to **temperance** because it helps the individual in moderating inordinate desire, emotions, or **appetites**, and it functions as a corrective to **pride**. False humility in belittling one's own talents, accomplishments, and so on, is contrary to true humility because that virtue aims primarily at giving an individual an honest picture of oneself so that she recognizes both strengths and weaknesses, talents, and defects, so that one can better rely on God for help in developing one's moral **character** (see James 4:6–7), and, modeling Jesus's own humility before God the Father (see Mt. 11:29), to receive the beatitude promised the humble (see Mt. 5:3).

Hürth, Francis (Franz), SJ (d. May 29, 1963), was a professor of moral theology (1915–35) at a Dutch Jesuit theologate before coming to Gregorian University as successor to **Arthur Vermeersch**. Hürth was a key consultor to the **Holy Office** (today the **CDF**) and important collaborator with **Pius XI** (on *Casti connubii*) and more extensively with **Pius XII**, helping to draft many of the pope's **occasional allocutions** on moral issues. Hürth's narrow interpretation of the **totality principle** in strict **physicalism** led him to condemn any **organ donation** of living tissue as forbidden self-mutilation (see *CC* #71).

I

N.B. Latin terms that might begin with "J" such as "*judicium*" or "*jus ad bellum*" are found under the letter "I" since there is no "J" in classical Latin, e.g., *ius ad bellum*.

ICSI (intracytoplasmic sperm injection) is an **IVF reproductive technology** procedure in which a single sperm is injected directly into an egg and then implanted in the uterus.

An **ideal** should not be confused or equated with an **absolute moral norm** or deontological duty since by definition an ideal represents a **teleological** goal that to some extent will never be fully realizable in concrete human life. **See also** *Zielgebot*.

Ignorance in the **manualist tradition** was seen as the cause of error, especially of an **erroneous conscience**. Invincible ignorance was that which could not be overcome by the person, and thus removed **culpability** for actions that otherwise would be objectively wrong. Vincible ignorance was that which could be remedied if the person were only to take sufficient effort. Crass or supine ignorance was a more serious form of vincible ignorance for which the individual had little excuse, for example, a confessor who did not know that a *latae sententiae* **canonical penalty** (e.g., for **abortion**) would not be applied if one or more of several factors outlined in *CIC* #1323 and 1324 were present. While a priest might genuinely be unaware of this basic point, his professional role would normally expect a working knowledge of **canon law**, so his ignorance would be termed "crass or supine."

Imago Dei (image of God) is the foundation of the Judeo-Christian theological **anthropology** that holds that we humans are made in the image of God (see Gen. 1:26), and through **ensoulment** we possess an immortal soul that gives us our basic **human dignity** as a sharing in God's life, who is our ***Summum Bonum***. For Christians this understanding also furnishes the core **vocation** to image God's own holiness in the world through following of

Christ (*sequela Christi*). The *imago Dei* also grounds Catholic **social teaching** inasmuch as all humans are created in the image of God, and they are therefore to be treated with dignity and accorded basic **human rights**.

Imitatio Christi (imitation of Christ). See *sequela Christi* (following of Christ) and **WWJD? (What would Jesus do?)**

Immunity (noncombatant). See **just war theory**

Impediment and irregularity is a complex and technical area in **canon law** that deals with things that restrict or suppress an individual's **capacity** or **freedom** in some area; for example, an existing **marital bond** would be an impediment to another **marriage** (unless an **annulment** were obtained) or to ordination to the priesthood (see *CIC* #1042), and so on. *For further reading*, consult commentaries on canon law such as the *New Commentary on the Code of Canon Law*, edited by John P. Beal, James A. Coriden, and Thomas J. Green (New York: Paulist Press, 2000).

Impossibility (physical versus moral) is an important distinction in both moral and pastoral theology. Physical impossibility is fairly clear: that which simply cannot be done due to our human **finitude**. For example, try as we might, we simply cannot fly unaided. Moral impossibility refers to that which would be exceedingly difficult and counter to human flourishing, even if physically possible. A **manualist tradition** example involved the **Easter duty** to confess one's serious sins if the only priest available (e.g., in a remote village) were one's own son. Physically going to **confession** to this priest would be "possible," yet psychologically it could be too difficult for some (though not all) parents. If going to confession to one's own son would be so difficult, then the manualists held that the individual was dispensed from this obligation due to moral impossibility. Moral impossibility is of its nature subjective, that is, it can only be discerned in relation to an individual subject, so its application will always be somewhat ambiguous at best. **See also** *epikeia* and *gradualism*.

Imputability. See **culpability**

Inclination. See **appetite** and **habit** and **virtue**

Inculturation. See **culture and inculturation**, *Evangelii nuntiandi*

Indirect moral act. See **direct and indirect**

Indissolubility of marriage. See **annulment** and **marriage**

Inductive approach. See **deductive and inductive**

Indulgences are the remission of temporal punishment of sins already for-given, either partial or plenary (i.e., total), which can be applied to oneself or as a suffrage (vicarious satisfaction) to a soul in purgatory. In the past partial indulgences indicated a certain number of "days" of remission of temporal punishment assigned for the successful completion of the pious, penitential, or charitable acts required by the indulgence (e.g., two hundred days for saying a certain prayer), but **Paul VI**'s 1967 apostolic constitution *Indulgen-tiarum doctrina* removed this temporal designation for partial indulgences and significantly reduced the number of plenary indulgences available. To obtain a plenary indulgence, one has "to perform the work to which the indulgence is attached and to fulfill three conditions: sacramental **confes-sion**, Eucharistic **Communion**, and prayer for the intentions of the Supreme Pontiff. It is further required that all attachment to **sin**, even to venial sin, be absent" (*ID* #7). The "works" attached to the indulgences often were par-ticipation in religious gatherings such as the World Meeting of Families or pilgrimages to certain sacred sites or churches. The practice of indulgences was sharply condemned by Luther and the Protestant reformers as examples of **works righteousness** and even as a form of **simony**, and they countered this theology with their doctrines of *sola fide*, *sola gratia*, and *solus Chris-tus*. The Council of Constance and **Council of Trent** reaffirmed the practice of indulgences, grounding it in an understanding of the Church's *munus* of sanctification and the "power of the keys" to forgive sins (see Mt. 18:18) in the **sacrament of reconciliation**. Applying indulgences for satisfaction of punishment incurred by a deceased person is likewise tied to the communion of saints united under Christ as head, and the notion of vicarious expiation and suffering spoken of by Paul in Colossians 1:24 and 1 John 2:2.

Infallibilism connotes an incorrect extension of the doctrine of papal **infal-libility** such that it would call faithful and "loyal" Catholics to believe or hold as absolutely unchangeable and true almost everything a pope would say in some official manner, even if these statements have not in fact been so defined by the **magisterium** of the Church. Both Church **Tradition** and **canon law** make it clear that this absolutist position is not **orthodox**: "No doctrine is understood as defined infallibly unless this is manifestly evident" (*CIC* #749 §3). *For further reading*, see *LG #25*, the 1973 **CDF** declaration *Mysterium ecclesiae*, and Cardinal Avery Dulles, "Moderate Infallibilism: An Ecumenical Approach," ch. 9 in *A Church to Believe In: Discipleship* *and the Dynamics of Freedom* (New York: Crossroad, 1982), 133–48. **See also** *charism of office, conscience, credenda, Lumen gentium, obsequium religiosum, Roma locuta causa finita, tenenda,* and *ultramontanism.*

Infallibility means "without error." Under certain conditions the pope in his *ex cathedra* exercise of the extraordinary magisterium invokes this infallibility as defined in **Vatican I**'s 1870 *Pastor aeternus*:

> It is a divinely revealed dogma that the Roman Pontiff, when he speaks *ex cathedra,* that is, when, acting in the office of shepherd and teacher of all Christians, he defines, by virtue of his supreme apostolic authority, a doctrine concerning faith or morals [*de fide vel moribus*] to be held [*tenenda*] by the universal Church, possesses through the divine assistance promised to him in the person of Blessed Peter, the infallibility with which the divine Redeemer willed his Church to be endowed in defining the doctrine concerning faith or morals; and that such definitions of the Roman Pontiff are therefore irreformable of themselves, not because of the consent of the Church (*ex sese, non autem ex consensu ecclesiae*). But if anyone presumes to contradict this our definition—which God forbid—*anathema sit.* (*PA*, ch. 4, para. 9 [*DS* #3074–3075])

First the pope has to explicitly invoke the claim of infallibility by speaking *ex cathedra* (from his chair as Bishop of Rome). Second, the object of his definition has to be a doctrine of **faith or morals**, and a discussion arises around "*vel moribus*" since the term could be rendered as either "morals" in the sense of objective morality or "mores" in the sense of customs. Third, what is infallibly proposed is to be "held" (*tenenda*) as opposed to calling for a faith "belief" (*credenda*). Fourth, such infallible definitions do not claim "absolute" fullness of truth or **certitude** but a more circumscribed and nuanced claim, namely, that these definitions would simply enjoy the same level of certainty that Christ willed his Church to have in this same area. Finally, and important ecclesially, the confirmation or validity of such papal definitions depends neither on subsequent conciliar approbation nor on reception of the faithful (*sensus fidelium*). Likewise, these definitions—like all doctrines defined as articles of the faith (*de fide definita*)—cannot be changed in their substance, though the explanations of such definitions can develop over time, as has been done in any number of dogmas such as with the doctrine on salvation outside of the Church (*extra ecclesiam nulla salus est*). **Vatican II**'s "Dogmatic Constitution on the Church," *Lumen gentium* #25, repeats the formulation of Vatican I, adding by way of explanation that under these conditions "the Roman Pontiff is not pronouncing judgment as a private person, but as the supreme teacher of the universal Church, in whom the charism of infallibility of the Church itself is individually present, he is expounding or defending a doctrine of Catholic faith." *Lumen gentium* #25 also adds that

> individual bishops do not enjoy the prerogative of infallibility, they nevertheless proclaim Christ's doctrine infallibly whenever, even though dispersed through the world, but still maintaining the bond of communion among themselves and with the successor of Peter, and authentically teaching matters of faith and morals, they are in agreement on one position as definitively to be held. This is even more clearly verified when, gathered together in an ecumenical council, they are teachers and judges of faith and morals for the universal Church, whose definitions must be adhered to with the submission of faith.

Thus, under certain conditions teachings proposed in the **ordinary magisterium** can enjoy infallibility if it is demonstrated that they are held by bishops "even though dispersed through the world, but still maintaining the bond of communion among themselves and with the successor of Peter." Verification of these conditions remains rather difficult, and while some moralists such as **John Ford, SJ**, and **Germain Grisez** have claimed infallibility for **Paul VI**'s 1968 **encyclical *Humanae vitae*** on **birth control**, to date no Vatican office or pope has explicitly endorsed this particular assertion. At the Vatican press conference upon the release of *Humanae vitae*, in response to a reporter's explicit question asking if the encyclical should be understood as being infallible, the clear answer given by the Vatican officials present was "no." *CIC* #749 §3 also states, "No doctrine is understood as defined infallibly unless this is manifestly evident." Thus, to date it seems that no doctrine dealing with moral matters has been proposed infallibly in the papal extraordinary magisterium and there is no clear consensus that any teaching in the ordinary magisterium claims infallibility. **John Paul II**'s 1995 *Evangelium vitae* did employ a new formula, stating that "by the authority which Christ conferred upon Peter and his Successors, and in communion with the Bishops of the Catholic Church, *I confirm that the direct and voluntary killing of an innocent human being is always gravely immoral,*" adding that this doctrine is discernible through **reason** as well as being "reaffirmed by Sacred Scripture, transmitted by the Tradition of the Church and taught by the ordinary and universal Magisterium" (*EV* #57; also used for a similar condemnation of **abortion** in #62). While it is unclear whether this formula meant to claim infallibility, the formula has not been employed further by

John Paul II or by his successor **Benedict XVI**. Even if a doctrine is not proposed infallible, it still should be received with the religious respect (*obsequium religiosum*) called for in *LG* #25. *For further reading*, see Cardinal Avery Dulles, "The Hermeneutics of Dogmatic Statements," ch. 11 in *The Survival of Dogma* (Garden City, NJ: Doubleday, 1971), 171–84. **See also** *ultramontanism*.

In forma communi **and** *in forma specifica* refers to one of two modes of indicating a level of papal approval or authorization for a document issued by a Vatican **dicastery** (such as the **CDF**). The usual mode is *in forma communi* ("in the common form"), which indicates that the pope has seen the document in question and authorized its release, but the document itself carries only the relative weight of the issuing office and does not constitute an exercise of the ordinary papal magisterium (such as an **encyclical** or apostolic exhortation). Examples of Vatican documents issued *in forma communi* include the CDF's two instructions on **reproductive technologies**, the 1987 *Donum vitae*, and the 2008 *Dignitas personae*. However, the other mode, *in forma specifica* ("in specific form"), is used for those documents that even though they originate with a Vatican office, the pope himself adds his own authority to the document and thus gives it added extrinsic authority. An example of an *in forma specifica* document is the 1997 Vatican "Instruction on Some Questions Regarding Collaboration of Nonordained Faithful in Priests' Sacred Ministry," which **John Paul II** commanded be issued *in forma specifica* largely due to the fact that this document had a number of liturgical norms. Thus, by attaching this added papal authority to it he gave it the equivalent force of papal law. **See also** *charism of office*, *credenda*, *encyclicals*, *ex cathedra*, *infallibilism*, *infallibility*, **Lumen gentium**, *magisterium*, and *tenenda*. *For further reading*, see Francis A. Sullivan, *Creative Fidelity: Weighing and Interpreting Documents of the Magisterium* (New York: Paulist Press, 1996).

Informed consent involves the moral and legal obligation on the part of those offering services (usually medical) or engaged in research on human subjects to make certain that the services, treatment, research, and so on are well understood by the patient or his proxy, especially in terms of risks, **burdens**, and costs in the light of potential benefits. After abuses in a number of highly questionable research experiments came to light, such as the Tuskegee Institute syphilis clinical study on poor, rural African Americans (1932–72), and the appropriation without sufficient notification of the cells of African American cancer patient Henrietta Lacks by George Gey at Johns Hopkins University in 1951, a variety of laws and research protocols have now been put into place to guard against such questionable practices in the future. **See also** *autonomy (bioethical principle)*, and *principlism*. **For further reading**, see Rebecca Skloot, *The Immortal Life of Henrietta Lacks* (New York: Random House, 2010, 2011).

Infused knowledge and infused virtues refer to God's special gifts that otherwise would be humanly unattainable. The **magisterium's charism of office** is not considered infused knowledge, as if God gave the bishops a special epistemological conduit unavailable to other humans. Examples of infused knowledge are mystical revelations received by some of the great saints, such as Teresa of Avila and Ignatius of Loyola, or the inspiration given to the biblical writers and prophets. Jesus Christ also had access to this kind of divine knowledge during his earthly life. The infused virtues likewise are special gifts of God and are also referred to as the **theological virtues** of faith, hope, and **charity** (or **love**). By contrast, **acquired knowledge and virtues** are the result of **human experience** and effort. **See also** *habit and virtue*.

Insemination. See **artificial insemination**; **see also** *reproductive technologies*.

The **inseparability principle** (procreative and unitive dimensions of the marital relation), first articulated in **Paul VI's** 1968 *Humanae vitae* and repeated regularly by **John Paul II** (see *FC* #32), holds that no form of **birth control** can be used in Christian **marriage** that would block, separate, or sacrifice either the procreative dimension or unitive (love) dimension of the conjugal act. **See also** *reproductive technologies* and *sterilization*.

Intention is often treated as if it were a singular motive, chosen by **reason** and **free will**, driving a moral choice, that is, the *finis operantis*. A moral act (*actus humanus*) requires an intention that in turn helps determine the **moral object** (*finis operis*) and the **species of moral act** (*ST II-I*, Q. 18, art. 6). But many decisions and their corresponding actions have a variety of intentions, and some of these may be in tension with the principal intention (*finis operantis*) or the *finis operis*. The plurality of intentions comes into play with **intrinsic evil**, which denotes moral objects that cannot be changed from evil to good simply by "*ulterior* intentions of the one acting and the circumstances" (*VS* #80). "Ulterior" here means "additional" or "further." Thus, if one chooses to directly terminate an otherwise viable fetus, the moral object (*finis operis*) is a **direct abortion**. Additional intentions, such as a desire to reduce economic hardship or psychological **suffering** due to an unwanted pregnancy may be "good" in abstract isolation, but in light of the **circumstances** and principal intention (*finis operantis*), these otherwise "good" intentions cannot transform the wrong act into a right act. On the other hand, if the circumstances and principal intention were to change, for example, as in an **ectopic pregnancy**, the termination of the fetal life is no longer "elective" but is medically required to save the life of the mother in a situation in which the fetus will die regardless of what is done or not done. In this case the *finis operantis* is to save the only life that can be saved, and the corresponding moral object (*finis operis*) is good and sanctioned by **proportionate reason** in light of these quite different circumstances, bearing out the Scholastic axiom "*Finis operis semper reducitur in finem operantis*" (The moral object [*finis operis*] ultimately comes down to [*semper reducitur*] the [principal] intention of the agent [*finem operantis*]), and bearing out the need to consider all of the **fonts of morality**.

Interdict. See **canonical penalties**

Interest-taking. See **usury and interest-taking**, and **capitalism**

Interim ethic is a term popularized by Albert Schweitzer for the interpretation of the **biblical ethics** contained in the New Testament, especially the **Sermon on the Mount**, which was considered to be a demanding yet provisional ethic for the early Church that would apply for the relatively short period envisioned before the definitive Second Coming. **See also** *Proprium* and *Zielgebot*.

Internal forum. See **forum, external and internal**

Intoxication. See **advertence** and **culpability**

Intrinsece inhonestum is used in **Paul VI's** 1968 **encyclical** *Humanae vitae* #14 to condemn artificial **birth control**: *Quapropter erret omnino, qui arbitretur coniugalem actum, sua fecunditate ex industria destitutum, ideoque intrinsece inhonestum, fecundis totius coniugum vitae congressionibus comprobari posse.* The term is quite difficult to translate accurately and concisely into precise idiomatic English without losing a good deal of nuance in the Latin original. The simplest cognate would be "intrinsically dishonest" and is so rendered in many English renditions of *Humanae vitae*, whereas others translate it as "intrinsically wrong" or "**intrinsically evil**" with the sentence appearing as "Consequently, it is a serious error to think that a whole married life of otherwise normal relations can justify sexual intercourse which is deliberately contraceptive and so intrinsically dishonest [wrong, evil]." The

Latin term for **intrinsic evil** (*intrinsece malum in se*) is widely established in the Catholic moral tradition, but *Humanae vitae* employed *inhonestum* instead. This vocabulary choice has been widely discussed among moralists since. *Inhonestum* in classical Latin carries the nuance of being "ignoble," "unworthy," or "less than ideal," such as might be used to describe a student who uses a study substitute such as *Cliff Notes* or *Wikipedia* instead of reading the assigned text. Such behavior would obviously fall far short of educational ideals but would not normally be viewed as serious as something like plagiarism.

Intrinsic evil (*intrinsece malum in se*, "intrinsically evil in itself") refers to the situation in which the evil occurs, including **circumstances** and **intention**. The **fonts of morality** require that every moral act, including intrinsic evil, has a human agent with **freedom** and intention (*finis operantis*) for the act to be a moral act (*actus humanus*). Circumstances are essential to the evaluation of every act since humans can act only in a particular time and space context. Taken together, the **action *in se***, the circumstances, and the intention produce the *finis operis* of the act as a whole. To claim that "intrinsically evil acts" pay no consideration to any circumstances or intention is seriously mistaken since an act devoid of circumstances and intention could never be a free human moral act. The concept "intrinsic evil" underscores that an act whose **moral object** (*finis operis*) is morally wrong could never be made morally right by ulterior ("further") consideration of mitigating circumstances or other intentions (see *VS* #70–72, 75, 78–82). For example, **direct abortion** is intrinsically evil by its object chosen, which is the intentional elective termination of an otherwise viable fetus. Other circumstances and intentions such as the economic status of the mother may lessen the **culpability** and evil of the act but will not make it morally good (see *VS* #81). Likewise, every homicide is a killing of a **human person**, but every killing is not the intrinsic evil of murder. What differentiates murder from other forms of killing? Intention and circumstances.

Intuitionism, a philosophical theory popular among some early-twentieth-century analytic philosophers, posits that an individual's own intuition is the fundamental mode of grasping moral knowledge and reality, including knowledge of God. This is much like the aesthetic judgment that "beauty is in the eye of the beholder," which presumes we can never arrive at facts about what constitutes true beauty. To call "X" a thing of beauty is ultimately a prejudice or intuition about someone's preferences since we can never come to an objective knowledge of, much less agreement on, what constitutes "beauty." Intuitionism is critiqued as falling into subjectivism and relativism, though another version, called "ethical intuitionism" or "moral intuitionism," does hold to the existence of objective facts of morality. Since these facts cannot be determined through scientific analysis, it is a human's intuitive **capacity** that furnishes evaluative ethical knowledge.

Invincible and vincible ignorance. See **ignorance** and **conscience (erroneous)**

In vitro fertilization (IVF). See **reproductive technologies**

Irregularity. See **impediment and irregularity**, and **canon law**

Is/ought distinction. See **naturalistic fallacy**

Iudicium de actu ponendo and *iudicium de positione actus* (judgment of the act to be undertaken and about the position of the act). See **conscience (faculty of)**

Ius ad bellum (justification for war), *ius in bello* (just conduct in war), *ius post bellum* (just conduct after the war, e.g., reconstruction) are three core criteria of **just war theory**. *Ius ad bellum* centers on establishing that there exists a truly just cause that is a last resort for going to war. *Ius in bello* focuses on the use of **proportionate means** in the prosecution of the war, for example, not targeting noncombatants. *Ius post bellum* is a more recent reflection on the responsibility of the party beginning the war to commit to rebuilding the society and its infrastructure that has borne the brunt of the war's damages and cost.

IVF (in vitro fertilization). See **reproductive technologies**

J

N.B. Latin terms that might begin with "J" such as *"judicium"* or *"jus ad bellum"* are found under the letter "I" since there is no "J" in classical Latin.

Jansenism is a movement that emphasized the power of **original sin** and human depravity, leading to great moral rigidity and excessive **scrupulosity**, and particularly opposed any **casuistry** or use of **probabilism** to argue for a looser interpretation of the moral law. Innocent X in 1653 condemned as heresy five core propositions taken from *Augustinus* by Belgian bishop Cornelius Jansen (1585–1638), including tenets such as that some of God's commandments are impossible to keep (see *Deus impossibilia non iubet*), that humans can never resist interior grace and must be free of all external constraint if they are to obtain merit for their good actions (see **free will**), and that Christ died for all. Though condemned, vestiges of Jansenism remain up to the present, especially in attitudes of great pessimism about the possibility of human **conversion**, and infrequency of **Communion** (until **Pius X**) and a stress on moral **rigorism** and **tutiorism**.

Janssens, Louis, is an important twentieth-century moral theologian on the faculty of Louvain (Leuven) who is best known as a major proponent of the notion of **personalism**.

John XXIII—Pope (November 25, 1881–June 3, 1963) was born Angelo Giuseppe Roncalli, was elected as a "transition successor" to **Pius XII** in 1958 one month shy of his seventy-seventh birthday, and was known affectionately as "Good Pope John" for his good-natured, easy-going manner. He surprised many with a number of bold moves in his brief reign, such as calling **Vatican II**, beginning the revision of the 1917 *Code of Canon Law* (completed in 1983), and establishing the **Pontifical Commission on Births** to reevaluate the Church's teaching on artificial birth control. He issued two **social encyclicals**, *Mater et magistra* (1961) and *Pacem in terris*, the latter issued just two months before his death, and the first **encyclical** addressed to "all men of good will," rather than the customary audience of just the bishops or laity of the Roman Catholic Church. His opening address of Vatican II, *Gaudet mater* *ecclesia* ("Mother Church Rejoices"), critiqued the "prophets of doom" who "in these modern times see nothing but prevarication and ruin. . . . The Church has always opposed . . . errors [but] nowadays . . . prefers to make use of the medicine of mercy rather than that of severity." He was beatified along with **Pius IX** by **John Paul II** in September 2000. *For further reading*, see his spiritual diary, *Journal of a Soul* (London: Geoffrey Chapman, 1965); and Peter Hebblethwaite and Margaret Hebblethwaite, *John XXIII: Pope of the Century* (New York: Continuum International, 2000).

John Paul II—Pope (May 18, 1920–April 2, 2005, beatified 2011), born Karol Józef Wojtyła, on October 16, 1978, succeeded John Paul I (Albino Luciani), who had reigned for just thirty-three days after the death of **Paul VI** on August 6, 1978. Reigning nearly twenty-seven years until April 2, 2005, only **Pius IX**'s pontificate was longer (1846–78). Trained in Rome as a philosopher, Wojtyła participated in **Vatican II** as archbishop of Krakow and became the first non-Italian pope since Dutch pope Adrian VI (1522–23). A pontiff of many records, he visited some 129 countries, beatified 1,340, and canonized 483—more than the combined tally of the previous five centuries—and he was beatified himself by his successor **Benedict XVI** on May 1, 2011. In moral theology his writings railed against what he saw to be modern philosophical and cultural errors of **relativism**, **secularism**, and what he termed a "**culture of death**" versus a "**culture of life**": of his fourteen **encyclicals**, see especially *Veritatis splendor* (1993), *Evangelium vitae* (1995), and *Fides et ratio* (1998). Theologically conservative, especially in matters of **sexual ethics**, he nevertheless articulated what he termed a modern **theology of the body** and was relatively liberal in his **social encyclicals**, such as *Laborem exercens* (1981), *Sollicitudo rei socialis* (1987), and *Centesimus annus* (1991). Critical of free-market **capitalism** and likewise suspicious of **socialism** and **liberation theology**, he was an implacable foe of **communism**. The **Solidarity** movement he supported in his native Poland helped bring an end to the **Communist** regimes in Eastern Europe. While not denying outright the **just war theory**, he was highly critical of the two Bush presidents' Iraq wars (1991 and 2003). He did modify the traditional teaching on **capital punishment**, stating that virtually no modern usage of it could be justified (see *EV* #56 and *CCC* #2267). *For further reading*, see Charles E. Curran, *The Moral Theology of Pope John Paul II* (Washington, DC: Georgetown University Press, 2005).

Jone, Heribert, OFM, Cap. See **manualist tradition**

Justice (*ius*) a complex polyvalent term that can connote **cardinal virtue**, fairness, **law**, a legal system, judgment, justification, rectitude, subjective right, retribution, restoration, and so on. **Thomas Aquinas** treats justice at length (see *ST II-II*, Q. 57–122). **See also** *affirmative action, communitarianism, contract justice, distributive justice, human rights, just war theory, principlism, reparation and restitution, restorative justice, retributive justice*, and *social encyclicals and social teaching*.

Justification. See **justice, justification by faith, reason**, and *simul iustus et peccator*

Justification by faith. See *sola scriptura, sola fide, sola gratia, solus Christus, and soli Deo gloria*

Just war theory is the set of criteria to guide an assessment of the moral legitimacy and urgency of deciding to go to war (*ius ad bellum*), the conduct of the war itself (*ius in bello*) including fair treatment of prisoners and protection of noncombatants, and the use of **proportionate means** in weapons, tactics, and so on. More recently, a third core criterion has been advanced (*ius post bellum*) that focuses on the responsibilities of the warring parties, and especially the victor, to restore the war-torn areas and to build a lasting peace. **Augustine** had outlined three key criteria: just cause, legitimate authority to wage war (e.g., by governments charged with maintaining public order), and right intention of those going to war. **Thomas Aquinas** further refined these criteria (see *ST II-II*, Q. 40) and, using the principle of the **double effect**, supported the legitimacy of using even deadly force to resist an unjust aggressor, although the force always had to be of proportionate means. Further reflection on this tradition added criteria of going to war only as a last resort after all other means had been exhausted to address a serious necessity (e.g., to restore a seriously egregious and enduring perversion of **justice**), a realistic and reasonable hope of success, and protection of noncombatants in the war zone. The US bishops issued a 1983 **pastoral letter**, *The Challenge of Peace*, and **John Paul II** discussed war extensively in his 1995 *Evangelium vitae*, while the *Catechism of the Catholic Church* summarizes the Catholic tradition on just war (see *CCC* 2302–17). Critiques of the just war theory are many and diverse but tend to center on one or more of the following themes:

- **Pacifism** is dictated by Jesus Christ and thus is the only legitimate Christian stance.
- It is practically impossible to determine whether all of the criteria for a just war are truly present in any given situation.
- The development of modern weapons such as nuclear arms, the difficulty of protecting noncombatants, and asymmetrical tactics (such as

terrorism and guerilla war) run the very serious risk of exacerbating any unjust situation.

- There is an ever-present danger of using just war discourse for propaganda purposes to rationalize or gain support for a nation's less-than-just political, economic, military, or imperial aims.

For further reading, see Lisa Sowle Cahill, *Love Your Enemies: Discipleship, Pacifism, and Just War Theory* (Minneapolis: Fortress, 1994); Jean Bethke Elshtain, ed. *Just War Theory: Readings in Social and Political Theory* (New York: New York University Press, 1992); Thomas Massaro and Thomas Shannon, *Catholic Perspectives on Peace and War* (Lanham MD: Sheed and Ward, 2003); James Turner Johnson, "Just War, As It Was and Is," *First Things* (January 2005): 14–24; and John Howard Yoder, *When War Is Unjust: Being Honest in Just-War Thinking*, rev. ed. (Maryknoll, NY: Orbis Books, 1996).

K

Kant, Immanuel (April 22, 1724–February 12, 1804), is the leading Enlightenment philosopher who strove in his 1781 *Critique of Pure Reason* to resolve what he considered metaphysics' failure to properly unite **reason** and **experience**. Three works expound his ethical philosophy: *Groundwork of the Metaphysic of Morals* (1785), *Critique of Practical Reason* (1788), and *Metaphysics of Morals* (1797). Kant's **deontology** holds that only actions done out of duty have true moral value, as formulated in his *Categorical Imperative*: "Act only according to that maxim whereby you can, at the same time, will that it should become a universal law." Two additional corollaries to this categorical imperative are that one must always treat another **human person** never simply as a means but always at the same time as an end, and that one should always act as if he were a **law**-making member of a kingdom of ends. Kant's stress on the **moral autonomy** of **conscience** and the minimal role he ascribed to religious **authority** led to strong critiques, especially in Church circles, that claimed his philosophy was grounded in epistemological **subjectivism** and **relativism**. More recently, **postmodernism** would condemn most Enlightenment thinkers, including Kant, as being excessively rationalistic.

Kelly, Gerald, SJ (1902–64), is an important pre-**Vatican II** moralist who taught at the Jesuit theologate in St. Marys, Kansas, and, in collaboration with **John Ford, SJ,** produced a considerable amount of the twentieth-century **manualist tradition**, such as their *Contemporary Moral Theology* (Westminster, MD: Newman Press, 1958–63). On his own, Kelly wrote what became a classic of pre-Vatican II **sexual ethics**, *Modern Youth and Chastity* (St. Louis: Queen's Work, 1941); a helpful book on **casuistry** in the **sacrament of reconciliation**, *The Good Confessor* (New York: Sentinel Press, 1951); and he was an early pioneer in **bioethics** with his *Medico-Moral Problems* (St. Louis: Catholic Hospital Association of the United States and Canada, 1958) as well as *Theological Studies'* annual "Notes on Moral Theology."

Kingdom of God/heaven (Greek: βασιλεία τοῦ θεοῦ, Basileia tou Theou/ Βασιλεία τῶν Οὐρανῶν, Basileia tōn Ouranōn) is central to Jesus's proclamation of the Gospel, especially in the **Sermon on the Mount**, and by extension to all of **biblical ethics** that elaborate what should characterize our relationship with **God**, one another (*koinonia*), and the rest of **creation**.

Koinonia (Greek, κοινωνία) signifies community in the sense of communion and fellowship that ideally should exist within the Church (see Acts 4:32–37). Those attitudes, behaviors, and **sins** that divide, strain, or break the bonds of *koinonia* need to be addressed and rectified. **See also** *liberation theology*, *restorative justice*, and *sacrament of reconciliation*.

L

Laborem exercens, *On Human Work*, is the 1981 **social encyclical** of **John Paul II** that asserts that a right to meaningful and dignified work is basic to human nature.

The **Lambeth Conference** is the major assembly of the **Anglican Communion** (including Episcopalians) held every ten years, originally at Lambeth Palace, the official London residence of the **Archbishop of Canterbury**, the Primate of England, and symbolic head of the Anglican Communion. Being the Protestant denomination closest to Roman Catholicism in liturgy and theology, its actions are watched with keen interest in the Vatican. For example, when the 1930 7th Lambeth Conference passed Resolution 15, which gave guarded approval to artificial **birth control**, this provided the impetus for **Pius XI**'s 1930 **encyclical *Casti connubii***, in which the pontiff reaffirmed the Catholic Church's ban on all artificial means to regulate births. The 1958 9th Lambeth Conference's call for respect for the **conscience**-based decisions of married couples using birth control added to the context of the discussion in **John XXIII**'s **Pontifical Commission on Births** as well as some of the negative reaction to **Paul VI**'s 1968 *Humanae vitae*. Other Lambeth Conferences supported **women's ordination** to the diaconate, priesthood, and episcopacy (1968 and 1978), and the conferences held in 1998 and 2008 were marked by considerable division over the acceptability of **homosexuality** and the ordination of active homosexuals as priests and bishops, which had been done by Episcopalian churches in the United States.

Latae sententiae are "automatic" **canonical penalties** and are distinguished from "declared" penalties (*ferendae sententiae*).

Law, according to **Thomas Aquinas** in his "Treatise on Law" (see *ST I-II* Q. 90–108), "is a rule and measure of acts, whereby man is induced to act or is restrained from acting: for *lex* [law] is derived from *ligare* [to bind], because it binds one to act." He elaborates further that law is an exercise of **reason**, ordered to the promotion of the **common good**, and promulgated

135

by a legitimate **authority**. He outlines various types of law (Q. 91), such as the eternal law (*lex aeterna*), **natural law** (the human participation in **God**'s eternal law, Q. 94), human law (Q. 95), and **divine law** as well as the laws of the Old Testament and New Testament (see Q. 98–108). **See also** *canon law*, *doubtful law*, *epikeia*, *positive law*, and *probabilism*.

Law and gospel. See **biblical ethics** and **Protestant ethics**

Laxism denotes the opposite of **rigorism, tutiorism,** and **probabiliorism,** which hold that the safer or stricter opinions should always be followed in situations of moral **doubt**. Laxism maintains that as long as there is at least some probability to the less safe course of action, this could then be followed with a clean **conscience**. Formally condemned by popes Alexander VII in 1665 (*DH #2021–65; ND #2005*) and Innocent XI in 1679 (*DH #2101–65; ND #2006*), no moral theologian ever formally espoused this position. Blaise Pascal accused Jesuit **casuistry** in his 1657 *Provincial Letters* as being a form of laxism, though the Church ultimately endorsed **Alphonsus Liguori**'s and the seventeenth-century Jesuit moralists' **probabilism**. See also *lex dubia non obligat*.

Lectio continua ("continued reading") is the Church's practice exemplified in the three-year Sunday cycle and the two-year daily cycle of the lectionary, which tries to read liturgically as much of the Bible as possible. *Lectio continua* also can be done as a part of the ancient tradition of *lectio divina*, in which scripture furnishes the basis for meditative prayer. *Lectio continua* responds to **Vatican II**'s *Optatam totius* mandate that scripture be the soul of all theology, and is especially important in **biblical ethics**. This practice also can function as a corrective to the natural tendency to remember or privilege just certain parts of the Bible and to overlook or neglect other passages.

Legalism is a pejorative term for making observance of the **law** an end in itself rather than a means to a larger goal, such as the **common good**, public order, or as an aid toward fostering a life of moral rectitude and **virtue**. Legalism is a perennial tension in any community, and Jesus himself inveighed against this attitude frequently in his encounters with Pharisees (see Mk. 7:5–13). The problem Jesus identified was the Pharisees' fundamental misunderstanding of God, whose nature is essentially **love** and not legalism. Theologically this problem surfaces in the dichotomy between **law and gospel**, and in problematic attitudes associated with **antinomianism** on one hand and **Voluntarism, rigorism,** and **tutiorism** on the other. **See also**

epikeia, lex dubia non obligat, positive law, probabilism and probabiliorism, and *works righteousness.*

Leo XIII—Pope (March 2, 1810–July 20, 1903), born Vincenzo Gioacchino Raffaele Luigi Pecci, succeeded **Pius IX** in 1878 and to date is the oldest and third-longest-reigning pontiff after his immediate predecessor, who ruled from 1846 to 1878, and **John Paul II**, who reigned from 1978 to 2005. He is best known for his 1891 *Rerum novarum*, the first **social encyclical** of modern times, which supported rights of labor to organize while rejecting **communism** and recognizing a legitimate role of **capitalism** and **private property**. Continuing Pius IX's protest against the Italian government for the loss of the Papal States, Leo never left the Vatican after his papal election. His 1880 encyclical *Arcanum Divinae Sapientiae* denounced the state's efforts to supplant the Church in the regulation of Christian **marriage**. His 1879 encyclical *Aeterni Patris* reinvigorated the use of **Scholasticism** and **Thomas Aquinas** in Christian philosophy in outlining the proper relationship between faith and philosophy while cautioning against **secularism**, and his 1893 encyclical *Providentissimus Deus* strengthened the use of Scripture in theology. His 1899 apostolic letter *Testem benevolentiae nostrae* inveighed against **Americanism**, which purportedly promoted anticlericalism, individualism, the rights of **conscience**, and free press over the legitimate **authority** and oversight of the Holy See. Leo also ended the practice of creating *castrati* for the Sistine Choir and was the first pontiff to have been filmed and recorded.

Lesser evil (Latin, *minus malum*) is an expression of **right reason** (*recta ratio*) put into practice. As the medieval theologian Thomas à Kempis put it, "*De duobus malis, minus est semper eligendum*" ("In matters concerning two evils, the lesser is always to be chosen"). This corresponds logically to **Thomas Aquinas**'s first principle of the **natural law**: *Bonum est faciendum et prosequendum, et malum vitandum* ("The good is to be done and fostered, and evil avoided"). If we cannot "avoid" **evil** entirely, then at least we should reduce the evil caused if this be in our power. The **manualist tradition casuistry** also held that one can "choose" to do a **moral evil** so a greater moral evil can be avoided: "It is always allowed materially to cooperate in another's **sin** to avoid a greater moral evil" (Anthony Browne, *Handbook of Notes on Theology* [St. Louis: Redemptorist Fathers, 1938], 10). This principle does not mean that as long as one could imagine a "greater" evil that might be done, somehow the "lesser" evil actually chosen is transformed from bad to good, for example, rationalizing that casual sex is somehow justified through a **safe-sex** practice of condom usage.

A quite different case arises if, instead of a college student's condom choice, public health officials are grappling with a public park haven for drug addicts. Efforts to clean up the park have been unsuccessful as well as attempts to get the individuals into effective rehabilitation. The addicts share used needles with each other, and this greatly facilitates the spread of a variety of diseases from hepatitis to HIV. The health officials decide that while they seemingly cannot eradicate this serious public health concern, they might be able to lessen its negative effects if they provided a clean needle-exchange program to the park's denizens. Under this policy anyone could get a sterile, fresh needle if they simply turned in a used needle in return. The hope then (borne out by several studies) is that at least some of the negative effects of illicit drug usage would be reduced.

While some argue this program would constitute **formal cooperation with evil**, most moralists hold the opposite view, that this remains **material cooperation** justified by **proportionate reason**. Care must be taken to avoid **scandal**, although few would mistakenly conclude that a needle-exchange policy means public officials are condoning recreational drug use. The drug addict's *finis operis* and *finis operantis* in using the clean needle is to get high, while a secondary **intention** may be to reduce the risk of a secondary infection. But the *finis operis* and *finis operantis* of the public health officials is only to reduce disease transmission in the most practical way possible. No one may ever personally commit a moral evil to avoid even a graver moral evil, but as the previous example illustrates, sometimes what may look like a very similar action from a photographic point of view may represent quite different moral goals and intentions. *For further reading*, see James T. Bretzke, "The Lesser Evil: Insights from the Catholic Moral Tradition," *America* (March 26, 2007): 16–18; Daniel P. Sulmasy, "Catholic Participation in Needle-and-Syringe-Exchange Programs for Injection-Drug Users: An Ethical-Analysis," *Theological Studies* 73 (June 2012): 422–41. **See also** *double effect*, *natural law*, and *tolerance*.

Lex aeterna (eternal law) expresses the **divine law** as contrasted with the other types of **law**, such as human law or the **natural law**. The precise nature of **God**'s eternal law remains an object of debate, especially among classical Protestant and Catholic approaches to theological ethics. **Thomas Aquinas** held that God's eternal law primarily was a *lex indita non scripta*, a law inscribed on the human heart and not "written" or promulgated in an external fashion as is a human law. The natural law is the human participation in the *lex aeterna*, and indeed, every proper law as an ordinance of **reason** comes from the *lex aeterna* (see *ST I-II*, Q. 93, art. 3). Other theologians, for example, **Karl Barth**, do not accept this understanding of the relation between the *lex aeterna* and the natural law, holding instead for a type of theonomy expressed as **divine command ethics**.

Lex dubia non obligat (a doubtful law does not oblige) is a key interpretive principle both in **canon law** and in moral theology, associated with *CIC* #18's *odia restringi* ("burdens are restricted") principle as well as Jesus's polemic against the Pharisees, who lay heavy burdens on others (see Mt. 23:3–5). In moral theology this principle is contrasted with **legalism**, **rigorism**, and **tutiorism**, and instead is closely allied with the doctrine of **probabilism** such that if a legitimate **doubt** exists regarding the application of a law or principle to a particular situation or case, then the law is "doubtful" and one could in **good faith** choose the path of greater **freedom**.

Lex indita non scripta (law is inscribed [on the human heart], not written down) is **Thomas Aquinas**'s expression to describe how humans come to grasp the **natural law**, that is, the human participation in **God**'s own *lex aeterna* (eternal law). The **human person** finds this **law** inscribed on her heart and uses **right reason** (*recta ratio*) to respond in **conscience** to what she understands that law requires. To do this in authentic **moral autonomy** is how **Vatican II** expressed the relationship of **conscience** to both God and the moral law: "In the depths of his conscience, man detects a law which he does not impose upon himself, but which holds him to obedience. Always summoning him to love **good** and avoid **evil**, the voice of conscience when necessary speaks to his heart: do this, shun that. For man has in his heart a law written by God; to obey it is the very dignity of man; according to it he will be judged" (*GS* #16).

Lex talionis, the law of retaliation or "an eye for an eye," is a **retributive justice** principle from the Latin *talio*, meaning a punishment equal to the injury sustained. This principle is often misunderstood as either requiring or justifying a punishment that is as harsh as the injury caused, when actually this principle was formulated to limit punishments so they could not go beyond the level of the original offense. This reciprocity principle is also found in both the Old Testament (Ex. 21:22–25; Lev. 24:19–21; Dt. 19:16–21) and the Code of Hammurabi (§230). The themes of mercy, **forgiveness**, and reconciliation drawn from New Testament **biblical ethics** such as Jesus's admonition in the **Sermon on the Mount** to turn the other cheek in Matthew 5:38–39 certainly challenge harsher applications of retributive justice and the *lex talionis*.

Lex valet ut in pluribus (the law holds in most cases) is an axiom that refers to the various levels of universality of **moral norms** derived from **Thomas Aquinas's natural law** treatise (see *ST I-II,* Q. 94, art. 4). Not all moral norms are absolute, nor do they bind in the same way. Those norms formulated in **speculative reason** can be universally or "necessarily" true, but as we descend to concrete application, then **practical reason** must be employed in making a **prudential judgment**, which due to **contingency and fallibility** may not be universally applicable in the same way in every situation. Such a **concrete material norm** holds *ut in pluribus* (in most cases) and still serves as a generally useful principle but should not be treated as if it binds absolutely in every case. For example, the obligation to preserve life is "law" (*lex*) that is *valet ut in pluribus*, which does not require **vitalism** but rather a **discernment** of **ordinary and extraordinary means** to determine legitimate circumstances in which life support systems are terminated.

Liberation theology focuses contextual theological reflection, especially on unjust and oppressive economic, political, and cultural systems that lead to structural evil and social sin with a view to transforming these through an orthopraxis that calls for **solidarity** with the oppressed, leading to adoption of the so-called preferential option for the poor. The term "liberation theology" was first used by African American Protestant theologian **James Cone** but gained greater awareness through the Peruvian Gustavo Gutiérrez's *A Theology of Liberation: History, Politics, and Salvation* (Maryknoll, NY: Orbis Books, 1973). The movement undeniably has been one of the most influential theological and ethical developments of the last half of the twentieth century, although it has also come under both ecclesial and political critique for its methods of critical social analysis, which critics said amounts to Marxist class struggle without the explicit atheistic charge against organized religion as the opiate of the masses. Liberation theologians were often charged as being with **Communist** regimes or political movements, especially in Latin America and Asia. During the pontificate of **John Paul II** the **CDF** under the leadership of **Cardinal Joseph Ratzinger** issued two critical Instructions on Certain Aspects of Liberation Theology. The first, in 1984, was quite severe, though the second, in 1986, acknowledged some positive aspects of liberation theology but reaffirmed problematic "ambiguities" in the movement as well as dangers that remained in the liberation approach. Several theologians such as Leonardo Boff, OP; Marciano Vidal, CSsR; Tissa Balasuriya, OMI; and Jon Sobrino, SJ, found certain of their works formally condemned by the CDF, and numerous others have been investigated. Liberation theology as a broad methodology—or what Robert Schreiter, CPPS, calls a "theological flow"—has been taken up in a variety of related disciplines such as **feminist ethics, biblical**

ethics, and **womanist**, **mujerista**, Korean **Minjung**, and **queer** theologies, to name a few. The bibliography on liberation theology is enormous, but *for further reading*, see Alfred T. Hennelly, ed., *Liberation Theology: A Documentary History* (Maryknoll, NY: Orbis Books, 1990); Ignacio Ellacuria and Jon Sobrino, eds., *Mysterium liberationis: Fundamental Concepts of Liberation* (Maryknoll, NY: Orbis Press, 1993); Robert Schreiter, *The New Catholicity: Theology between the Global and the Local* (Maryknoll, NY: Orbis, 1997); Antônio Moser and Bernardino Leers, *Moral Theology: Dead Ends and Ways Forward* (Wellwood, UK: Burns & Oates, 1990); and Christopher Rowland, ed., *The Cambridge Companion to Liberation Theology*, 2nd ed. (New York: Cambridge University Press, 1999, 2007).

Liguori, Alphonsus, CSsR (1696–1787), was the founder of the Congregation of the Most Holy Redeemer (Redemptorists) and one of the greatest moral theologians in the period between the **Council of Trent** and **Vatican II**. He suffered from **scrupulosity** but always sought to mediate the Gospel compassion in his practical pastoral approach to the problems and practical questions posed by the laity. He steered a middle course between **laxism** and the **rigorism** associated with **Jansenism**. His doctrine of **probabilism** (technically called equiprobabilism) was attacked by those who espoused a stricter **probabiliorism** or **tutiorism**, but ultimately his theory became the established Catholic moral position. He was canonized in 1839 and in 1871 proclaimed a Doctor of the Church and patron saint of moral theologians.

Living in sin is the colloquial term used in the pre-**Vatican II** Church for cohabitating couples, either in irregular **marriage** or in what came to be called a **domestic partner** relationship. Based on the *parvitas materiae in Sexto* view that any transgression against the Sixth Commandment represented at least **grave matter** and a probability of **mortal sin**, the common judgment was that such couples were likely not living in the **state of grace** but rather of sin and would possibly be condemned to hell if they should die unrepentant. Post–Vatican II moral theologians largely, though not universally, offer a more nuanced understanding of these complex realities. *For further reading*, see *Catechism of the Catholic Church*, especially #2353, and #2360–67; the **CDF**'s 1975 "Declaration on Certain Problems of Sexual Ethics," *Persona humana* #1–7; and Kevin Kelly, *New Directions in Sexual Ethics: Moral Theology and the Challenge to AIDS* (London: Geoffrey Chapman, 1998).

Living will. See **advance health care directive, ANH, autonomy (bioethical principle), death with dignity, euthanasia, ordinary and extraordinary means, PVS**, and **vitalism**

Locked-in syndrome. See **states of consciousness: brain death, coma, PVS, MCS, and locked-in syndrome**

Locutio contra mentem (Latin, "speech against what is in the mind") is an intentional violation of what one believed to be "true" (regardless of whether this was actually the case), that is, lying. In the **manualist tradition**, violating the **faculty** of speech was *contra naturam* and **intrinsically evil**. However, its **casuistry** also placed great emphasis on the context of any supposedly "false" speech, allowing for employment of the so-called **mental reservation** or basic etiquette that did not reasonably demand the full truth and nothing but the truth. In responding to the greeting, "How are you?" one who was in fact suffering from minor malady could respond, "Fine, and you?" without this considered a *locutio contra mentem*. More acrimonious debates still arise over **truth and truthfulness** in more complex situations, such as shielding innocent people from a murderous mob. Some moral theologians, following **Augustine**, maintain that even in such situations a person must always answer "truthfully" to questions like "Are you harboring such people?" whereas other theologians, following the Blessed John Henry Cardinal Newman (as expressed in his *Apologia pro vita sua*), distinguish between what objectively might be a "lie" from what would also be a "**sin**." Owing to **moral impossibility** of a given circumstance Newman argued what might objectively be a "lie" would not in every instance also translate into a "sin." Still other moral theologians would hold that using misleading and even downright false speech in such situations to mislead the rampaging mob and save the innocents would not be a violation of truth but would actually be using speech in its higher moral end of communicating the truth that innocent life ought to be protected.

Logical positivism. See **positivism** and **emotivism**

Love. See **charity**; **marriage**; **sexuality, gender, sexual orientation, and sexual ethics**; and **situation ethics**.

Lumen gentium, **Vatican II**'s "Dogmatic Constitution on the Church" in which the primary metaphor employed for the Church is the "People of God," all of whom are called to the universal vocation of holiness (ch. 5). *Lumen gentium* also articulates the notion of the **magisterium** as moral teacher, calling all faithful Catholics to a respectful religious consideration (*obsequium religiosum*) of even those propositions put forward in the **ordinary magisterium** and therefore not enjoying the specific claim of **infallibility** that would be the case of an *ex cathedra* declaration or a conciliar dogma presented as a *de fide definita* (defined article of the faith). To judge the appropriate level of **assent** being called for, the faithful are enjoined to consider the triple criteria of **character, manner,** and **frequency** in their **discernment** of how to receive a particular teaching of the magisterium.

Lust. See **capital sins** and **concupiscence**

Lying. See **confidentiality and secrecy,** *locutio contra mentem,* **mental reservation,** and **truth and truthfulness**

M

Magisterium, from the Latin *magister*, indicates one who has teaching **authority** (*auctoritas*) as distinguished from dominion, which exercised governing power (*potestas*). **Thomas Aquinas** spoke of twin magisteria, that of the Church hierarchy (primarily governing) and that of the theologians (primarily teaching, though faculties such as the University of Paris handed down **excommunications** and defined heresies). After the **Council of Trent** and with the growth and centralization of the ecclesial bureaucracy in Rome, the magisterium increasingly became identified with the pope and bishops, but it was not until the nineteenth century that the current sense of the term crystalized as an exercise of the *munera* of teaching, governing, and sanctifying that is aided by **charism of office** given with episcopal ordination. The teaching *munus* is exercised in either the ordinary or extraordinary magisterium. "Ordinary" here connotes "usual" or "customary," and does not mean "everyday" or "unexceptional," whereas "extraordinary" means "special" or "supplemental" and does not signify "astounding" or "rare," even though concrete instances of the *ex cathedra* extraordinary magisterium have been quite infrequent. The ordinary magisterium does not claim **infallibility** but asks of the faithful a reception of religious respect (***obsequium religiosum***) discerned through *Lumen gentium* #25's **character, manner, and frequency criteria**. By contrast, the extraordinary magisterium invokes the claim of both infallibility and irreformability of doctrines solemnly proposed *de fide definita*. A nonexhaustive list of forms of magisterial teaching includes conciliar documents, papal **encyclicals**, apostolic exhortations, **allocutions** (addresses), documents of various Vatican **dicasteries** (such as the **CDF**), and **pastoral letters** of individual bishops and bishops conferences. *For further reading*, see John P. Boyle, *Church Teaching Authority: Historical and Theological Studies* (Notre Dame, IN: University of Notre Dame Press, 1995); Charles E. Curran and Richard A. McCormick, eds., *Readings in Moral Theology, No. 3: The Magisterium and Morality* (New York: Paulist Press, 1982); and Francis A. Sullivan, *Magisterium: Teaching Authority in the Catholic Church* (Dublin: Gill and Macmillan, 1983). Because the theme of the magisterium as been extensively treated in other entries, **see also** *credenda* and *tenenda, de fide vel moribus, deposit of faith, dissent, ecclesia discens and ecclesia docens, expert in humanity, faith*

and morals, in forma communi and in forma specifica, infallibilism, papal pri-macy, Responsum ad dubium, Roma locuta causa finita, and *ultramontanism.*

Malum in se (evil in itself). See **intrinsic evil**

Malum/mala (evil/evils). See **evil**

Malum physicum (physical evil). See **ontic evil**

The **manualist tradition** dates back to the seventeenth century, when moral theology became established as a recognizable discipline and was marked by series of **moral manuals** written primarily for the training of priests to hear **confessions**. The most important manualists were Jesuits, Redemptorists, and Dominicans, and although there were differences in organizational approaches and particular judgments of **casuistry**, in general there was a great deal of agreement regarding the articulation of general themes as well as the exposition of various principles such as the **double effect, cooperation with evil, totality**, and so on. Until the twentieth century virtually all of the moral manuals were written in Latin, although in the period shortly before and after World War II, the manuals appeared in the vernacular, such as those of Henry Davis, SJ, **John Ford, SJ**, **Gerald Kelly, SJ**, Edwin Healy, SJ, and the very popular *vademecum* of Heribert Jone, OFM, Cap. In the 1950s the manualist approach waned as the leading moral theologians such as **Bernard Häring, CSsR**, and Gérard Gillemann, SJ, began to formulate a moral theology grounded more in scriptural themes. The contemporary moral philosopher **Germain Grisez** has attempted to continue the older genre of the moral manual with his three-volume *Way of the Lord Jesus* (Chicago: Franciscan Herald Press, 1983, 1993, 1997). *For further reading*, see John A. Gallagher, *Time Past, Time Future: An Historical Study of Catholic Moral Theology* (New York: Paulist Press, 1990); and James F. Keenan, *A History of Catholic Moral Theology in the Twentieth Century: From Confessing Sins to Liberating Consciences* (New York: Continuum, 2010).

Marriage in Catholic sacramental theology requires the free consent of a baptized man and woman, each of whom is free to marry (e.g., neither has a prior marital bond or **impediment** that has not been resolved according to **canon law**). The core marks of sacramental marriage are unity of the spouses, indissolubility of the bond until one dies, openness to procreation, and the ability to complete the marital act that is per se apt for procreation (even if for any number of reasons procreation would be unlikely or even impossible). The theology of marriage has undergone considerable **historical development** from the time of **Augustine**, who posited three chief ends of marriage: *bonum prolix* (procreative good), *bonum fidei* (good of fidelity and stability), and *bonum sacramenti* (good of the sacrament). While sexual pleasure was not listed as a positive good of marriage in its own right, secondary goods such as a *remedium concupiscientiae* and paying the *debitum* acknowledged this contractual aspect of the marital union, which was also reflected in the 1917 **canon law** code. The "constancy of **Tradition**" held as the sole primary end of marriage the procreation and rearing of children, and this procreative end could never be sacrificed for any other end. This tradition was significantly modified in **Vatican II**'s *Gaudium et spes*, which affirmed that the unitive dimension of marriage is of equal dignity and that married couples had a duty to exercise **responsible parenthood** in the number and spacing of children (see *GS* #47–52), and the 1983 *Code of Canon Law* added the metaphor of **covenant** (see *CIC* #1055). **See also** *ABC*, *AIH*, *birth control*, *gender*, *inseparability principle*, *natural family planning*, *privilege (Pauline and Petrine)*, and *safe sex*. **For further reading**, see Charles E. Curran and Julie Hanlon Rubio, eds., *Readings in Moral Theology No. 15: Marriage* (New York: Paulist, 2009); and Joseph A. Selling, "Magisterial Teaching on Marriage, 1880–1968: Historical Constancy or Radical Development? *Studia Moralia* 28 (1990): 439–90.

Masturbation is defined by **Thomas Aquinas** as the "unnatural vice" and a species of the **capital sin** of **lust**, contrary to both **reason** and the natural order (*contra naturam*), and as such, after bestiality and sodomy, the gravest sexual sin ("*hoc peccatum est gravissimum*"), ranking ahead of (in descending order of gravity) incest, rape, **adultery**, **seduction**, and **fornication** (*ST II-II* Q. 154, art. 11 and 12). More recently, the *Catechism of the Catholic Church* defines masturbation as "the deliberate stimulation of the genital organs in order to derive sexual pleasure," about which (quoting *PH* #9) the **magisterium**, "constant **Tradition**, and the moral sense of the faithful [*sensus fidelium*] have been in no doubt and have firmly maintained that masturbation is an intrinsically and gravely **disordered** action." Without using Thomas's gravity rank order but again quoting *PH* #9, the primary moral defect is seeking venereal pleasure "outside of 'the sexual relationship which is demanded by the moral order and in which the total meaning of mutual self-giving and human **procreation** in the context of true love is achieved'"; the section concludes with a pastoral note on assessing relative moral **culpability** for individual masturbatory acts: "To form an equitable judgment about the subjects' moral responsibility and to guide pastoral action, one must take into account the affective immaturity, force of acquired

habit, conditions of anxiety, or other psychological or social factors that lessen or even extenuate moral culpability" (*CCC* #2352).

While as a *quaestio disputata* the topic of masturbation has not generated a great deal of contemporary discussion, some moral theologians question whether semen procurement for fertility treatments or use in **reproductive technologies** truly constitutes "masturbation" from a moral perspective, and others who note the relatively high statistical incidence of the practice among teenagers and those in situations of enforced **celibacy** question whether these **circumstances** might have a bearing on its moral meaning that might moderate the position of Thomas Aquinas. This last concern does seem to be reflected in the *Catechism*'s observation about "other psychological or social factors that lessen or even extenuate moral culpability" of the act. *For further reading*, representing sharply contrasting views (although both publications have a *nihil obstat* and an *imprimatur*), see Charles E. Curran, "Masturbation and Objectively Grave Matter," ch. 8 in *A New Look at Christian Morality*, 201–21 (Notre Dame, IN: Fides Publishers, 1968); and Ronald Lawler, Joseph M. Boyle Jr., and William E. May, "Masturbation" in *Catholic Sexual Ethics: A Summary, Explanation, and Defense* (Charlotte, NC: Our Sunday Visitor, 1985), reprinted as ch. 27 in Charles E. Curran and Richard A. McCormick, eds., *Readings in Moral Theology No. 8: Dialogue about Catholic Sexual Teaching* (New York: Paulist Press, 1993), 361–71.

Mater et magistra is the 1961 **social encyclical** of **John XXIII** on Christianity and social progress.

Material cooperation. See **compromise and compromise/cooperation with evil**. For the distinction between formal and material cooperation, see **causality.**

Material norms. See **concrete material norms**

Material sin refers to the commission of an objective moral evil by an agent that may not necessarily involve the moral culpability of formal sin if the individual lacked sufficient knowledge or consent for the sinful action. See also **sin** and **causality.**

McCormick, Richard A., SJ (October 3, 1922–February 12, 2000), gained his S.T.D. at Rome's Pontifical Gregorian University in 1957, then taught in Jesuit theologates until 1974, when he became the Rose F. Kennedy Professor of Christian Ethics at Georgetown University, and in 1986 the John A. O'Brien Professor of Christian Ethics at the University of

Notre Dame, remaining there until his death. A leader in **revisionist moral theology**, **proportionalism**, and dialogue with Protestants in **ecumenical ethics**, McCormick authored the annual "Notes on Moral Theology" in *Theological Studies* from 1965 to 1984, critically analyzing virtually all of the major developments in the field from around the world. A prolific author, he published six additional books, began and coedited with **Charles Curran** the first eleven volumes of the influential Readings in Moral Theology series while also penning numerous other articles and op-ed pieces, especially in the Jesuit weekly *America*. The son of a prominent physician, McCormick was a leader in **bioethics**, although in this area as well as in the controversy over **birth control** and *Humanae vitae*, some of his positions were in tension with those of the **magisterium**. McCormick was never publicly censured by the Vatican. *For further reading*, see Charles E. Curran, "Notes on Richard McCormick," *Theological Studies* 61 (2000): 533–42; see also McCormick's principal works: *Ambiguity in Moral Choice* (Milwaukee: Marquette University Press, 1973); *Doing Evil to Achieve Good: Moral Choice in Conflict Situations*, coedited with Paul Ramsey (Chicago: Loyola University Press, 1978); *Notes on Moral Theology: 1965 through 1980* and *Notes on Moral Theology: 1981 through 1984* (both Boston: University Press of America, 1981, 1984); *How Brave a New World?: Dilemmas in Bioethics* (Garden City, NJ: Doubleday, 1981); *Health and Medicine in the Catholic Tradition: Tradition in Transition* (New York: Crossroad, 1984); *The Critical Calling: Reflections on Moral Dilemmas since Vatican II* (Washington, DC: Georgetown University Press, 1989); *Corrective Vision: Explorations in Moral Theology* (Kansas City, MO: Sheed & Ward, 1994).

MCS (minimally conscious state). See **states of consciousness: brain death, coma, PVS, MCS, and locked-in syndrome**

Mental reservation (*mentalis restrictio*) justifies certain forms of nonmalicious deception that otherwise would be classed as *locutio contra mentem* or even outright lies. Such **casuistry** reasoned that only a partial **truth** need be verbally expressed as long as the mind told the whole truth to God. Thus, responding to a salesman's query "Is your mother home?" a child could reply "No" with the added but unverbalized mental reservation ("she's not available to you"). Legitimate canons of **confidentiality and secrecy**, especially as required by the **seal of the confessional**, expanded the moral description of truth-telling and lying so that withholding factual truth from someone who lacked either the right or the need to know would not constitute the **intrinsic evil** of lying.

Metanoia (μετανοια) is the Greek word used in the New Testament for **conversion**.

Methotrexate is a drug used to end an **ectopic pregnancy**.

Middle axiom has somewhat different meanings depending on context. In moral theology it is usually employed to denote what **Thomas Aquinas** terms a *lex valet ut in pluribus* (law binds in most [but not all] cases; see *ST I-II*, Q. 94, art. 4). Specifying a **moral norm** helps navigate the terrain between a **universal moral norm**, which is absolute and has no exceptions, and **concrete material norms**, which may have a number of legitimate exceptions or may be valid in one time or place but not in another. For example, the moral norm "Drive safely" may be seen as universal, and the speed limit of 55 mph is a concrete material norm that is appropriate for a freeway but that would hardly work for a suburban cul de sac! "Drive according to the posted speed limit" would be a middle axiom: it is true in most cases, but there are foreseeable legitimate exceptions, such as transporting a heart-attack victim from a rural farm to a local hospital in the middle of the night when no reliable and timely ambulance service would be available. In this case, using *epikeia* one concludes the speed limit is a middle axiom that could be sacrificed in this particular instance. The exception, however, would not destroy the existence or value of the moral norm as a middle axiom but would actually strengthen it by allowing for the limited exception.

Minjung theology emerged in the 1970s as an Asian form of **liberation theology** engaged in theological and political resistance against the military dictatorships and economic oppression in South Korea. *Minjung* denotes the common people as distinguished from the social and economic *yangban* elite (similar to the Mandarin class in China) and is an exemplar of **inculturation** in theology. *For further reading*, see James T. Bretzke, "Cracking the Code: Minjung Theology as an Expression of the Holy Spirit in Korea," *Pacifica* 10 (October 1997): 319–30; Commission on Theological Concerns of the Christian Conference of Asia, ed. *Minjung Theology: People as the Subjects of History* (Maryknoll, NY: Orbis Books, 1983); and Jung Young Lee, ed., *An Emerging Theology in World Perspective: Commentary on Korean Minjung Theology* (Mystic, CT: Twenty-Third Publications, 1988).

Minus malum (lesser evil) expresses the accepted **moral principle** that in situations in which it is altogether impossible to persuade another to forgo evil, and if given a choice among the possible evils, **reason** would dictate that one should always elect to do the lesser evil. Thus, **premarital sex** is morally wrong, but if the fornicating individuals cannot be dissuaded from this activity one could at least enjoin them to practice **safe sex**, which would involve "lesser evils" than unprotected sex.

Mirari vos (*You Wonder*), the papal encyclical "On Liberalism and Religious Indifferentism" issued by Gregory XVI in 1832 (one of the first papal **encyclicals**). It condemned indifferentism as an "absurd and erroneous proposition which claims that liberty of **conscience** must be maintained for everyone" (*MV* #14). The encyclical's position on **religious liberty** was repeated by Gregory XVI's successor, **Pius IX**, in his 1864 *Quanta cura* and became an important example of the **history and development of moral theology and doctrine** when the position was essentially reversed in **Vatican II**'s 1965 *Dignitatis humanae*, "Declaration on Religious Freedom."

Modernism is a vaguely defined theory of adaptation to the modern world condemned by **Pius X** in his 1907 **encyclical** *Pascendi Dominici gregis*. This led to harsh hunts to root out supposed modernists that might be teaching in seminaries or holding various ecclesiastical offices. Even the future pope **John XXIII** (Angelo Roncalli) was suspected by the **Holy Office** (today the **CDF**) of being a modernist. Seminarians and their professors had to take a yearly oath against modernism up to the time of **Vatican II**, and even up to the 1990s in some parts of the world. The "errors" that modernism was supposed to espouse included the historical–critical method of biblical study, Enlightenment philosophy, and a **secularism** that downplayed the role of faith and organized religion in the public sphere. One archbishop described the legacy of modernism's "fervor for **orthodoxy**" as an atmosphere in which "amateurs—turned theologians—easily became headhunters and leaders were picked, not by their ability to work toward a synthesis of the new knowledge and the **Tradition**, but by the rigidity of their orthodoxy, so that often second-rate and repressive minds, riding on the waves of that fear, took over" (Archbishop Rembert Weakland, OSB, *Milwaukee Catholic Herald*, September 11, 1986). Ultraconservatives often claim that Vatican II was infused with modernism and thus was not a legitimate Church Council.

Moral absolutes. See **absolutes**

Moral acts and moral agency. See *actus hominis and actus humanus*, and *finis operis and finis operantis*

Moral autonomy. See **autonomy (moral)**

The **Moral Autonomy school and Faith Ethics school** debate over **scripture and ethics** developed in the two decades after **Vatican II**. The Moral Autonomy school held that while scripture is important primarily on the level of *paranesis* and to support growth in moral **character** and **virtue**, the Bible itself adds no new moral content. Therefore, Christians have no special commands nor special revelation (*Proprium*) that would go beyond the **natural law** already inscribed on the hearts and **conscience** of each person (the *lex indita non scripta* of **Thomas Aquinas**). Each person should earnestly seek with discerning **reason** first to discover in conscience that inner law that *GS* #16 highlighted and then to hold herself accountable to obedience to that law. This is true autonomy and avoids the problems associated with **heteronomy** and **Voluntarism**. Major theologians associated with this school include Alfons Auer, Klaus Demmer, MSC, **Josef Fuchs, SJ**, **Richard McCormick, SJ**, and Bruno Schüller, SJ. Classic **Protestant ethics** would counter their view by recalling our fallenness due to **original sin**, which requires scripture (e.g., *sola scriptura*) and **biblical ethics** to aid Christians in living authentic moral lives. Some contours of this position were adopted by a group of Catholic theologians called the *Glaubensethik* or the Faith Ethics school, including **Bernard Häring, CSsR**, Hans Urs von Balthasar, Heinz Schürmann, and **Joseph Ratzinger (Benedict XVI)**. For them the Bible is an indispensable source of moral teaching to aid human reason, which may be clouded by sin or unconsciously influenced by other pressures and factors in contemporary secular society. Ratzinger also stressed the role of the **magisterium** and its *munus* of preserving and transmitting the **deposit of faith**, which in turn aids human reason. *For further reading*, see Charles E. Curran and Richard A. McCormick, eds., *Readings in Moral Theology, No. 2: The Distinctiveness of Christian Ethics* (New York: Paulist Press, 1980); and Vincent MacNamara, *Faith and Ethics* (Dublin: Gill and Macmillan, 1985).

Moral evil. See **evil (moral)**

Moral impossibility. See **impossibility (physical versus moral)**

Moralism is generally a pejorative term distinguished from genuine morality, which focuses on passing judgments, usually negative, on the choices or actions of others—often accusing them of offending **God** as well. Striking condemnations of moralism are found in Jesus's parables and rebukes against the Pharisees (see the story of the Pharisee and tax collector in Luke 18:9–14).

Morality (independent). See heteronomy and theonomy, Moral Autonomy school and Faith Ethics school, and *Proprium*

Moral manuals were standardized seminary texts used in the **manualist tradition**.

Moral norms, as opposed to a guideline, counsel, or suggestion, require strict observance. **Thomas Aquinas**'s *Treatise on the Natural Law* (see *ST I-II*, Q. 94) delineates three levels of moral norms: (1) **universal moral norms** that hold in all times, places, and situations; (2) **middle axioms** that are generally true (*lex valet ut in pluribus* "the law holds in most [but not all] cases"); and (3) **concrete material norms** that apply to very specific situations but that, due to Thomas's notions of **contingency and fallibility**, are less universal and may change over time or may not be applicable in a wider variety of **circumstances** (see *ST I-II*, Q. 94, art. 4). *For further reading*, see Charles E. Curran and Richard A. McCormick, eds., *Readings in Moral Theology, No. 1: Moral Norms and Catholic Tradition* (New York: Paulist Press, 1979); and Richard M. Gula, *What Are They Saying about Moral Norms?* (New York: Paulist Press, 1982).

Moral object. See action *in se, finis operis and finis operantis,* and **fonts of morality**

Moral principles such as the **double effect, lesser evil** (*minus malum*), and **totality** (*pars propter totum*) are ethical propositions grounded in truth claims that help the application of **reason** to a concrete moral decision, action, or evaluation. For example, the truth claim that "life is sacred from the moment of conception to natural death" leads to several moral principles expressed as **moral norms**—such as "**euthanasia** and **direct abortion** are morally wrong"—that help guide one to come to a morally correct decision in a particular case. Often, moral principles seem to overlap and even conflict with one another, and in these sorts of cases the discipline of **casuistry** is helpful in determining which particular moral principle applies or has precedent in this or that particular case.

The **mores versus morals distinction** arises from the linguistic ambiguity in the translation of the Latin word "*mores*" used in the expression "*de fide vel* *moribus*" (*mores*, *moribus*, "concerning faith or morals/mores"). The Latin root word is "*mos*," which means custom, guide, practice, fashion, or **moral norm**. In English this same range of ideas is expressed as "morals" or "mores." For example, in the 1950s, wearing blue jeans to a college class would have been a clear violation of community standards (i.e., "mores"), whereas today such attire is acceptable. However, at neither point would it be "immoral" to wear blue jeans to class. This example underscores some of the difficulty in assessing the precise meaning of the term "*de fide vel moribus*" given in **Vatican I**'s 1870 definition of papal **infallibility** in *Pastor aeternus*, and by extension to the exercise of the *munus docendi* of the pope and bishops to teach authoritatively even in its **ordinary magisterium**. Some commentators would interpret *moribus* to refer to matters of custom and law (liturgical rules), whereas others maintain the magisterium can pronounce definitively even on **concrete material norms** contained in the **natural law**, and still others adopt a middle position that holds that the magisterium can certainly articulate the general **moral principles** of the natural law, but concrete specification of details, for example, public policy initiatives and so on, are more a matter of **prudential judgment, conscience**, or **subsidiarity**. The magisterium does distinguish teachings that must be definitively believed (*credenda* for a *de fide definita* dogma) from those that must be held (*tenenda*) even though in the latter case an **assent** of faith is not called for in the *obsequium religiosum* stance articulated in *LG* #25's **character, manner, and frequency criteria**.

Mortal sin. See **sin**

Mortification. See **asceticism**

Mosaic Law. See **Decalogue** and **Holiness Code**; **see also** *biblical ethics* and *covenant*

Mujerista theology is a form of **feminist** and **liberation theology** that prioritizes the experiences of Hispanic and Latina women along with other women of color. The term is primarily associated with Cuban Catholic theologian Ada María Isasi-Díaz (March 22, 1943–May 13, 2012).

Munus (plural, *munera*, Latin for mission, ministry, office) is used in ecclesiastical contexts to denote the various roles of the **magisterium**, whose **charism of office** enjoys the "**special assistance of the Holy Spirit**" in fulfilling the ministries of teaching (*munus docendi*), governing (*munus gubernandi* or *regendi*), and sanctifying (*munus sanctificandi*) the members of the Church (see *LG*

#21). The ordained also share in these ministries, especially that of sanctification through the celebration of the sacraments. The Munus Petrinium (Petrine, i.e., papal ministry) specifies the particular functions, powers, and privileges the pope receives as the successor of Peter, including being the supreme legislator for the Church and being able to claim **infallibility** for specific teachings on **faith and morals** when delivered *ex cathedra* as an exercise of the **extraordinary magisterium**. In liturgical contexts *munus/munera* can mean "gift" or "gifts," and in Christology the *munus triplex* connotes the threefold ministry of Jesus Christ as priest, prophet, and king, which all Christians have a share in by virtue of their baptism (see *LG* #12). **See also** *sensus fidelium*.

Murray, John Courtney, SJ (September 12, 1904–August 16, 1967), was originally silenced by his Jesuit superiors at the behest of the Vatican for his writings on **religious liberty** and pluralism in the American democratic context, which were viewed as **dissent** from the **ordinary magisterium** and **Tradition**. He went on to serve as a *peritus* (theological expert) at **Vatican II** in the drafting of the conciliar "Declaration on Religious Liberty," *Dignitatis humanae*. *For further reading*, see his *We Hold These Truths: Catholic Reflections on the American Proposition* (Kansas City, MO: Sheed & Ward, 1960).

Mysterium ecclesiae, the "Declaration in Defense of the Catholic Doctrine on the Church against Certain Errors of the Present Day" issued on June 24, 1973, by the **CDF**, defends the ministerial priesthood and the **infallibility** of both the Universal Church and the **magisterium**.

N

NARTH (National Association for Research and Therapy of Homosexuality). See **reparative therapy**

Natural family planning (NFP) was viewed with considerable suspicion in the **manualist tradition** inasmuch as both the *finis operis and finis operantis* seemed aimed at **birth control** contrary both to the "constant **Tradition**" as well as to the *bonum prolix* regarded as the greatest good and the primary end of **marriage**. NFP also might challenge **divine sovereignty**, since the number of children born to a couple should be entirely **God**'s will, and human efforts to influence this would be morally suspect. **Continence** and **abstinence** were counseled, although in the 1930s the use of the so-called rhythm method or Billings Method was allowed for couples who experienced serious need to limit children. **Pius XI**'s 1930 *Casti connubii* gave tacit acceptance of NFP (see *CC* #13, 18, 37), and **Pius XII**'s 1951 **Address to Italian Midwives** made this permission explicit for "serious motives . . . which can arise from medical, eugenic, economic and social so-called 'indications,' [which] may exempt husband and wife from the obligatory, positive debt [*debitum*] for a long period or even for the entire period of matrimonial life." **Paul VI**'s 1968 *Humanae vitae* (see *HV* #16) gave this position added **authority**, and support for NFP was a frequent theme in **John Paul II**'s teaching on **marriage** and the **family** (see *FC* #32). While many couples find NFP effective and supportive of their marriage, others experience significant difficulties. *For further reading* on two married people who had problems with NFP, see Janet Claussen, "My Argument with Natural Family Planning," *America* (February 11, 1995): 20–22; and Mitch Finley, "The Dark Side of Natural Family Planning," *America* (February 23, 1991): 206–7. For a defense of NFP, see Germain Grisez, Joseph Boyle, John Finnis, and William E. May, "NFP: Not Contralife," in *The Teaching of Humanae vitae: A Defense* (San Francisco: Ignatius Press, 1988), 81–92, also found in *Readings in Moral Theology No. 8: Dialogue about Catholic Sexual Teaching*, edited by Charles E. Curran and Richard A. McCormick, 126–34 (New York: Paulist Press, 1993). For a theological critique of NFP, see Peter A. Kwasniewski, "The Primacy of Charity in the Question of Family Size," *Homiletic & Pastoral Review* (December 2010): 22–28.

Naturalistic fallacy connotes a philosophical category error in moral reasoning that has two principal varieties. One is a form of ethical naturalism, which holds that in certain situations the use of "artificial means" are immoral when "natural means" are available. In this view it is the "artificiality" that renders the "means" problematic, and this argument is advanced by some for the supposed superiority of **NFP** over artificial **birth control**. However, if it were true that the artificiality is what renders birth control **intrinsically evil**, then by logical extension other artificial means such as heating, shelter, clothing, and so on would at least be morally suspect because of their artificiality. The other variety of naturalistic fallacy as articulated by British philosopher G. E. Moore involves Hume's Guillotine of the "is/ought problem." This error can be made both in terms of natural properties (e.g., the "is" of procreative possibility of the sexual faculty demands morally the "ought" that one therefore must procreate—highly problematic for consecrated **celibacy**) or in terms of equating the notion of "truth" with some other property such as "beauty" so that "beauty" always fully signifies "truth" and vice versa (*pace* Keats's "Ode on a Grecian Urn"). *For further reading*, see Josef Fuchs, "Natural Law or Naturalistic Fallacy?" ch. 2 in *Moral Demands and Personal Obligations*, 30–51 (Washington, DC: Georgetown University Press, 1993).

Natural law has two foundational premises: ontological and epistemological. The ontological premise holds that there is an objective moral order of right and wrong that is not of human devising and that can be at least partially expressed in ethical **norms** to which humans are held accountable. The epistemological premise postulates that humans can come to know on their own, at least partially, the nature and demands of this objective moral order. History shows a variety of natural law theories such as Roman (e.g., Ulpian), Confucian (e.g., Mandate of Heaven), and various Christian theories. Foremost among Christian natural law theorists is **Thomas Aquinas**, who describes the natural law as the human participation in **God**'s *lex aeterna* (see *ST I-II*, Q. 94). Common misperceptions of the natural law include the following:

- Identifying the natural law with the laws of nature such that what is observable in nature becomes somehow morally obligatory. Some of the problems associated with **physicalism** and the **naturalistic fallacy** are linked to this misunderstanding.

- Identifying the natural law as something inflexibly posited "out there," such as the periodic table of elements, which is divorced from or exists absolutely independently of human interaction. Thomas's notion of the moral law as a *lex indita non scripta* partially corrects this misperception, as does his position on **moral norms** that hold in some but not all cases (*lex valet ut in pluribus*), which counters the mistaken view that every moral norm is universally absolute regardless of the concrete situations marked by **contingency and fallibility**.
- Confusing or equating a particular theory (whether that of Thomas Aquinas, **Suárez**, or Confucius, and so on) with the existence of the natural law itself.

For further reading, see James T. Bretzke, *A Morally Complex World: Engaging Contemporary Moral Theology* (Collegeville, MN: Liturgical Press, 2004); Michael Betram Crowe, *The Changing Profile of Natural Law* (The Hague: Martinus Nihoff, 1977); Charles E. Curran and Richard A. McCormick, eds., *Readings in Moral Theology, No. 7: Natural Law and Theology* (Mahwah, NJ: Paulist Press, 1991); Jean Porter, *Natural and Divine Law: Reclaiming the Tradition for Christian Ethics* (Grand Rapids, MI: Eerdmans, 1999); Jean Porter, *Nature as Reason: A Thomistic Theory of the Natural Law* (Grand Rapids, MI: Eerdmans, 2005); Martin Rhonheimer, *Natural Law and Practical Reason: A Thomist View of Moral Autonomy* (New York: Fordham University Press, 2000); and Cristina L. H. Traina, *Feminist Ethics and Natural Law: The End of the Anathemas* (Washington, DC: Georgetown University Press, 1999).

The **NCCB (National Conference of Catholic Bishops)** is the US Episcopal Conference founded in 1966 in response to **Vatican II**'s "Decree on the Pastoral Office of Bishops," *Christus Dominus*, and **Paul VI**'s 1966 apostolic letter, *Ecclesiae sanctae*. The NCCB issued a number of important **pastoral letters** until **John Paul II**'s 1998 apostolic letter *Apostolos suos* sharply constrained this practice. The NCCB was reconfigured in 2001 as the **USCCB**.

Needle-exchange programs. See **lesser evil**

Negative duties (*semper et pro semper*). See **duties (negative and positive)**

Nemo tenetur ad impossibile (No one is held to the impossible) is one of several variations of a basic principle in **discernment** of both human and **natural law** that holds that one cannot predicate a moral "ought" or duty except upon a reasonable expectation that the corresponding duty, action, and so on can be performed without reaching the limits of **physical** or **moral impossibility**. In other words, no one is called upon to attempt what for them would be morally impossible. For example, someone "constitutionally" homosexual could not be morally enjoined to enter into a heterosexual **marriage** relationship since this would be for that individual repugnant. **See also** *self-preservation*.

Neuner-Dupuis. See *Enchiridion symbolorum definitionum et declarationum de rebus fidei et morum*

Newman, Blessed Cardinal John Henry (February 21, 1801–August 11, 1890, beatified 2010), was an important English theologian who taught at Oxford, converted to Catholicism in 1845, and joined the Oratorians. His writings on moral themes such as the **primacy and sanctuary of conscience**, **history and development of doctrine**, *locutio contra mentem*, **magisterium**, and the *sensus fidelium* had been especially influential in the period leading up to **Vatican II**. *For further reading*, see Ian Ker and Terrence Merrigan, eds., *The Cambridge Companion to John Henry Newman* (Cambridge: Cambridge University Press, 2009).

New Testament ethics. See **biblical ethics**

NFP. See **natural family planning**

Nicomachean Ethics is the major text of **Aristotle** on ethics and the **virtues**.

Nihilism is a philosophical tradition that holds that life ultimately lacks any purpose, meaning, or intrinsic value. Moral nihilism denies the objective moral order foundational to the **natural law** and holds that the notions of "morality" and "moral right/wrong" are merely abstract conventions that enjoy a certain amount of societal success. While certain strains of deconstruction in **postmodernism** have been associated with nihilism, the terms certainly are not synonymous and in fact often deal with quite different issues. A more existential type of nihilism can be a symptom of psychological depression and, as with any illness, needs to be treated (rather than simply condemned).

Nominalism in metaphysics holds that there are no true universals or abstract objects and that such terms merely are the "names" (*nomina* in Latin) conventionally given to these concepts. This theory is identified with **Wil-**

liam of Ockham (c. 1288–c. 1348) and closely intertwined with the theory of **Voluntarism**, which holds that "goodness" depends solely on **God**'s sovereign will, and that, if God so desired, what we now call "good" could be "bad." This theory emphasized **divine command** morality and held that our highest moral duty was not the use of **reason** to **discern** the good but rather obedience to God as the Supreme Law-Giver. *For further reading*, see Servais Pinckaers, "Moral Theology in the Late Middle Ages: The Nominalist Revolution," ch. 10 in *The Sources of Christian Ethics*, 240–53 (Washington, DC: Catholic University of America Press, 1995). **See also** *legalism* and *lex aeterna*.

Nonmaleficence, do no harm (*primum non nocere*), is one of the four bioethical tenets of **principlism.**

Norm. See **moral norms**

Norma normans non normata ("Norming norm not itself normed") denoted a foundational theological norm that grounds itself and does not depend on a higher principle or **authority** for its legitimacy. Scripture is one such example, as described in **Vatican II**'s *Dei Verbum* treatment of the **magisterium**, whose "teaching office is not above the word of God, but serves it, teaching only what has been handed on, listening to it devoutly, guarding it scrupulously and explaining it faithfully in accord with a divine commission and with the help of the Holy Spirit" (*DV* #10).

O

Obsequium religiosum (religious submission [of the will]) appeared just once, in ***Lumen gentium*** #25, in all the documents of **Vatican II**. The full expression is *religiosum voluntatis et intellectus obsequium*, and the shorthand *obsequium religiosum* is used also in **canon law** (see *CIC* #725) and the **CDF**'s 1990 ***Donum veritatis***, "Instruction on the Ecclesial Vocation of the Theologian." "*Voluntatis et intellectus*" refers to the "will" (*voluntas*) and the "intellect" (*intellectus*) or "mind" (*mentem*, which is used in the phrase that follows). Application depends much on just how one translates this phrase. Clearly, some prefer "submission" to translate *obsequium* (e.g., *Donum veritatis* #23), which would effectively rule out any public disagreement, much less any **dissent**, with even the teachings of the **ordinary magisterium**. Others note, though, that if this were truly the intent of the Vatican II council fathers, other terms such as *submissio* (submission) or *oboedientia* (obedience) would have indicated this nuance more precisely. The other major interpretation of "religious submission" holds it as a fundamental attitude of loyal openness to accept and evaluate the teaching of the **magisterium**, especially when not proposed with **infallibility** as in the ***ex cathedra*** form of the **extraordinary magisterium**. *CIC* #752 seems to reflect this view by stating that "although not an **assent** of faith, a religious submission of the intellect and will must be given to a doctrine which the Supreme Pontiff or the college of bishops declares concerning faith or morals when they exercise the authentic magisterium, even if they do not intend to proclaim it by definitive act; therefore, the Christian faithful are to take care to avoid those things which do not agree with it," and *CIC* #749 §3 adds that "no doctrine is understood as defined infallibly unless this is manifestly evident." Respected canonist Ladislas Orsy, SJ, and ecclesiologist Francis Sullivan, SJ (both former professors at Rome's Pontifical Gregorian University), suggest that "respect" as opposed to "rejection" better characterizes the attitude of *obsequium religiosum*, though this does not mean simple blind acceptance. ***For further reading***, see Ladislas Orsy, "Magisterium: Assent and Dissent," *Theological Studies* 48 (1987): 473–97; Francis A. Sullivan, *Creative Fidelity: Weighing and Interpreting Documents of the Magisterium* (New York: Paulist Press, 1996); and Francis Sullivan, "The Theologian's Ecclesial

Vocation and the 1990 CDF Instruction," *Theological Studies* 52 (1991): 51–68. **See also** *conscience (forming and informing)*, *primacy of conscience*, *de fide definita*, *ex cathedra*, *mores versus morals distinction*, *munus*, *sensus fidelium*, and *ultramontanism*.

Obsessive-compulsive disorder (OCD) is often related to **scrupulosity**, in which the individual suffers from the obsession of having sinned, which in turns triggers the compulsion to confess frequently (sometimes even daily). Scrupulosity is a very difficult ailment to treat, but as with other forms of OCD behavior (such as excessive hand washing), the more successful approach is to block recourse to the compulsion after the obsession has been triggered (e.g., for someone with the hand washing disorder, they might be encouraged to handle something dirty and then be prevented from immediately being able to wash their hands). While scruples cannot always be treated in exactly the same way, the traditional approach has been for the scrupulous person to trust the advice of his or her confessor, especially when being instructed that a particular action is either not a **sin** or, if a sin, that it has been forgiven and so should not be confessed again. *For further reading*, see Joseph W. Ciarrocchi, *The Doubting Disease* (Mahwah, NJ: Paulist Press, 1995).

An **occasional allocution** is a speech given on a specific occasion or event (and does not mean "episodic" or "every now and then"). See also *allocutions (occasional and papal)*.

"Occasions of sin" is the traditional term used primarily along with the promise of a firm purpose of **amendment** in conjunction with the **sacrament of reconciliation** to refer to those external **circumstances** that might lead an individual into **sin**—even if the "occasion" itself was not sinful. Traditional **casuistry** distinguished between proximate (or "near") and remote occasions of sin. These are not objective, geographical terms but rather expressive of subjective probability to incite or weaken one so that the particular sin is more likely to be committed than if the occasion had been avoided. For example, if an alcoholic deliberately took a route that he knew would lead past a bar, this might be a near occasion for sin, whereas for another individual this would lead to no special difficulty. On the other hand, going to a shopping mall that also includes restaurants that serve alcohol would be classed only as a remote occasion of sin since the chances of that leading the person to drink would be less likely. No one can reasonably avoid every possible occasion for sin, and even the proximate or near occasion of sin might be impossible to avoid if one's duties required exposure to that occasion. For example, if one has a weakness for internet pornography but also has a job that requires internet access and usage, such an individual cannot be counseled to avoid using the internet altogether but rather should devise various other measures to prevent falling into this sin. It may be helpful to recall that the mere fact of temptation is not necessarily evidence of a disposition to sin because even Jesus was tempted. The Greek word "πειρασμοσ" (peirasmos) has its primary definition "testing" and lists "temptation" only as a secondary meaning. The key is not a futile search never to experience temptation but rather to resist temptation by following Jesus's example. Temptation that does lead to sin can always be dealt with in the sacrament of reconciliation as well as through prayer, **asceticism**, and good works.

Occult compensation. See **compensation** and **occult compensation** and **reparation and restitution**

Ockham's Razor. See **William of Ockham**

Octogesima adveniens ("The Coming Eightieth [Anniversary]") is the 1971 apostolic letter of **Paul VI** commemorating **Leo XIII**'s 1891 *Rerum novarum*. It is usually included with the **social encyclicals**, even though a letter ranks below an **encyclical** in terms of *Lumen gentium*'s **character, manner, and frequency criteria**. Highlighting the theme of promoting the **common good** in new problems such as urbanization, workers, the roles of women, youth, media, ideology, and so on, the pope noted intrinsic limitations in the papal **magisterium**'s role in light of moral complexity in the concrete world: "In the face of such widely varying situations it is difficult for us to utter a unified message and to put forward a solution which has universal validity. Such is not our ambition, nor is it our mission" (*OA* #4). Echoing *Gaudium et spes*, he added that there would always be a legitimate range of pluralism and options in the Christian responses since in "concrete situations, and taking account of **solidarity** in each person's life, one must recognize a legitimate variety of possible options. The same Christian faith can lead to different commitments" (*OA* #50). This was also the first papal document to reference **environmental ethics**.

Odia restringi is a long-standing interpretive principle of **canon law**, especially **canonical penalties**, that mandates, according to *CIC* #18, that all laws "which establish, restrict the free exercise of rights, or contain an exception from the law, are subject to strict interpretation." This principle is very important when considering issues such as who is barred from the sacraments, especially **communion**. The full formulation of the traditional principle is *odia restringi, et favores convenit ampliari*, which could be translated as burdens (i.e., "odious" things) are to be restricted, and favors (e.g., privileges) are to be multiplied (or extended). **See also** *lex dubia non obligat*.

Old Testament ethics. See **biblical ethics**

Omission and commission (sins of). See **sin** and **euthanasia**

Onanism is the older term used either for **masturbation** or coitus interruptus (e.g., withdrawal during sexual intercourse with seminal ejaculation outside of the vagina). The term is based on a very problematic **exegesis** of Genesis 38:8–10, which recounts the refusal of Judah's second son, Onan, to raise up offspring for his dead brother, Er, in Levirate marriage with his brother's widow, Tamar. To prevent conceiving offspring that would not be counted as his own, Onan spilled his seed on the ground, thus offending **God**, who then punished Onan with death. For centuries, any intentional seminal ejaculation that was done outside of the vagina was therefore considered *contra naturam* and a serious **sin**. **Pius XI**, quoting **Augustine**, condemned artificial **birth control** as onanism in his 1930 *Casti connubii*, stating, "the Divine Majesty regards with greatest detestation this horrible crime and at times has punished it with death" (*CC* #55). Most biblical experts agree, however, that Onan's sin was not masturbation but rather a serious violation of filial duty to continue his deceased brother's line. Nevertheless, onanism was the usual term employed in the **moral manuals** and Church documents until the mid-twentieth century.

Oncofertility. See **reproductive technologies**

Ontic evil, also termed *malum physicum* (physical evil) in the **manualist tradition** and **"premoral evil"** by some contemporary authors, represents nonmoral **evil** as distinguished from a *malum morale* (moral evil). Noted Louvain moralist **Louis Janssens** described ontic evil as "any lack of a perfection at which we aim, any lack of fulfillment which frustrates our natural urges and makes us suffer. It is essentially the natural consequences of our limitation" (Janssens, "Ontic Evil and Moral Evil," *Readings in Moral Theology, No. 1: Moral Norms and Catholic Tradition*, edited by Charles E. Curran and Richard A. McCormick [New York: Paulist Press, 1979], 60). Thus, due to our **finitude** and sinfulness, every concrete action will involve the commission of a certain amount of ontic evil, or the omission of doing some good, or the relieving of some other evil. Responding using **practical reason** to **Thomas Aquinas**'s first principle of the **natural law** to do and foster the good while minimizing and avoiding the evil (***Bonum est faciendum . . .***) therefore obliges us to discern the **proportionate reason** in avoiding or reducing as far as possible ontic evil that arises from our actions. As Janssens observes, "If our actions contain more ontic evil than they must have to be the proper means, they are not ordered properly to the goals of man and society. Consequently, they are immoral" (ibid., 80). A proper understanding of ontic evil is crucial, especially in situations involving the principles of **cooperation with evil, double effect, lesser evil,** *minus malum*, and **totality**, and is also a key concept in the theory of **proportionalism**. For example, surgery to correct a serious issue will unavoidably involve some pain, **suffering**, cost, and so on, and these are all ontic evils if the surgery is truly necessary. However, to choose a procedure or therapy that would cause more suffering than is medically necessary would lack proportionate reason and therefore would no longer be ontic evil but moral evil. Debate remains among moral theologians about the nature of evil in certain actions, for example, whether using the less invasive laparoscopic surgery to resolve an **ectopic pregnancy** rather than the more serious removal of the whole fallopian tube represents an ontic evil and an **indirect abortion** justified by proportionate reason, or whether this would be an **intrinsic evil** of a **direct abortion**.

Optatam totius ("Desired by All"), **Vatican II**'s 1965 "Decree on the Training of Priests," called for "a most careful training in holy Scripture, which should be the soul, as it were, of all theology." Instead of just repeating older approaches, seminarians "should learn to seek the solution of human problems in the light of revelation, to apply its eternal truths to the changing conditions of human affairs, and to express them in language which people of the modern world will understand." The reform of the discipline of moral theology "should draw more fully on the teaching of holy Scripture," which helped support a Catholic growth in **biblical ethics**.

Option for the poor. See **liberation theology**

Order of nature and order of reason. See **physicalism and personalism**

Ordinary and extraordinary means is the principle of health care treatment **discernment** dating back to sixteenth-century **casuistry**. The decision is made primarily by the patient herself or by a designated proxy, who ideally follows the wishes of the patient, which may have been expressed in an **AHCD** (living will). Pioneer medical ethician **Gerald Kelly**'s 1958 definition still is serviceable today: Ordinary means of preserving life are "all medicines, treatments, and operations, which offer a reasonable hope of benefit for the patient and which can be obtained and used without excessive expense, pain, or other inconvenience." By contrast, extraordinary means would be "all medicines, treatments, and operations, which cannot be obtained or used without excessive expense, pain, or other inconvenience, or which, if used, would not offer a reasonable hope of benefit" (Kelly, *Medico-Moral Problems* [St. Louis: Catholic Hospital Association of the United States and Canada, 1958, 129]). It is important to note that this definition is intentionally "relative" and "subjective" in that it relates to the patient as subject. Thus, neither the **ERD** nor any other health care manual lists procedures that would always be "ordinary" and others that would always be "extraordinary," since such determination must be made on a case-by-case basis. Surgery to treat a perforated stomach in a twenty-year-old would generally be considered "ordinary" and therefore morally obligatory, while the same procedure in a ninety-year-old heart attack victim would likely be "extraordinary" and optional (or even counterindicated). Kelly's view, confirmed by the Catholic moral tradition and relevant teachings of the **magisterium**, is that no one is morally obligated to use any means—natural or artificial—that are or that have become disproportionate to the goal of ameliorating or maintaining the patient's condition. **Palliative care**, distinguished from **euthanasia**, belongs with ordinary means since effective pain management should be available to all patients. For key magisterial teachings, see the 1980 **CDF**, *Iura et bona*, "Declaration on Euthanasia" (Sec. 4), **John Paul II**'s encyclical *Evangelium vitae* (especially *EV* #2, 65), *CCC* #2278, and *ERD* #32 (5th ed., 2009). *For further reading*, see Kevin Wildes, "Ordinary and Extraordinary Means and the Quality of Life," *Theological Studies* 57 (1996): 500–512; Thomas R. Kopfensteiner, "Death with Dignity: A Roman Catholic Perspective," *Linacre Quarterly* 63 (November 1996): 64–75; Dolores L. Christie, *Last Rights: A Catholic Perspective on End-of-Life Decisions* (Lanham, MD: Rowman and Littlefield, 2003). **See also** *allocutions (occasional and papal)*, *ANH*, *autonomy (bioethical principle)*, *death with dignity*, *informed consent*, *principlism*, *probabilism*, and *PVS*.

Ordinary magisterium is an expression first used by **Pius IX** in his 1863 letter to the archbishop of Munich, *Tuas libenter*, which countered the view of some German theologians that Catholics were bound to hold only those truths of the faith that had been formally defined *de fide definita*. See the fuller discussions under **charism of office**, **magisterium**, and *obsequium religiosum*.

Ordinatio sacerdotalis (*On Ordination to the Priesthood*) is the 1994 apostolic letter of **John Paul II** that restates the position of the 1976 **CDF**'s declaration *Inter Insigniores* ("On the Question of the Admission of Women to the Ministerial Priesthood") that the Catholic Church "has no authority whatsoever to confer priestly ordination on women, and that this judgment is to be definitively held [*definitive tenenda*] by all the Church's faithful." As an exercise of the **ordinary magisterium**, rather than the **extraordinary magisterium**, it does not have the latter's claim of **infallibility**, but a 1995 CDF *Responsum ad dubium* about the status of this teaching stated that it belonged to the **deposit of faith**, which requires that the **assent** of faith must be "definitively held" [*definitive tenenda*]. The precise requirements of assent on the part of the faithful involve a careful understanding of the distinction between propositions to be "believed" (*credenda*) and those to be "held" (*tenenda*). While sharply criticized by many, especially in the context of **feminism and feminist ethics**, the text itself simply states that the Church lacks the permission or authority from Jesus to ordain women and so should not be considered as an instance of **sexism** or **gender** discrimination, and that, moreover, ordination is not a **human right** but a divinely given **vocation**.

Organ donation and transplantation. See **totality (principle of)** and **Hürth, Francis**

Orientation (sexual). See **sexuality, gender, sexual orientation, and sexual ethics**

Original sin is the ancient Christian doctrine that holds that the **sin** of our first parents destroyed or at least seriously compromised humanity's natural **justice** and goodness. New Testament references are found in Romans 5:12–21 and 1 Corinthians 15:22. Classic Protestant theology holds that original sin has so destroyed or distorted the power of **reason** that reliance on a **natural law** approach to morality is methodologically suspect, and **biblical ethics** and *sola scriptura* are preferred. The Catholic position accepts that reason has been compromised by the Fall, but it still is basically trustworthy, especially when aided by grace with proper attention to scripture, **Tradition**, and the **magisterium**. **Augustine** developed the doctrine of original sin that accounted for the transmission of the effects of the sin, though not its **guilt**, onto the descendants of Adam and Eve through the **concupiscence** associated with the sexual act. More contemporary theological reflection speaks of original sin in terms of the sin in the world that cannot be entirely explained as the result of personal sins for which individuals have **culpability** but that manifest themselves as **social sin and structural evil**.

Orthodoxy (Greek, *orthos*, "true" or "straight" + *doxa*, "belief" or "opinion") holds to the truths of the Christian faith coming from scripture (see Tit. 2:1; 2 Tm. 1:13), **Tradition**, and the **magisterium**'s **authority** expressed in its teaching as well as in conciliar creeds and defined articles of the faith (*de fide definita*) listed in the *Enchiridion symbolorum definitionum et declarationum de rebus fidei et morum* [*Denzinger* or *Neuner-Dupuis*]). **Liberation theology** also insists as a necessary correlation the related term "*orthopraxis*" to highlight the necessity of committed right action to promote social **justice**. **Heterodoxy** is opinions contrary to accepted normative teaching that, if expressed, become heresy or schism, leading to **canonical penalties** such as **excommunication**. However, many contested or debated topics have not yet been definitively settled, so there is a legitimate range of opinions in such instances, often expressed theologically in the form of a *quaestio disputata* and *status quaestionis*, which should be carried on respectfully in **charity**. **Cardinal Avery Dulles** also cautions that merely "to parrot the words of an old definition in a new situation is a false and inauthentic form of orthodoxy. When the sociocultural context has changed, further progress is demanded in order not to lose sight of the truth conveyed by an earlier formulation. In order to develop the Church's teaching as the times require, we have to take a somewhat critical stance toward the formulas handed down to us from the past." (Dulles, "The 'Irreformability' of Dogma," ch. 12 in *Survival of Dogma* [Garden City, NJ: Doubleday, 1971], 198). **See also** *Congregation for the Doctrine of the Faith*, *history and development of moral theology and doctrine*, *probabilism*, and *Roma locuta causa finita*.

Orthopraxis ("right practice"). See **liberation theology** and **orthodoxy**

P

Pacem in terris (*Peace on Earth*) is the last **encyclical** by **John XXIII**, issued April 11, 1963, just two months before his death. It was also the first encyclical explicitly addressed to all people of good will, rather than just to the Catholic bishops or faithful, who were exhorted to assist non-Catholics and non-Christians in building a just peace. Written in the context of the Cold War, the pope did not advocate **pacifism** but called for conflicts to be resolved through negotiation rather than arms, and emphasized Catholic **social teaching**, especially respect for **human rights**, which include "the right to life, to bodily integrity, and to the means which are suitable for the proper development of life, particularly food, clothing, shelter, medical care, rest, and, finally, the necessary social services. In consequence, he has the right to be looked after in the event of ill-health; disability stemming from his work; widowhood; old age; enforced unemployment; or whenever through no fault of his own he is deprived of the means of livelihood" (*PT* #8).

Pacifism holds that neither violence nor war is ever justified. See the section on "critiques" in the entry for **just war theory**. See also *Hauerwas, Stanley*; and *Yoder, John Howard*.

Palliative care refers to pain alleviation or management, which is not only *always* allowed in the **ordinary and extraordinary means** principle but is a form of "disinterested charity" that "should be encouraged" (*CCC* #2279). Therefore, it cannot be legitimately interrupted except with the **informed consent** of the patient, even if it is foreseen that palliative care will shorten a patient's life (see *EV* #65). However, direct euthanasia is not licit to end pain (*CCC* #2277).

Papal primacy holds that the pope as bishop of Rome is *primus inter pares* ("first among equals"), the vicar of Christ, and his *servus servorum* (servant of servants). He is the reference point of unity for the entire college of bishops (see *LV* #25). **Vatican I**'s *Pastor aeternus* defined the conditions for the *ex cathedra* exercise of papal **infallibility** in the extraordinary magisterium.

Paranesis (παραίνεσις, Greek, "exhortation"), in **biblical ethics**, refers to the hortatory nature of scripture's moral focus and is closely tied to the *Proprium* (distinctiveness) of **Christian ethics**, the stance of the **Faith Ethics school** and the motivation for popular movements such as **WWJD?** Some in the **Moral Autonomy school** evidence a suspicion bordering on disdain for a perceived overreliance on scripture for ethical norms that would be better arrived at through **reason**-based reflection and would avoid risking a "Christonomous **positivism**" associated with **Karl Barth**. "There are really only relatively few individual **precepts** that the NT sets forth explicitly. To the extent that the word of revelation does contain individual precepts of the law of Christ, it probably intends to help people out at those points where they have not yet managed to apprehend moral precepts on their intrinsic grounds. Even if human beings should never manage to dispense with this assistance totally, nonetheless they should strive to require it as little as possible" (Bruno Schüller, "A Contribution to the Theological Discussion of Natural Law," in *Readings in Moral Theology, No. 7: Natural Law and Theology*, edited by Charles E. Curran and Richard A. McCormick [Mahwah, NJ: Paulist Press, 1991], 89). A helpful counterbalance to this view is offered in a classroom anecdote by James Gaffney of a pro-choice coed who changed her view on permitting case-by-case **abortions** in non–life-threatening **circumstances** after realizing that Jesus would not have condoned such a position, and that she "admired" Jesus for his ethical stance. What seemed to convince this individual was not ethical normative reasoning as such but rather the appeal (*paranesis*) that she felt Jesus would have made in this case. Gaffney concludes that we simply cannot draw a complete and sharp dichotomy between *paranesis* and ethical norms since every ethical norm is also paranetic. "Pure paranesis is moral vapor; the only response to 'I exhort' is a look of expectation: the verb requires a direct and indirect object." James Gaffney, "On Paranesis and Fundamental Moral Theology," *Journal of Religious Ethics* 11 (1983): 31; also published as ch. 10 in Gaffney's *Matters of Faith and Morals* (Kansas City, MO: Sheed & Ward, 1987), 134–51. **See also** *Proprium* and *Zielgebot*.

Pardon. See **absolution** and **sacrament of reconciliation**

Pars propter totum (part sacrificed for the whole). See **totality (principle of)**

Parvitas materiae in Sexto, the shortened form of the fuller axiom "*Nulla parvitas materiae in Sexto*" (there is no paucity of matter in the Sixth Commandment), held that its sinful matter *ex toto genere suo* was grave and never light, and if done with **sufficient knowledge and consent, mortal sin** was presumed. Much **casuistry** of the **moral manuals** was devoted to answering the perennial question "How far can you go?" Detailed discussions can be found regarding what types of dancing would be allowed, whether hand-holding or a light kiss were licit, and so on. In 1612, the superior general of the Society of Jesus, Claudio Acquaviva, issued a decree forbidding all Jesuits from teaching that some pleasure in sexual matters (*re venerea*) was slight, which could be excused from being considered **mortal sin** even if deliberately sought. The Dominican Charles-René Billaurt (1685–1757) proposed an important distinction between **direct and indirect** pleasure, judging that only sexual pleasure directly sought as an end in itself was sinful but that indirect pleasure, though foreseen and voluntary, would be licit if it was intended for some other end, for example, hand-holding in the context of courtship that might lead to **marriage** and legitimate sexual activity aimed at **procreation**, or as a remedy for **concupiscence**. These sorts of debates certainly led not only to an overpreoccupation with sexual matters but also a good deal of excessive **scrupulosity** and a rather pessimistic view of **sexuality** as a whole. *For further reading*, see Patrick J. Boyle, *Parvitas materiae in Sexto in Contemporary Catholic Thought* (Lanham, MD: University Press of America, 1987). **See also** *Decalogue, delectatio morosa, fornication and adultery, living in sin*, and *premarital sex*.

PAS, physician-assisted suicide, is a form of **euthanasia** as distinguished from either the legitimate termination of **extraordinary means** or **palliative care**. Euthanasia, regardless of whether it is active, passive, voluntary, or involuntary, is considered **intrinsically evil** and thus always morally wrong even if the **intention** would seem to be "good" in the sense of seeking to end pain and **suffering**. **See also** *advance health care directive, autonomy (bioethical principle), death with dignity, Evangelium vitae, ordinary and extraordinary means, suicide*, and *vitalism*. **For further reading**, see the **Catechism of the Catholic Church** #2278 and the United States Catholic Bishops 2011 statement *To Live Each Day with Dignity: A Statement on Physician-Assisted Suicide*.

Passion. See **anger, appetite, concupiscence, culpability**, and **habit and virtue**

Pastor aeternus (*Eternal Pastor*), **Vatican I**'s 1870 dogmatic constitution on the Church of Christ, after a long debate formally defined papal **infallibility**. Some believed this conciliar definition would render future ecumenical councils unnecessary since the pope could pronounce infallibly on all matters of **faith and morals** (*de fide vel moribus*). So far, this power has been invoked twice:

Pius IX's 1854 definition of the Immaculate Conception and **Pius XII**'s 1950 definition of the Assumption. To date, no *ex cathedra* infallible pronouncement has been given on a concrete moral issue, and the popes continue to use vehicles of the **ordinary magisterium** such as **encyclicals**, apostolic exhortations, **occasional allocutions**, homilies, and so on to exercise their teaching **authority**. See also *charism of authority*, *infallibilism*, and *munus*.

Pastoral letters can be issued by local bishops as part of their exercise of the **ordinary magisterium**. The **NCCB** (reconfigured in 2001 as the **USCCB**) issued a number of important pastoral letters, such as *Always Our Children*, *The Challenge of Peace* (1983), and *Economic Justice for All* (1986), until **John Paul II**'s 1998 apostolic letter *Apostolos suos* curtailed their use by requiring either unanimous consent or a *recognitio* (recognition and approval) given by the Holy See for bishops' conferences pastoral letters.

Patriarchy. See **feminism and feminist ethics**, and **sexism**

Paul VI—Pope (September 26, 1897–August 6, 1978), born Giovanni Battista Montini, succeeded **John XXIII** on June 21, 1963, and reigned until he died on August 6, 1978. He was ultimately succeeded by Karol Wojtyła (**John Paul II**) following the thirty-three-day reign of Albino Luciani (John Paul I). Created a cardinal in John XXIII's first consistory in 1958, Paul VI remained committed to John XXIII's vision of *aggiornamento* ("adaptation" or "renewal"), continuing **Vatican II** and the revision of **canon law**, expanding the **Pontifical Commission on Births**, and maintaining a stance of openness to **ecumenism** and interreligious dialogue. Choosing the name Paul indicated his desire to mirror the Apostle's missionary evangelization, and for a pope of that era, he traveled widely, visiting six continents, delivering a memorable plea in New York to the United Nations in October 1965: "No more war, never again war. Peace, it is peace that must guide the destinies of people and of all mankind." His 1967 **social encyclical** *Populorum progressio* ("On the Progress of Peoples") linked true peace going beyond the absence of war with the establishment of a more just order (see *PP* #76, 83, 87). The 1968 *Humanae vitae* on **marriage** and **birth control** remained his last **encyclical**, although he was to reign another decade. The resulting controversy and **dissent** to that encyclical may be one reason Paul VI did not return to this genre of the papal **magisterium**.

Pauline privilege. See **privilege (Pauline and Petrine)**

PDE (principle of double effect). See **double effect principle**

Pecca fortiter ("sin boldly," or sometimes termed "brave sinning") is an expression used by Martin Luther to underscore salvation by faith (sola fide) in **God**'s grace (*sola gratia*) rather than by our own actions or efforts (**works righteousness**). The full aphorism, *"Pecca fortiter sed fortius fide et gaude in Christo"* ("Sin boldly, but believe and rejoice in Christ more boldly still"), expresses the hallmark of Protestant theology of **justification by faith** as opposed to **works righteousness** and contrasted with the perceived view of Catholicism's obsession with **casuistry**, degrees of gravity of **sin**, and so on.

Peccatum (Latin for "sin as crime"). See **sin**, *adikia* (αδκια, unrighteousness), **hamartia** (*'αμαρτια,* missing the mark), and **hubris** (*ὕβρις,* **pride**).

PEG tube, or percutaneous endoscopic gastrostomy tube, aka feeding tube, used in **ANH**. **See also** *ordinary and extraordinary means.*

Penance. See **sacrament of reconciliation**

Persistent/permanent vegetative state (PVS) refers to the reduced clinical state of consciousness in which the patient exhibits no purposeful awareness or interaction with her environment, although she has sleep/wake cycles and involuntary reaction to external stimuli such as noise. See **states of consciousness: brain death, coma, PVS, MCS, and locked-in syndrome**

Person. See **human person** and *imago Dei*; see also *conscience* and *culture and inculturation*

Persona humana (*Human Person*), the **CDF**'s 1975 "Declaration on Certain Problems of Sexual Ethics," was originally entrusted to a committee of moral theologians who disagreed on the basic approach, so the resulting declaration was mainly the work of Father Lio, OFM, Cardinal Pietro Palazzini, and Father Visser, CSsR, reproducing in large part a chapter from Palazzini's 1975 *Vita e virtù cristiane* (*Christian Life and Virtue*). Both the declaration and book use a **deductive** methodology in which principles are put forth and conclusions drawn from them with less explicit attention to an **inductive** investigation associated with **personalism**. A whole range of sexual practices such as **masturbation** are condemned as exemplars of "grave moral disorder" (*PH #9*) too frequently understated in the contemporary world. *Persona humana* breaks new ground in some key areas: it is the first major Vatican document that uses the concept of human **sexuality** without reducing it to sexual activity (see *PH #1, 5, 9, 10, 13*), and it accepts the notion of "constitutional **homosexuality**," acknowledging a "distinction . . . between homosexuals whose tendency comes from a false education, from a lack of normal sexual development, from **habit**, from bad example, or from other similar causes, and is transitory or at least not incurable; and homosexuals who are definitively such because of some kind of innate instinct or a pathological constitution judged to be incurable" (*PH* #8). The declaration also condemns what it considers unsound expressions of **fundamental option theory** (see *PH* #10). *For further reading*, see James McManus, "Moral Theology Forum: The 'Declaration on Certain Questions concerning Sexual Ethics,' a Discussion [with Sean O'Riordan, CSsR, and Henry Stratton]," *The Clergy Review* 61 (1976): 231–37; and for official commentaries published by the Vatican, see *Declaration on Sexual Ethics: Commentaries* (Washington, DC: United States Catholic Conference, 1977).

Personalism, personalist approach. See **physicalism and personalism**

Petrine privilege. See **privilege (Pauline and Petrine)**

PGD (preimplantation genetic diagnosis) is a procedure to select embryos fertilized in vitro that are free of obvious defects and that have the greatest potential for successful implantation in **IVF**. **See also** *Dignitas personae*

Philia. See **agape, eros, and** *philia*, and see **love**

Phronesis (Greek: φρονησις) is the term used by **Aristotle** in his *Nicomachean Ethics* to denote the **virtue** of **prudence**.

Physical impossibility. See **impossibility (physical versus moral)**

Physicalism and personalism are two paradigms for framing and evaluating complex moral actions as they relate to ethical values, **moral norms**, understandings of the **human person**, and the interpretation of the **natural law** and the **fonts of morality**. It is crucial to realize that these are paradigms, that is, ways of modeling and viewing reality, and there is a certain amount of overlap between these two models. Each has its own particular strengths and weaknesses, and each needs the strengths of the other to compensate for its own weaknesses. Thus, it is not an "either/or" choice of physicalism versus personalism. The **physicalist** paradigm, coming out of neo-Scholasticism, is primarily a classicist, essentialist method that in turn stresses faculties and finalities in interpreting the natural law. Sometimes these paradigms are also called the order of nature and the order of reason, although this expression falls into the same difficulty of presenting a clear-cut dichotomy that does not exist so neatly in reality.

In physicalism the content of moral norms is derived in a **deductive** manner from structures of nature, which are considered as **God's** will revealed in the corresponding faculties or finalities of the acts themselves. Since the sexual faculty has the capacity, among other things, for **procreation (*bonum prolix*)**, anything that would intentionally frustrate that faculty and finality is deemed *contra naturam* and ipso facto immoral. While physicalism has the strength of clear parameters and criteria for establishing moral norms, it has been criticized for so narrowly focusing on the exterior, observable aspects of the physical act as to equate the physical with the moral act while largely ignoring subjective factors of **intention, character** of the agent, **virtue, reason, conscience**, and the relative amount of **freedom** involved in light of the **circumstances** in which the physical act was performed. Its validity seems grounded largely in the **classicist worldview** and shares the weaknesses of that perspective. Another critical weakness is the greater propensity to fall into the so-called **naturalistic fallacy** and to identify a physicalist "is" and then posit a moral "ought" as with the moral norm that because conjugal acts can be procreative (the "is") this therefore morally demands a corresponding "ought" that holds that each and every conjugal act must be left fecund (see *HV* #14).

While physicalism marked both the Scholastic and **manualist tradition** of moral theology, **Vatican II** showed a paradigm shift toward the personalist approach, for example, in treatment of the principle of **totality** in **marriage** (*GS* #51). In this context, using as the fundamental moral criterion the **human person** "integrally and adequately considered," Louvain moralist Louis Janssens outlined eight key dimensions: (1) subject; (2) embodied subject; (3) part of the material world; (4) interrelational with other persons; (5) an interdependent social being; (6) historical; (7) equal but unique; and (8) called to know and worship God. These in turn were **discerned** primarily in an **inductive** manner consonant with a **historical worldview** and using the principle of the **hierarchy of values** to resolve any **conflict of duties**. Much of the teaching of the **magisterium** since Vatican II, including **John Paul II's "theology of the body,"** uses personalist categories. While personalism is better at lifting up the morally relevant features in a thicker description of both the moral act and the agent, this paradigm also has significant weaknesses. It often is rather vague and indeterminate, especially when one is trying to concretize or specify material norms, the real "dos and don'ts" of the moral life. It can be more easily "abused" and is perhaps more open to the deceptive processes of human **rationalization**: "My conscience says it is okay" or "No one is being hurt by this." Thus, many authors have begun to suggest that while personalism is clearly important for fundamental moral theology, by itself it is insufficient to ground a full consideration of the natural law and moral norms. *For further reading*, see Louis Janssens, "Artificial Insemination: Ethical Considerations," *Louvain Studies* 5 (1980): 3–29; also published more recently as "Personalism in Moral Theology," in *Moral Theology: Challenges for the Future. Essays in Honor of Richard A. McCormick, SJ*, edited by Charles E. Curran (New York: Paulist Press, 1990), 94–107; and Brian V. Johnstone, "From Physicalism to Personalism," *Studia Moralia* 30 (1992): 71–96.

Physicalist. See **physicalism and personalism**

Physician-assisted suicide. See **PAS**

Pius IX—Pope (May 13, 1792–February 7, 1878; beatified 2000), born Giovanni Maria Mastai-Ferretti, has had the longest pontificate to date (1846–78), with **John Paul II**'s coming in next. He defined the dogma of the Immaculate Conception in 1854 and called **Vatican I**, which defined papal **infallibility**. His thirty-eight **encyclicals** established this genre for the papal **ordinary magisterium**, of which the 1864 *Quanta cura* with its accompanying *Syllabus of Errors* are most remembered for the condemnation of a host of propositions including **religious liberty**, freedom of speech, and the separation of Church and state. He was the last temporal ruler of the Papal States, which fell in the 1870 Italian Risorgimento, forcing a suspension of Vatican I and forcing the pope to flee his Quirinale Palace to take up residence in St. Peter's as the "prisoner of the Vatican," which continued for his successors until **Pius XI**'s 1929 *Lateran concordat* established the Vatican City State. He was beatified in 2000 by John Paul II.

Pius X—Pope (June 2, 1835–August 20, 1914), born Giuseppe Melchiorre Sarto, succeeded **Leo XIII**, reigning from 1903 to 1914. He countered the spirit of **Jansenism** by encouraging more frequent reception of Holy **Communion**, and he promoted Thomism and was a strong opponent of **modernism**, condemning it in his 1907 **encyclical** *Pascendi Dominici gregis*. He commissioned the first complete codification of **canon law**, though the project was completed in 1917 by his successor Benedict XV. Canonized by **Pius XII** in 1954, he was the first pope to be made a saint since Pius V (1566–72), who had excommunicated Elizabeth I of England.

Pius XI—Pope (May 31, 1857–February 10, 1939), born Ambrogio Damiano Achille Ratti, was elected Benedict XV's successor on February 6, 1922.

He advocated the participation of laypeople in the Catholic Action movement under the supervision of the **magisterium**. He was strongly opposed to both **communism** and fascism, as evidenced by his forceful 1937 **encyclical** *Mit brennender Sorge* (German, "With burning concern") against Nazism, although he also established a diplomatic concordat with Hitler's regime. His *Lateran concordat* with the Italian government established the Vatican City State and ended the period of the pope as "prisoner of the Vatican" dating back to the 1870 Risorgimento takeover of the Papal States during the reign of **Pius IX**. In moral theology he is most remembered for two encyclicals, the 1930 *Casti connubii*, which condmned **artificial contraception** as the grievous **sin** of **onanism** (*CC* #55–56), and a year later his 1931 **social encyclical** *Quadragesimo anno*, which critiqued **socialism**, **communism**, and **capitalism** and articulated the principle of **subsidiarity** (*QA* #79).

Pius XII—Pope (March 2, 1876–October 9, 1958), born Eugenio Pacelli, was elected March 2, 1939, to succeed **Pius XI** on the eve of World War II. In addition to his efforts to end war and promote peace, in the area of moral theology a number of his **occasional allocutions** (many written with **Hürth**'s assistance), such as the 1951 **Address to Italian Midwives**, were important in the **history and development of moral theology** in the areas of **responsible parenthood**, the moral legitimacy of **NFP**, and the **ordinary and extraordinary means** principle of health care **discernment**. He was the first (and to date only) pope after **Vatican I**'s definition in *Pastor aeternus* of papal **infallibility** to use this **extraordinary magisterium** to proclaim the Marian dogma of the Assumption as *de fide definita*. His 1943 **encyclical** *Divino afflante Spiritu* sanctioned the use of the historical-critical method in biblical **exegesis** and **hermeneutics**. His 1950 encyclical *Humani generis* gave guarded acceptance of the theory of evolution but sharply criticized the French Nouvelle Théologie for its departure from Thomism in using **existentialism** and its supposed **relativism** and neomodernism, adding that once the pope has "passed judgment" on an issue, even in the **ordinary magisterium**, this matter "cannot be any longer considered a question open to discussion among theologians" (*HG* #20). **See also** *obsequium religiosum*, *quaestio disputata*, *Roma locuta causa finita*, and *status quaestionis*.

Plus tenetur homo vitae suae providere quam vitae alienate (One is required to take more care of one's own life than that of another). See the discussion under **self-preservation**.

The term "**political correctness**" is usually employed pejoratively for attempts to force changes in established patterns that are deemed discriminatory in social conventions, language, policies, and even ideas, especially regarding **gender**, race, ethnicity, and **sexual orientation**. For example, the traditional etiquette of a man holding a door open for a woman could be held as offensive by some, while others could still consider it a form of basic politeness. Certainly unjust discrimination is always to be corrected where possible, and this is an area that requires a great deal of **wisdom** and **prudence** in **discernment** of the **signs of the times** as contrasted with **Zeitgeist**. **See also** *white privilege*.

Pontifical Commission on Births, formally the Pontifical Commission on Population, Family, and Birth, was constituted by **John XXIII** in 1959 and greatly expanded by **Paul VI** in 1963 to include seventy-two members from five continents, including a number of lay men and women. Some of the leading theologians were the Redemptorist **Bernard Häring, CSsR**; Jesuit moralists **Josef Fuchs, SJ**, and **Marcelino Zalba, SJ**, professors at the Pontifical Gregorian University; and **John Ford, SJ**, moralist at Weston College (today the Boston College School of Theology and Ministry). Father Fuchs was one of the leaders of the contingent whose Final Report, usually termed the "Majority Report," was ultimately approved in 1966 by an overwhelming majority of the commission members. Fathers Zalba and Ford, joined by the French Jesuit Stanislas de Lestapis and the Dutch Redemptorist Jan Visser, were the four theologians who **dissented** from the Final Report and who, with the help of a young American moral philosopher, **Germain Grisez**, drafted a "minority report" secretly submitted to Paul VI, which ultimately furnished the groundwork for the 1968 **encyclical** *Humanae vitae*. Both reports were leaked to the press, fueling speculation that the pope might indeed change the Church's teaching on **birth control**. An excellent journalistic account of the deliberations of the commission along with the text of the Final Report was published by Robert Blair Kaiser under the titles *The Politics of Sex & Religion* (1985; 2nd ed. e-book, 2012) and *The Encyclical That Never Was: The Story of the Pontifical Commission on Population, Family and Birth, 1964–66* (London: Sheed and Ward, 1987).

The summary of the Final Report (also termed the Majority Report) goes beyond **physicalism** and primarily uses **personalism** to describe the **vocation** of **marriage**. **Human persons** are described as being cocreators with **God**, and a key aspect of this is seen in humanity's "tremendous progress in control of matter by technical means" (Kaiser, *Encyclical That Never Was*, 11). **Moral norms** are certainly acknowledged, but "since moral obligations can never be detailed in all their concrete particularities, the personal responsibility of each individual must always be called into play. This is even clear today because of the complexities of modern life: the concrete moral norms to be followed must not be pushed to an extreme" (ibid., 4). In the chapter titled "Fundamental Values of Marriage," the married couple "ought to be considered above all a community of persons which has in itself the beginning of new human life," and this community must be strengthened (ibid., 5). The key duty in the regulation of **procreation** is **responsible parenthood**, which is a **prudent** and generous "fundamental requirement of a married couple's true mission" (ibid., 6). **Conflicts of duties** are resolved through **discernment** in **conscience** with attention to a **hierarchy of values** such that "the married couples take care to consider all values and to seek to realize them harmoniously in the best way they can, with proper reverence toward each other as persons and according to the concrete **circumstances** of their life. They will make a judgment in conscience before God about the number of children to have and educate according to the objective criteria indicated by **Vatican Council II**" (*GS* # 50 and #80) (ibid., 6–7). Thus, "to observe and cultivate all the essential values of marriage, married people need decent and human means for the regulation of conception," and science should help provide "means agreeable and worthy of man in the fulfilling of his responsible parenthood" (ibid., 8).

The principle of **totality** "does not depend upon the direct fecundity of each and every particular act. Moreover, the morality of every marital act depends upon the requirements of mutual **love** in all its aspects" (ibid., 9). The Majority Report acknowledges that this teaching represents a **development of moral doctrine** but is required by

> social changes in matrimony and the family, especially in the role of the woman; lowering of the infant mortality rate; new bodies of knowledge in biology, psychology, **sexuality** and demography; a changed estimation of the value and meaning of human sexuality and of conjugal relations; most of all, a better grasp of the duty of man to humanize and to bring to greater perfection for the life of man what is given in nature. Then must be considered the sense of the faithful [*sensus fidelium*]: according to it condemnation of a couple to a long and often heroic **abstinence** as the means to regulate conception, cannot be founded on the truth. . . . The doctrine on marriage and its essential values remains the same and whole, but it is now applied differently out of a deeper understanding (ibid., 10).

Viewed in this perspective, "the substance of tradition stands in continuity and is respected. . . . In light of the new data, these elements are being explained and made more precise. The moral obligation of following fundamental norms and fostering all the essential values in a balanced fashion is strengthened and not weakened" (ibid., 11). Objective moral criteria and norms exist, but these "are to be applied by the couples, acting from a rightly formed conscience and according to their concrete situation. . . . It is impossible to determine exhaustively by a general judgment and ahead of time for each individual case what these objective criteria will demand in the concrete situation of a couple" (ibid., 12). Finally, the fundamental criterion for the interpretation of the **natural law** is that "the action must correspond to the nature of the person and of his acts so that the whole meaning of the mutual giving and of human procreation is kept in a context of true love" (*GS* #51) (ibid., 13). A second criterion is **proportionate reason** in determining whether conception is to be avoided "temporarily or permanently" (ibid.). A third criterion considers the "physical [**ontic**] evil" present in *all* forms of **contraception**, including "periodic or absolute **abstinence**" and the fourth and last criterion concerns the choice made according to availability of means and other considerations, including cost.

The main objections of the minority report are found in *Humanae vitae* itself, although the minority report added a further rationale not contained in the encyclical that follows principally the argument of Father Zalba as chronicled in the various accounts of the commission and published reminiscences of other members, which can be summarized in three points:

•   The Majority Report would constitute untenable ecclesiological acknowledgment that the Holy Spirit somehow was more active in the **Anglican Communion**'s 1930 **Lambeth Conference** vote to accept artificial contraction than it was in **Pius XI**'s encyclical *Casti connubii*, which was issued as a response later that same year, or that the **special assistance of the Holy Spirit** to the **ordinary magisterium** was somehow again lacking in **Pius XII**'s 1951 "**Address to the Italian Midwives**" that allowed for **NFP** but not for **artificial contraception**.
•   It would raise a huge difficulty of seemingly having condemned to eternal damnation Catholics who had knowingly violated this teaching of the **magisterium**—a practice that now would be deemed licit.
•   If the magisterium were to change its position on such a substantive matter, could it be deemed a trustworthy and binding guide in subsequent issues that dealt with **faith or morals**?

Certainly these three arguments seemed ultimately to have been very persuasive with Paul VI, although the debate obviously has continued unresolved elsewhere.

Pontifical Council. See **dicastery**

Populorum progressio is the 1967 **social encyclical** of **Paul VI**, "On the Progress of Peoples," that first used the expression that the Church was an **expert in humanity**.

Positive duties (*semper sed non pro semper*). See **duties (negative and positive)**

Positive law is not to be confused with **positivism** since its most basic meaning simply refers to human laws that are "posited" or promulgated for the community. Positive law (*ius positum*) is distinct from either the **natural law** or **God's eternal law**, but, like all laws, it too should be an ordinance of **reason**, in service to the **common good**, established by the competent **authority**, and promulgated. Since positive law is fashioned by humans oriented toward some concrete and specific goal or need, it is more subject to **contingency and fallibility**. For example, we cannot hope to arrive at a concrete tax code that would be both perfect and unchanging over the years. *Epikeia* is also used to deal with unforeseen **circumstances** and imperfections in human law. **See also** *legalism*.

Positivism is a philosophical theory associated with empiricism combined with rationalism; positivism prioritizes observable evidence for moral analysis. Positivism has been attacked by critical theorists for producing a false universalism based on its distorted representation of human action that fails to take into adequate account how human consciousness itself is historically and socially conditioned. Another critique deals with positivism's opposition to abstract **moral norms** and principles that go beyond observable facts and details. Positivism would have great difficulty accepting the validity of concepts such as "human nature" and the **natural law** and thus is a theory certainly at odds with much of the Christian philosophical and theological tradition.

Postmodernism has a spectrum of meanings ranging from denial of any possibility of universal claims, **moral norms**, and objective truth found in ethical theories such as **emotivism**, **relativism**, and subjectivism, to a more nuanced emphasis on the need to reconsider the exaggerated Enlightenment claims of the modern era for the power of **reason** to ascertain all truth, calling for a more careful consideration of the roles of **culture**, history, language, social constructs such as power and **gender** in the **creation** of meaning—especially various worldviews. **See also** *classicist and historical worldviews*; *feminism and feminist ethics*; *Fides et ratio*; *Kant, Immanuel*; *liberation theology*; *physicalism and personalism*.

Practical reason is employed by **Thomas Aquinas** in his *Treatise on the Natural Law* (see *ST I-II*, Q. 94) to denote **right reason**'s (*recta ratio*) application of moral principles grasped through **speculative reason** to concrete situations using **prudential judgment** to best realize the foundational principle of **natural law**: *bonum est faciendum et prosequendum et malum vitandum*. Thomas says that "speculative reason is busied chiefly with the necessary things, which cannot be otherwise than they are, its proper conclusions, like the universal principles, contain the truth without fail." Thus, a triangle "necessarily" will be a three-sided polygon with the sum of its internal angles totaling 180 degrees. This is necessarily, absolutely, and universally "true" (at least in Euclidian geometry). But practical reason "is busied with contingent matters about which human actions are concerned: and consequently, although there is necessity in the general principles, the more we descend to matters of detail, the more frequently we encounter defects." These "defects" or deficiencies are due to **contingency and fallibility**, which means that, unlike speculative reason, practical reason cannot hope to be as universal or **infallible**; or, as Thomas puts it, "in matters of action, truth or practical rectitude is not the same for all, as to matters of detail, but only as to the general principles: and where there is the same rectitude in matters of detail, it is not equally known to all" (*ST I-II*, Q, 94, art. 4). It is important not to confuse practical reason with "being practical-minded" or the philosophical theory of **pragmatism**. See also *deductive and inductive*.

Pragmatism features a process by which theory is somehow extracted from practice and then applied back onto that practice; it suggests that moral truth is found in terms of "what works best." Leading pragmatists include Charles Sanders Peirce, William James, John Dewey, Josiah Royce, and later twentieth-century thinkers such as Richard Rorty. Bertrand Russell critiqued pragmatism as being a form of **relativism** that overvalued practicalism in its moral analysis. Pragmatism should not be identified with **Thomas Aquinas**'s notion of **practical reason** in the **natural law**.

Precept and precepts of the Church (*præceptum*, "command") is a term used variously in the **manualist tradition**. Some, for example, Henry Davis, SJ, include the **Decalogue** under the umbrella of precepts, whereas others, for example, Cardinal Giuseppe Palazzini, differentiate precepts from **law** (which always binds unless it is abrogated), restricting its usage to questions of jurisdiction aimed at an individual. A good deal of **canon law casuistry** held that precepts given by an **authority** (e.g., a religious superior) ceased when that person died or left office. Six precepts of the Church drawn from the *Roman Catechism of the Council of Trent* were traditionally enjoined upon all Catholics: (1) to attend Mass on Sundays and Holy Days of Obligation; (2) to observe the laws of fast and **abstinence**; (3) to receive the sacrament of **penance (reconciliation)** once a year; (4) to receive Holy **Communion** at least once during Easter time (see **Easter duty**); (5) to contribute to the support of the pastor; and (6) to observe the **marriage** laws of the Church. The precepts of the Church were widely discussed in the division of the **moral manuals** on "special" or "applied" ethics.

Preferential option for the poor. See **liberation theology**

Preimplantation genetic diagnosis or screening. See **PGD**

Premarital sex in most contemporary **sexual ethics** is distinguished from nonmarital sex because the former term has come to refer to sexual activity of a couple that fully intends to marry but has not yet celebrated their Church wedding. **Domestic partners** would be another example of a more committed but not-yet-married sexual relationship. Nonmarital sex, by contrast, refers to sexual activity not only outside of **marriage** but without the presumed commitment to marry within the foreseeable future. A type of nonmarital sex is sometimes called "casual sex," "hooking up," or any number of other idiomatic expressions that fall in and out of popular usage. Both premarital sex and nonmarital sex are considered to be **fornication** (or **adultery** if one or both partners is married), which is condemned by the Church's **Tradition** and **magisterium**. The expression **living in sin** was employed not only for these sorts of ongoing relationships but also for irregular marriages that might be civilly valid but that would not be allowed in **canon law** for a variety of possible reasons and therefore could not be solemnized by the Church. Consideration of all three **fonts of morality** helps in weighing the gravity of a possible offense in the sexual realm to distinguish between, for example, a sexual act between an engaged couple soon to be married and that of a very casual "one-night stand." A few moral theologians, such as Michael Lawler and Todd Salzman, have argued for the moral acceptability of premarital sexual relationships either when the couple finds it difficult to marry at the moment or when they have made an expressed commitment to marry in the future (e.g., by getting engaged), but this position had been strongly critiqued by the magisterium and has not been widely adopted by most other theologians. **See also** *parvitas materiae in Sexto* and *re venerea*. *For further reading* from a spectrum of views, see Todd A. Salzman and Michael G. Lawler, *The Sexual Person: Toward a Renewed Catholic Anthropology* (Washington, DC: Georgetown University Press, 2008); Kevin Kelly, *New Directions in Sexual Ethics: Moral Theology and the Challenge* *to AIDS* (London: Geoffrey Chapman, 1998); and Ronald Lawler, Joseph M. Boyle Jr., and William E. May, *Catholic Sexual Ethics: A Summary, Explanation, and Defense*, rev. ed. (Huntington, IN: Our Sunday Visitor, 1985, 1996).

Premoral evil is an alternative term for **ontic evil**.

Prescriptions and proscriptions are those **moral norms** that indicate actions that either must be done (i.e., that are prescribed) or that must be absolutely avoided (i.e., prohibited). These terms are sometimes also referred to as **positive or negative duties**. A positive duty is a prescription binding *semper sed non pro semper* (always but not in every instance). It can be universally true yet still admit legitimate exceptions, such as the maxim "Pray always," which expresses an **ideal** that no one can fulfill in each and every moment of daily existence. A negative duty, though, is held to be a valid moral **absolute**, allowing for no legitimate exceptions (*semper et pro semper*, always and in every instance), such as the prohibition against murder expressed in the **Decalogue**. **See also** *deontology* and *epikeia*.

Presupposition of St. Ignatius of Loyola (*SpirEx.* #22). See **rash judgment**

Pride. See **hubris** and **capital sins**

Primacy of conscience. See **conscience (primacy and sanctuary)**

Primacy (papal). See **papal primacy**

Primum non nocere (First do no harm) is the traditional first principle of medical care, which enjoins health care professionals not to make matters worse through their interventions, recognizing there are limitations (**finitude**) to what will be medically possible, and taking into account especially the **burden** criterion in the **ordinary and extraordinary means** principle. This principle is also included in the Hippocratic Oath as well as in **principlism**'s principles of **beneficence** and **nonmaleficence**.

Principles (moral). See **moral principles**

Principlism in **bioethics** is heavily indebted to the seminal work of Tom L. Beauchamp and James F. Childress, *Principles of Biomedical Ethics*, 6th ed. (Oxford: Oxford University Press, 1979, 2008) and is recognized by the

National Commission for the Protection of Human Subjects of Biomedical and Behavioral Research in its 1979 Belmont Report. Four key principles to guide decisions in patient health care, biomedical research, health care public policy, and so on are (1) **autonomy**, that, as far as possible, the individual (patient, research subject, etc.) be able to make and give an **informed consent** for treatment; (2) **beneficence**, that the primary **intention** and goal of any medical therapy, treatment, research, and so on be to do good; (3) **nonmaleficence**, that no unnecessary harm be caused; and (4) **justice**, especially **distributive justice**, that the social benefits, burdens, and risks be shared throughout society rather than benefits given just to those more able to pay, or burdens and risks borne by those who are more disadvantaged. "Autonomy" in principlism is not the same as **moral autonomy** but rather indicates that decision-making authority and responsibility reside primarily with the individual most affected by the biomedical decisions. The individual has the freedom to designate a health care proxy or to indicate preferred treatment options in advance of an actual decision using something like an **AHCD**. Beneficence and nonmaleficence are in accord with the foundational principle of the **natural law** as articulated by **Thomas Aquinas**, namely, that good is to be done and evil avoided (***Bonum est faciendum . . .***). These two principles are also implied in the Hippocratic Oath and in the medical dictum of *primum non nocere* (first do no harm).

Private property. See **capitalism** and **property rights**

Privilege (Pauline and Petrine) is invoked for decrees of nullity in certain types of nonsacramental **marriages**. Drawn from 1 Corinthians 7:12–15, the Pauline **privilege** can dissolve a marriage between two people, neither of whom was a baptized Christian at the time of the union. When one of the two converts to Christianity and the other neither wishes to convert nor to remain in the marriage, then Paul held the marriage to be no longer binding, leaving the convert free to marry a Christian (the so-called privilege of the faith). Pauline privilege cases can be adjudicated at the diocesan level since it involves primarily a finding of facts: (1) that both parties were unbaptized at the time of their marriage; (2) that the marriage has ended (e.g., by **divorce**); (3) that the party desiring to marry the Catholic party has converted; and (4) that the Catholic party is otherwise free to marry (i.e., has no existing bond or **impediment**) (see *CIC* #1143–48). The Petrine privilege is an extension of the Pauline privilege, but it involves situations that can be considerably more complicated, the adjudication of which is reserved to the Holy See (thus the term "Petrine"). In a Petrine privilege case, the first marriage was contracted between a baptized Christian and a nonbaptized person and during the marriage the nonbaptized person did not convert. This type of marriage is not considered absolutely indissoluble since it was not completely "ratified" (*ratus* as in ***ratum et consummatum***) and "for a just cause" can be dissolved by the pope "in favor of the faith" (see *CIC* #1142 and 1149).

Probabilism and probabiliorism are two opposing theories much debated in the seventeenth century as to the course of action to be followed in cases of a doubtful law, which does not oblige (*lex dubia non obligat*) either in the **external forum** or the **internal forum** of **conscience**. Probabiliorism, coming from the Latin comparative form, held that in cases of doubt one must always follow either the "safer" (**tutiorist**) course or the "more certain" view (e.g., the one that had more proponents, arguments, etc.). Probabilism (or equiprobabilism), on the other hand, held that as long as the arguments themselves (intrinsic probabilism) or the authorities that held this position (extrinsic probabilism) were well founded and more or less equal in terms of strength of arguments or **authority**, then one could in good conscience choose the course of action that had greater **freedom**. This approach should not be confused with **laxism**, but rather should be seen as the exercise of the **virtue** of **prudence**. The theory of probabilism was formulated by the founder of the Redemptorists, **Alphonsus Liguori**, Doctor of the Church and patron saint of moral theologians; it was commonly taught by both the Redemptorists and the Jesuits while the Dominicans tended to favor the theory of probabiliorism. **Bernard Häring, CSsR,** defined equiprobabilism as "when an upright conscience has equally or almost equally good reasons for creative use of freedom in view of present needs, it is not bound by law which is, in itself or in its concrete application, doubtful. Law should have no right to stifle creative freedom unless it has clearly stronger reasons for doing so" (Häring, *Free and Faithful in Christ: Moral Theology for Priests and Laity, Volume I: General Moral Theology* [Middlegreen, Slough: St. Paul Publications, 1978], 50). Although the theoretical debate of the legitimacy has been decided, great tensions remain on its application in a range of concrete cases, especially in **bioethics**, such as determining what differentiates **ordinary and extraordinary means** in certain end-of-life cases. **See also** *quaestio disputata and status quaestionis.*

Procreative and unitive dimension. See **birth control, inseparability principle, natural family planning**, and **marriage**

Proof-texting takes isolated passages, for example, a biblical verse, out of context in order to "prove" the validity of a proposition in a manner that reflects neither the intent of the author nor the content of the document as a whole. While proof-texting can be done with virtually any written work, it is particularly problematic in the misuse of authoritative texts such as scripture or the writings of revered authors such as **Thomas Aquinas**, or even quotations from documents of the **magisterium**. The placard "God hates fags! Lev. 18:22" would be a most odious example since it asserts that somehow **God** has a special hatred for his creatures, which is contradicted by the bulk of scripture and also is a serious misapplication of the **Holiness Code**, as is made evident in the counter placard "God hates shrimp! Lev. 11:9–12." Countless other examples abound, such as the supposed biblical support of **capital punishment** and **retributive justice**: "Let he who lives by the sword, die by the sword" (Mt. 26:52), and so on. Not all proof-texting need be intentionally vicious, as is evidenced in **John Paul II**'s exegetically problematic use in his 1979 post-synodal apostolic exhortation "Catechesis in Our Time" (*Catechesi tradendae* #64): "I beg you, ministers of Jesus Christ: Do not, for lack of zeal or because of some unfortunate pre-conceived idea, leave the faithful without catechesis. Let it not be said that 'the children beg for food, but no one gives to them' [Lam. 4:4]." Lamentations 4:4, however, speaks of the context of exile and ruin in Israel, not of catechesis, as the two verses that frame the pope's citation make abundantly clear: "Even the jackals offer the breast and nurse their young, but my people has become cruel, like the ostriches in the wilderness. / The tongue of the infant sticks to the roof of its mouth for thirst; the children beg for food, but no one gives them anything. Those who feasted on delicacies perish in the streets; those who were brought up in purple cling to ash heaps." (Lam. 4:3–5 *NRSV*). While the intent of the employment of the scriptural verse is admirable, nevertheless such proof-texting risks blunting, skewing, or spiritualizing the biblical message. This is why good **hermeneutics** and sound **exegesis** are critical in the methodology of using **scripture and ethics**. However, not every brief use of scripture is methodologically incorrect, as often a single verse such as "God is love" (1 Jn. 4:8) can in fact illustrate and confirm a much larger theme that in turn could easily be "proved" by reference to a good deal of the biblical corpus.

Property rights and private property are not *absolute*, even in **contract justice**, but are only relative rights subordinated to the **common good** and the other demands of **justice**, especially **distributive justice** (see *ST II-II*, Q. 66). **See also** *capitalism*, *Centesimus annus*, *Rerum novarum*, *social encyclicals and social teaching*, *socialism*, and *Sollicitudo rei socialis*.

Prophylaxis means prevention, for example, of disease, and is an important consideration in concrete issues such as **condom use** and **safe sex** as well as in helping to determine the moral meaning of contested practices such as safe **needle-exchange programs, tubal ligations** when future pregnancies would pose a serious health risk, and the like.

Proportionalism is associated with some **revisionist moral theologians**, such as **Richard McCormick, SJ**, who highlight the use of **proportionate reason** in moral dilemmas such as those employing the **double effect** and **totality principles**. Key to the proportionalist methodology is the distinction between **moral evil** and **ontic evil** (the latter also termed "premoral" or "physical"). In cases such as an **ectopic pregnancy**, proportionalists hold that the inevitable death of the fetus lodged in the fallopian tube is an ontic evil and thus may be excised since there is clear proportionate reason present (nonaction risks the life of the mother and in every case the fetus will die). Moral evil, though, may never be done, and this crucial distinction often escapes critics of proportionalism who inaccurately accuse proportionalists as denying all moral **absolutes**, the concept of **intrinsic evil**, and espousing instead a form of **consequentialism** or **utilitarianism**. An example of this latter critique is found in **John Paul II**'s 1993 **encyclical** "On Fundamental Moral Theology," *Veritatis splendor* (see *VS* # 75), although no individuals are identified who supposedly hold the condemned version of proportionalism. *For further reading*, see Bernard Hoose, *Proportionalism: The American Debate and Its European Roots* (Washington, DC: Georgetown University Press, 1987).

Proportionate and disproportionate means. See **proportionate reason** and **ordinary and extraordinary means**

Proportionate reason is a judgment of **practical reason** that **discerns** the balance (or proportion) between the end (**moral object**, *finis operis*) and the means chosen to achieve that end. For example, if outpatient laparoscopic surgery were sufficient for correcting a hernia, the **ontic evil** of pain would be morally justified since the means chosen were proportionate. On the other hand, if the older, more invasive major surgery were employed, the excess pain and injury would be disproportionate and not morally justified. Proportionate reason is a foundational criterion in the principle of the **double effect**, in distinguishing between **ordinary and extraordinary means** in health care, and in the *ius in bello* principle of **just war theory**. Proportionate reason has long been established in the Catholic moral tradition since the time of **Thomas Aquinas**. While proportionate reason is an important element in the moral theory of **proportionalism**, it is incorrect to identify every use of proportionate reason as thereby indicating that the mode of moral analysis employed is proportionalism.

Proprium (Latin for "proper" or "distinctive") refers to that which comes from divine revelation, especially regarding what is communicated about the content of morality that would otherwise not be fully accessible to usual ways of human knowing or **reason**. See **Moral Autonomy school and Faith Ethics school**; see also *biblical ethics*, *Fides et ratio*, *sola scriptura*, *WWJD?*, and *Zielgebot*.

Proscriptions. See **prescriptions and proscriptions**

Protestant ethics, in contrast with the **manualist tradition** and classic approaches of Roman Catholic moral theology, tends to be suspicious of what it considers an overreliance on **reason** and the **natural law**, especially as applied in **casuistry** and practiced in the sacraments, especially the **sacrament of reconciliation**, which were often decried as a form of **works righteousness**. Instead, Protestant ethics focused much more on a **biblical ethics** approach and themes such as law and gospel, which in turn are grounded in the five *solas* of *sola scriptura*, *sola fide*, *sola gratia*, *solus Christus*, and *soli Deo gloria*. The time from **Vatican II** onward has been marked by greater respect and collaboration with Roman Catholic moral theologians as seen in the work of Protestant ethics such as **James Gustafson**, Paul Ramsey, **Stanley Hauerwas**, and **John Howard Yoder**, as well as in the movements such as **ecumenical ethics** and cooperation with the **WCC**. *For further reading*, see Waldo Beach, *Christian Ethics in the Protestant Tradition* (Atlanta: John Knox Press, 1988); James M. Gustafson, *Protestant and Roman Catholic Ethics: Prospects for Rapprochement* (Chicago and London: The University of Chicago Press, 1978); Roger Mehl, *Catholic Ethics and Protestant Ethics*, The Warfield Lectures, Princeton Theological Seminary, 1968 (Philadelphia: Westminster Press, 1971); and J. Philip Wogaman, *Christian Ethics: A Historical Introduction* (Louisville: Westminster John Knox Press, 1993). **See also** *law and gospel* and *pecca fortiter.*

Providentissimus Deus is the 1893 **encyclical** of **Leo XIII** on the use of scripture in theological studies. **See also** *biblical ethics*, *Divino afflante Spiritu*, and *Optatam totius*.

Prudence and prudential judgment (*prudentia*, from *providentia*, "seeing ahead") is termed *phronesis* (φρονησις) by **Aristotle** in his *Nicomachean Ethics*, and by **Thomas Aquinas** as the **cardinal virtue** that is exercised by *recta ratio*'s **practical reason** to provide the form of the content of the other virtues (see *ST II-II*, Q. 47–56). For example, the decision whether to stand and fight or beat a tactical retreat is a prudential judgment decision that wisely **discerns** whether the choice would constitute **courage** to be embraced or foolhardiness to be avoided. The great majority of our everyday moral decisions are prudential judgments that usually do not involve a clear-cut differentiation between good and bad, right and wrong. Thus, two people with properly formed and informed **consciences** can in **good faith** in light of the relevant **circumstances** come to divergent decisions about the wisdom of a particular choice—whether it be for a political party or candidate, for a course of treatment in **ordinary and extraordinary means**, or for myriad other possibilities. *For further reading*, see Richard R. Gaillardetz, "Prudential Judgment and Catholic Teaching," ch. 5 in *Voting and Holiness*, edited by Nicholas P. Cafardi, 66–80 (New York: Paulist Press, 2012).

Punishment (capital). See **capital punishment**

PVS (persistent/permanent vegetative state). See **states of consciousness: brain death, coma, PVS, MCS, and locked-in syndrome**

Q

Quadragesimo anno ("Fortieth Anniversary [of *Rerum novarum*]) is the 1931 **social encyclical** of **Pius XI** on the moral duty of living wages and articulation of the principle of **subsidiarity**.

Quaestio disputata and *status quaestionis* (disputed question and state of the question/debate) are two genres of theological discourse on issues that lack either a strong consensus or a definitive pronouncement by the legitimate **authority** (for example, the so-called *Roma locuta causa finita* principle). The *quaestio disputata* usually involves a more narrowly focused issue, such as the time range for the **ensoulment** of the fetus, while a *status quaestionis* covers an issue that is more complex or includes a broader range of related concerns, such as the proper public policies that should be promoted to deal with the pandemic of **HIV/AIDS**. Unfortunately, there is a tendency of each side to accuse the other of **heterodoxy** on important issues that either have not been definitively resolved, or over which there is an honest difference of opinion as to the best **prudential judgment**. **See also** *Congregation for the Doctrine of the Faith* and *probabilism*.

Quanta cura refers to two papal **encyclicals**: one by **Benedict XIV** (1741) on **simony** and related abuses in trafficking in Mass stipends, and the other by **Pius IX** issued December 8, 1864, which contained a *Syllabus of Errors* condemning a number of modern "errors," such as freedom of speech, separation of Church and state, indifferentism, and religious liberty previously condemned in Gregory XVI's 1832 *Mirari vos*. **Vatican II**'s *Dignitatis humanae*, "Declaration on Religious Liberty," essentially would reverse this latter position, thus raising issues regarding **development of moral doctrine** as well as the response of *obsequium religiosum* required by *Lumen gentium* (#25) of Catholics to all teachings of the **ordinary magisterium** such as encyclicals. **See also** *modernism*.

Queer theory/theology is allied with **postmodernism** and aspects of **feminism** and **liberation theology** that consider **gender** as a nonconstructed essential part of **sexuality**. Originally focusing primarily on challenging assertions that **homosexual** activity is *contra naturam* and therefore immoral, more recently queer theory engages **heterosexism** in challenging condemnations of sexual identity or activity judged to be nonnormative or "deviant."

R

Racism is a bias that results in attitudes, discriminatory practices, and actions based on the mistaken and sinful belief that certain human races are inherently inferior or superior, or that they may possess innate positive or negative characteristics that differentiate them from other races. Racism provided a false legitimatization for slavery and had even been supported by the **magisterium** well into the nineteenth century, but since then has been strongly condemned as an **intrinsic evil**. *For further reading*, see Bryan N. Massingale, "What Is Racism?" ch. 1 in *Racial Justice and the Catholic Church* (Maryknoll, NY: Orbis Books, 2010), 1–42. **See also** *affirmative action*; *Cone, James*; *justice*; *liberation theology*; *restorative justice*; *white privilege*; and *womanist theology*.

Rash judgment is defined by the ***Catechism of the Catholic Church*** (see #2477–2478) as assuming as true, even if only tacitly, a judgment about the moral fault of another. This fault is often related to **calumny**, *delectatio morosa*, **detraction**, and even **slander**, and like them, is a violation of **charity**. To counter the possibility of rash judgment, the *Catechism* counsels adoption of the presupposition of St. Ignatius of Loyola given in his *Spiritual Exercises* #22: "Every good Christian ought to be more ready to give a favorable interpretation to another's statement than to condemn it. But if he cannot do so, let him ask how the other understands it, and if the latter understands it badly, let the former correct him with **love**. If that does not suffice, let the Christian try all suitable ways to bring the other to a correct interpretation so that he may be saved."

Rationalization. See **reason**

Ratum et consummatum (ratified and consummated) are two indispensable requirements for a valid sacramental **marriage**, namely (1) the free and **informed consent** and exchange of vows by a baptized man and woman free to marry, performed according to proper canonical form, and (2) confirmed by the subsequent conjugal act performed in a manner per se open to **procreation**. Once a marriage is validly ratified and consummated, it remains indissoluble until the death of one of the partners (see *CIC* #1141). **Annulments** could be granted if the ecclesiastical tribunal determines that one or more of the required elements for a valid marriage were absent or defective at the time of the union. **See also** *privilege (Pauline and Petrine)*.

Ratzinger, Joseph, was born April 16, 1927, in Bavaria, drafted into Hitler's army as a youth, and ordained a priest after World War II. He became an important *peritus* (theological expert) at **Vatican II**. He also was a noted author and professor of systematic theology at various German universities before being named archbishop of Munich by **Paul VI** in 1977. Ratzinger was named the cardinal prefect for the **CDF** under **John Paul II** in 1981, whom he served as a key advisor for most of that pontificate until being elected pope himself upon the former's death in 2005, taking the name **Benedict XVI** and reigning until his resignation on February 28, 2013.

Rauschenbusch, Walter (October 4, 1861–July 25, 1918), was a key Protestant Christian theologian and Baptist minister whose social action and writings, such as his 1907 *Christianity and the Social Crisis*, helped animate the Social Gospel movement in the United States to respond to the myriad social ills caused by rapid industrialization and urbanization at the turn of the twentieth century. **See also** *WWJD*.

(In) **re venerea** translates literally as "in venereal matters" but refers primarily to the whole area of human activity that might result in some sort of sexual stimulation and attendant pleasure. Guided by the principles of **ex toto genere suo** (from the totality of its nature) and **parvitas materiae in Sexto** (no paucity of matter in the Sixth Commandment), the **moral manuals** devoted considerable attention and **casuistry** as to what could be considered legitimate or illegitimate sexual activity, although the strong opinion was that most forms of sexual activity if directly sought for pleasure outside of **marriage** were seriously sinful. **See also** *Decalogue*, *direct and indirect*, *sexuality*, and *sin*.

Reason used colloquially expresses the justifying motive or **intention** for a choice or action: "The reason I hit Johnny was because he was teasing me." Rationalization is a form of **vincible ignorance** to justify actions that upon closer examination are clearly wrong. In **Thomas Aquinas**, the Scholastic, and the **manualist tradition**, "reason" is the human **faculty of conscience** that employs the intellect's power of *recta ratio* (right reason) to make morally correct judgments. Thomas further distinguishes *recta ratio* as **specula-**

tive reason, used in abstract judgments, and **practical reason**, used in light of concrete **circumstances** to make **prudential judgments**.

Reconciliation (sacrament of). See **sacrament of reconciliation**

Recta ratio (right reason). See **reason**

Regicide is the killing of an unjust king. **See also** *tyrannicide.*

Relativism and **subjectivism** are variations of a theory that denies objective or absolute moral truth and holds that ethical values are only subjective to an individual's own perceptions or relative to a particular situation, time, or place. These approaches bear similarities to **emotivism, intuitionism, post-modernism**, and **situation ethics** and run counter to the foundational prem-ises of the **natural law** and most of the Catholic moral tradition. As such, relativism and subjectivism have been the particular focus of criticism by recent popes, especially **John Paul II** and **Benedict XVI**, and of **encyclicals** such as *Veritatis splendor* and *Fides et ratio*. A particularly strong variant of these theories is cultural relativism, which holds that "truth" is so condi-tioned by time, place, and **culture** as to render **universal moral norms** vir-tually impossible to know or apply. However, it is important not to confuse relativism with a legitimate taking into account the relevant moral features of circumstances in moral decisions, and similarly not to confuse subjec-tivism with proper attention to the necessary subjective aspects of moral evaluation that are found in a person's **intention** and in established concepts such as **sufficient knowledge** and **freedom** that by their very nature will be "subjective" inasmuch as these focus on the particular aspects of the moral subject in what she thinks or perceives rather than the external objective aspects of the **action** *in se.*

Religious liberty. See *Dignitatis humanae* and *Quanta cura*

Remedium concupiscientiae (remedy for concupiscence). See **concupis-cence**, *debitum*, and **marriage**

Remote, mediate, and immediate cooperation with evil. See **cooperation with evil**

Reparation and restitution are two aspects of both **commutative** and **re-storative justice** that require efforts as far as reasonably possible to address the injustices caused by sinful acts. Since commutative justice holds that each one should have what belongs to him, any violation of this requires that what was taken be restored as far as possible (see *ST II-II*, Q. 62). Restitution is not just physical, as in repaying a sum stolen, but can also include reparation in repairing injury done to another's reputation through **gossip, calumny**, or **slander**. Satisfaction of the requirements of restitution in the context of **sacrament of reconciliation** was extensively treated in **manualist tradition casuistry**. Occult restitution, for example, an anonymous repayment, could be counseled so the penitent would not risk legal repercussions, and partial or symbolic restitution could satisfy the moral debt if it were very difficult or impossible to make full repayment either because of lack of resources or because of the nature of the injury caused, for example, restitution in the strict sense could not be made for **adultery**. **See also** *compensation and occult compensation.*

Reparative therapy, also called "sexual reorientation" or "conversion" therapy, is a highly controversial movement that believes **homosexuality** is a disease that can be cured through aggressive treatment. A leading proponent of this movement is NARTH (the National Association for Research and Therapy of Homosexuality), which has been strongly allied with a number of conservative advocacy groups, including a number of religious-based organizations. While the therapy movement claimed significant success in turning people into "ex-gays," subsequent investigation has challenged many of these claims and most psychiatrists challenge its claims, including an influential former backer of the movement, Dr. Robert Spitzer, who publicly recanted his support for the movement in 2012. It is important to note that neither reparative therapy nor NARTH is endorsed by an official organ of the Catholic Church although some groups, such as **Courage**, recommend it. Indeed, the teaching of the **magisterium** as expressed in documents such as the US bishops' 1998 **pastoral letter** *Always Our Children, The Catechism of the Catholic Church*, and the **CDF**'s 1975 "Declaration on Certain Questions Concerning Sexual Ethics," *Persona humana* (*PH* #8), all acknowledge that for many, if not most, individuals with a same-sex orientation, this is constitutional in nature, that gay men and women should live out their sexual identity in **chastity** (*CCC* #2333), that they should be treated with compassion and respect, and that any unjust discrimination must be avoided (*CCC* #2333).

Reproductive technologies include a wide range of therapies aimed at assisting **procreation**, from fertility treatment to forms of assisted reproduction such as **artificial insemination (AID/AIH), GIFT, ICSI,** and **IVF.**

Cloning, although morally unobjectionable in animal husbandry, is the most objectionable of all forms of human reproductive technology. **Pius XII** addressed sterility and fertility treatments in several **occasional allocutions** (1949–56), forbidding artificial fertilization but allowing "artificial means" used to "facilitate" the natural and primary end of the conjugal act ("il fine principale del matrimonio"), which is procreation (*bonum prolix*). *CCC* #2373–79 as well as two **CDF** instructions, the 1987 *Donum vitae* and the 2008 *Dignitas personae*, outline objections to all forms of assisted reproduction because they compromise the **physicalist** dimensions of the conjugal act expressed in the **inseparability principle** of the unitive and procreative **ends of marriage**, adding that sterility is neither a **sin** nor an absolute **evil**. A child is always a gift and never a "right" (*CCC* #2379), and those unable to conceive naturally "should unite themselves with the Lord's Cross, the source of all spiritual fecundity. They can give expression to their generosity by adopting abandoned children or performing demanding services for others" (*CCC* #2379). These positions are not yet proposed **infallibly** but still are subject to the *obsequium religiosum* due to the **ordinary magisterium**. The issue, though, remains a serious *quaestio disputata* among many theologians, and the widespread use of these prohibited technologies seems to indicate some lack of reception on the part of the faithful (see *sensus fidelium*). New bioethical problems and possibilities, such as treatments for oncofertility, will likely continue to expand discussion in this arena. *For further reading*, see Thomas A. Shannon, ed., *Reproductive Technologies: A Reader* (Lanham, MD: Rowman and Littlefield, 2003); Edmund D. Pellegrino, John Collins Harvey, and John P. Langan, eds., *Gift of Life: Catholic Scholars Respond to the Vatican Instruction* (Washington, DC: Georgetown University Press, 1990); Maura A. Ryan, *Ethics and Economics of Assisted Reproduction: The Cost of Longing* (Washington, DC: Georgetown University Press, 2001); and Paul Lauritzen and Andrea Vicini, "Oncofertility and the Boundaries of Moral Reflection," *Theological Studies* 72 (2011): 116–30.

Rerum novarum, issued in 1891 by **Leo XIII**, is considered the first **social encyclical** in that it addressed in positive terms the rights of labor to organize in unions for collective bargaining while rejecting **communism** and recognizing a legitimate role of **capitalism** and **private property**.

Responsible parenthood is an aspect of family planning that takes into account a married couple's desire and ability to conceive, nurture, and educate children in light of their financial, emotional, and medical resources. The **Anglican Communion**'s 1930 **Lambeth Conference** Resolution 15 first spoke of the possibility of "a clearly felt moral obligation to limit or avoid parenthood," and while **artificial contraception** was firmly rejected that same year in **Pius XI**'s *Casti connubii*, the basic duty to exercise responsible parenthood was implicitly accepted (see *CC* #13, 18, 37). **Pius XII**'s 1951 **Address to Italian Midwives** explicitly noted that for serious reasons **procreation** could be delayed, limited, or even avoided for the duration of a **marriage**. Vatican II's *Gaudium et spes* likewise accepted this concept (*GS* #51–52), and the **Pontifical Commission on Births** established by **John XXIII** and expanded by **Paul VI** studied a number of factors, including multigenerational systemic poverty linked to the inability to control family size, before concluding in its "Majority Report" that **discernment** of how best to meet the concrete obligations of responsible parenthood should be left to the couples themselves to decide in **conscience**. Although Paul VI's 1968 *Humanae vitae* once again reaffirmed the Church's rejection of artificial contraception, he did clearly accept the notion of responsible parenthood (see *HV* #7, 10). Likewise, the subsequent pontificates have continued to affirm the moral obligation of responsible parenthood, although at the same time condemning artificial contraception. *For further reading*, see Jo McGowan, "Simplifying Sex: What Some Priests Don't Understand about Contraception," *Commonweal* (April 20, 2012): 6. **See also** *reproductive technologies* and *sterilization*.

Responsum ad dubium (response to a doubt/question) is a form of teaching or governance used primarily by the Vatican **dicasteries** such as the **CDF**. The *dubium* is usually sent to the appropriate dicastery by a bishop or conference of bishops (although others could submit a *dubium* as well), and if the issue is deemed of sufficient importance and capable of being resolved, then the dicastery issues a response. However, many questions forwarded are not answered or might only be answered after some considerable time. In this manner the relevant office of the **magisterium** functions a bit like the US Supreme Court, which can choose which cases to take up or not. Some examples of moral matters treated in this manner are the moral liceity of **uterine isolation** when any future pregnancy is medically counterindicated (1993) and the continuance of **ANH** in **PVS** cases (2007). While in the past such Vatican pronouncements usually closed further discussion of the disputed point (see *Roma locuta causa finita*), this has been less the case in the present, especially if new or convincing arguments have not been added. One such issue that remains discussed is the precise doctrinal weight of **John Paul II**'s 1994 apostolic letter *Ordinatio sacerdotalis* on **women's ordination**, which reiterated that women could never be ordained priests. In 1995, the CDF issued a *responsum* in the affirmative to the *dubium* of whether this papal teaching must be definitively held (*tenenda*) even though the pope did not invoke the usual formula for **infallibility** as an exercise of his **extraordinary magisterium** that would normally be expected for a defined doctrine (*de fide definita*). *For further reading* on this point, see Ladislas Orsy, "The Congregation's 'Response': Its Authority and Meaning," *America* 173 (December 9, 1995): 4–5; Francis A. Sullivan, "Guideposts from Catholic Tradition" *America* 173 (December 9, 1995): 5–6. **See also** *probabilism* and *status quaestionis*.

Restitution. See **reparation and restitution**

Restorative justice focuses on repairing **justice** that has been wounded or fractured by **sin** (often social or structural) and injustice. This restoration can involve many facets, including the **reconciliation** and healing of the wounds suffered both by the victims of injustice as well as by the offenders, or the rectification of systemic injustice that has arisen from social sin such as **racism** through programs such as **affirmative action**. Taking responsibility for sinful actions as well as suffering some possible punishment, **reparation** and **restitution** are required from those guilty of the violations of justice. This approach differs from **retributive justice**'s use of the *lex talionis* standard of "an eye for an eye and a tooth for a tooth." Restorative justice recognizes that it is usually impossible to go back to a true *status quo ante* that existed prior to the offense and instead uses the Christian themes of redemption and reconciliation to restore the community relationships fractured by the injustices caused. The victims then must be able to extend real **forgiveness**, and the offenders must seek genuine **conversion** in the process of moving forward into healing. *For further reading*, see Stephen Pope, "From Condemnation to Conversion: Seeking Restorative Justice in the Prison System," *America* (November 21, 2011): 13–16.

Retributive justice, expressed in the so-called *lex talionis*, metes out proportionate punishment to fit the offense as in "an eye for an eye, a tooth for a tooth." Retributive justice is designed to limit excessive punishment. Retributive justice was also used as a justification for **capital punishment**. As an example of the **history and development of moral theology**, the current teaching of the Catholic Church based on **John Paul II**'s 1995 *Evangelium vitae* and the subsequent revision of the *Catechism of the Catholic Church* no longer employs retributive justice. Retributive justice is notoriously difficult to limit in the concrete, and most ethicians today focus instead on **restorative justice** as being more appropriate to address serious wrongs.

Revisionist moral theology is a loosely defined term employed for some post–**Vatican II** moral theologians who question the **deductive, classicist,** and **physicalist** aspects of the **manualist tradition,** positing instead an approach that is more **inductive, historical,** and **personalist** both in theory (e.g., **moral norms** and the **natural law**) and in application, for example, in contested issues in **sexual ethics.** This approach often leads either to an authentic **historical development of moral theology** in the view of its proponents or to a posture of unacceptable **dissent** from the perspective of its opponents. *For further reading,* see Kenneth R. Melchin, "Revisionists, Deontologists, and the Structure of Moral Understanding," *Theological Studies* 51 (1990): 389–416; and Todd Salzman, *What Are They Saying about Catholic Ethical Method?* (Mahwah, NJ: Paulist Press, 2003).

Rhythm method. See **birth control** and **natural family planning**

Righteousness. See *adikia* (αδκια, unrighteousness) and **works righteousness**

Rightness and goodness. See **goodness and rightness distinction**

Right reason (*recta ratio*). See **reason**

Rights. See **canon law, human person, dignity, and rights;** and **white privilege**

Rigorism is associated with **Jansenism** and closely aligned with **tutiorism** and **probabiliorism,** which hold that in cases of moral **doubt** or disagreement about the liceity of a certain course of action, one should always follow at least the "safer" opinion, if not the absolutely "safest" possible opinion. Rigorism also stressed a value in following the "harder" or more rigorous interpretation as somehow being more likely to be more pleasing to **God.** However, the Church ultimately condemned Jansenism as heresy and adopted the counterposition of **probabilism** held by **Alphonsus Liguori, CSsR,** and the Jesuits. Liguori was later canonized and declared a Doctor of the Church and patron saint of moral theologians. See also *epikeia, legalism, lex dubia non obligat,* and *Voluntarism.*

Roma locuta causa finita translates as "Rome has spoken, the case is closed (or perhaps as "the cause is finished"). Based on **Augustine**'s "Sermon 131 Pelagius," this aphorism underscores the role of the **magisterium** to pronounce authoritatively on disputed matters (*quaestio disputata*). In the modern era this principle is tied to a number of magisterial documents such as

Pius XII's 1950 encyclical *Humani generis*, John Paul II's 1994 *Ordinatio sacerdotalis* on the impossibility of women being admitted to the ordained priesthood, and the **CDF**'s 1990 *Donum veritatis* "On the Ecclesial Vocation of the Theologian." The proper *obsequium religiosum* (religious respect) requested for any Church pronouncement comes from a consideration of the **character, manner, and frequency** criteria outlined in *Lumen gentium* #25, especially since the **history and development of moral doctrine** has shown that a number of teachings and pronouncements offered at one point in time are later refined and even changed, such as the Church's teachings on **capital punishment, religious liberty**, slavery, **torture, usury**, and so on. *For further reading*, see Maureen Fiedler and Linda Rabben, eds., *Rome Has Spoken: A Guide to Forgotten Papal Statements and How They Have Changed through the Centuries* (New York: Crossroad, 1998); Richard A. McCormick, "Matters of Free Theological Debate," ch. 9 in *The Critical Calling: Reflections on Moral Dilemmas since Vatican II*, 163–70 (Washington, DC: Georgetown University Press, 1989); and Karl Rahner, "Open Questions in Dogma Considered by the Institutional Church as Definitively Answered," in *Readings in Moral Theology, No. 3: The Magisterium and Morality*, edited by Charles E. Curran and Richard A. McCormick, 129–50 (New York: Paulist Press, 1982). **See also** *desuetude, infallibility, infallibilism, papal primacy, status quaestionis*, and *ultramontanism*.

The **Roman Rota** is the highest appellate court in the legal system of the Holy See, although the **Apostolic Signatura** functions like the US Supreme Court in that it can reverse decisions of the Rota and can judge its members (see *CIC* #1443–45). However, the ultimate **authority** in the Holy See's legal system is vested not in a constitution but rather the pope himself (see *CIC* #1442). The court dates back to the thirteenth century. *Rota*, Latin for "wheel," refers to the round room in which the court originially sat. Most of the cases that come before the Rota deal with disputes over decisions made by lower diocesan tribunals in marriage **annulment** cases although it can also hear any number of other judicial and nonadministrative cases that might arise in **canon law**.

S

A **sacrament** is a visible outward sign instituted by Christ and entrusted by him to the sanctifying mission of the Church to give God's grace. The **Council of Trent** (1545–63) defined seven sacraments (baptism, confirmation, Eucharist, **reconciliation**, **marriage**, anointing of the sick, and Holy Orders), although most Protestants hold only baptism and Eucharist as sacraments.

The **sacrament of reconciliation** is the sacrament with the greatest **historical development** over time. Originally, it was a once-in-a-lifetime "nonrepeatable" sacrament like baptism and employed only for **forgiveness** of serious **sin**, was usually public, and had a corresponding long public penance (although a public confession of sin was not required). After completion of this penance the forgiven sinner was ritually brought back into the Christian community with a celebration of **God**'s mercy and reconciliation with the community. Over time, individual confession became part of spiritual direction, especially in Irish monasteries, and tariff penances were outlined for various sins in manuals called penitentials. The exacting of a penance to "pay" for the sin committed heightened the perception of sin as individual crime rather than as disease and weakened the social dimensions of the earlier celebration of the sacrament. In the **manualist tradition**, **casuistry** gained greater prominence in training of priests to serve as confessional judges, assessing the nature of the crime, the relative **culpability** of the sinner, and the appropriate penance to be assigned for satisfaction of the sin. Great attention was also focused on helping the penitent make an "integral confession," that is, one in which sins were confessed according to "species and number" along with at least imperfect **contrition** and "firm purpose of amendment" to avoid the "near **occasions of sin**" in the future before **absolution** could be imparted. In 1215 the Fourth Lateran Council mandated the so-called **Easter duty**, and over the succeeding centuries the practice grew up that strongly counseled going to confession before any reception of the Eucharist. Long lines for Saturday afternoon confessions marked most parishes up to **Vatican II**, after which the sacrament was thoroughly reformed. Three rites were promulgated by **Paul VI** in 1972–73: Rite 1, reconciliation of individual penitents (the so-called traditional rite); Rite 2, reconciliation of several penitents with individual confession (as is commonly practiced in Advent and Lenten parish reconciliation services); and Rite 3, reconciliation of several penitents with general confession and absolution. Before this, Rite 3 promulgation of general absolution could be administered only in danger of death (e.g., on a sinking ship or in time of war), and Rite 3 broadened its application to include other situations of "grave need," such as large numbers of penitents present with insufficient numbers of confessors. Both Rites 2 and 3 lift up the communal nature of sin, **forgiveness**, and reconciliation in addition to the necessity for individual **conversion**. **John Paul II**, especially after the promulgation of the new *Code of Canon Law* (see *CIC* # 959–97) and the **Synod of Bishops** on penance (both in 1983), in his subsequent 1984 apostolic exhortation *Reconciliatio et paenitentia* ("On Reconciliation and Penance"), raised concerns that Rite 3 could be abused and that the traditional Rite 1 practice of individual confession was sharply declining, so he tightened up the conditions under which Rite 3 could be used, charging the local bishops with responsibility to limit its practice to truly extraordinary circumstances. *For further reading*, see James Dallen, *The Reconciling Community: The Rite of Penance* (New York: Pueblo Publishing, 1986); Kurt Stasiak, *The Confessor's Handbook* (New York: Paulist Press, 2010). See also *seal of confession*.

Safe sex is an expression that arose in the 1980s with the explosion of the **HIV/AIDS** virus and after discovering that **condom use** in sexual intercourse significantly reduced the transmission of this virus as well as other **STDs** (sexually transmitted diseases). While condom use has been decried by many Church officials who believed that promoting this usage would encourage illicit sexual behavior, subsequently **Benedict XVI** noted that condom usage by an infected individual who was unlikely to be persuaded to sexual **abstinence** would, according to **gradualism**, represent at least some level of responsibility and therefore could be accepted. Safe-sex practices cannot transform an immoral action into a moral action, but in accord with the established principle of the **lesser evil**, it is always desirable to lessen the evil effects of even immoral actions wherever possible. While safe sex is generally understood to refer to practices among nonmarried partners, a difficult issue has arisen in the moral analysis of so-called discordant couples, the medical term for a married couple in which one person is HIV positive and the other is HIV negative. The morality of the usage of condoms by such discordant couples is a much debated *status quaestionis* among moral theologians; at this writing (2012) the question has been under study by the **CDF** for several years and so remains open to **probabilism**. *For further reading*, see Benedict Guevin and Martin Rhonheimer, "On the Use of Condoms to Prevent Acquired Immunity Deficiency Syndrome," *National Catholic Bioethics Quarterly* (Spring 2005): 37–48; James F. Keenan with Jon D. Fuller, Lisa Sowle Cahill, and Kevin Kelly, eds., *Catholic Ethicists and HIV/AIDS Prevention* (New York: Continuum, 2000); and Pope Benedict XVI, *Light for the World: The Pope, The Church and the Signs of the Times. A Conversation with Peter Seewald* (San Francisco: Ignatius Press, 2010). **See also** *ABC, compromise with evil, contraception, natural law, Roma locuta causa finita, self-preservation, sexual ethics,* and *tolerance.*

SALIGIA. See **capital sins**

Salpingectomy/salpingotomy. See **ectopic pregnancy**

Same-sex unions, also called "gay marriage," are unions that seek to realize legal recognition equivalent to heterosexual **marriage** for same-sex couples going beyond **domestic partners** legislation. While social acceptance of such unions is growing and several states now legally recognize gay marriages, the Church's definition of marriage as a union between a man and a woman open to the physical possibility of **procreation** (see *CCC* #2360–69) precludes the possibility of celebrating sacramentally such unions. Nevertheless, arguments for some sort of ecclesial recognition for such unions continue to be discussed by some theologians and other religious denominations such as the **Anglican Communion.**

Sanctuary of conscience. See **conscience**

Satisfaction for sin. See **sin** and **reparation and restitution**

Scandal (from the Greek for putting a "stumbling block" in another's way) in itself is not inherently good or bad. St. Paul, for example, speaks of the Cross of Christ as a scandal (or stumbling block) for the Jews and a folly for the Gentiles, but to those called to salvation, Christ is indeed **God**'s power and wisdom (see 1 Cor. 1:23–25). Paul, however, cautions against *scandalum pusillorum* ("scandal of the weak") by unnecessarily scandalizing some in eating food ritually sacrificed to idols (see 1 Cor. 8) even though Christians secure in their faith realize that no such idols exist and thus could eat with a clear **conscience.** However, **charity** demands special care for those not yet able to make this important theological distinction. If they saw other Christians eating ritually sacrificed food, they might misjudge them to have fallen into idol worship. A contemporary example of avoiding *scandalum* *pusillorum* might be that of a priest-chaplain serving on a cruise ship who has the same **dispensation** in **canon law** from the Good Friday fast and **abstinence** regulations that all those on the ship enjoy (whether crew or passengers). While the priest "could" choose the prime rib entrée on the menu, care not to scandalize the other passengers who likely would be unaware of this special dispensation would suggest the **prudential judgment** of the choice of the fish course instead.

Passive scandal is the unjust taking of offense against the just actions of another, such as the Pharisees' condemnation of Jesus's healing on the Sabbath, and could be a **sin** of **rash judgment** against charity (see Mt. 18:6–7). **Thomas Aquinas** defined "active scandal" as a word or action that is evil in itself and that works toward causing spiritual or moral detriment of another (see *ST II-II*, Q. 53, art. 1) and bears a certain similarity to **seduction**. If a priest wore his Roman collar to a strip club, this would be an example of active scandal, even if the priest himself did not engage in any other immoral activity. The **moral manuals** often treated the terms "scandal" and "seduction" together and developed a fairly complex **casuistry** for granting permission to risk giving scandal to others. Seduction, however, would never be morally allowed. For example, a wife and her children were permitted to miss Sunday Mass if their attendance might unjustly provoke the fury of the husband and father. The "sin" would be the father's anger, but this "stumbling" could be related to the wife and children's attendance at Mass. While the wife and children are not **culpable** for the husband's sin, it might be a prudential judgment done in charity to help this man, and thus the confessor could be counseled to so advise the wife or children so they would not suffer from the burden of any false **guilt** about having missed Mass on Sunday. Finally, in the moral sense "scandal" does not include simple shock or dismay. If the pope were to utter an untoward remark in public upon painfully stubbing his toe, it would not be technically correct to accuse him of causing scandal—even if his particular choice of vocabulary might be infelicitous on this occasion. On the other hand, if he were to engage in telling bawdy stories or off-color jokes, this might indeed be a case of giving scandal since others within hearing might conclude that he in fact did not believe the strictures against improper speech.

Schiavo, Terri, was a Florida woman who died in 2005 after being in **PVS** for more than fourteen years; her family and husband battled over whether to end **ANH**. Ultimately the husband prevailed after a protracted court battle, and the **PEG** feeding tube was removed. **See also** *ordinary and extraordinary means*; *states of consciousness: brain death, coma, PVS, MCS, and locked-in syndrome*; and *vitalism*.

Scholasticism is the term used for the conceptual approach to philosophy or theology that predominated in the universities of the Middle Ages from about 1100 to 1500. Key Scholastic figures include **William of Ockham**, Bonaventure, Duns Scotus, Albertus Magnus, and **Thomas Aquinas**, whose masterpiece the *Summa theologiae* is generally regarded as the apogee of Scholasticism. **Leo XIII**'s 1879 encyclical *Aeterni Patris* called for a return to the use of Scholasticism in seminary training.

Scripture and ethics refer to how the Bible is used methodologically as a resource for the discipline of moral theology while avoiding pitfalls such as poor **exegesis**, **proof-texting**, and the like. See the longer entry under **biblical ethics** and see also *Proprium*. *For further reading*, see James T. Bretzke, *Bibliography on Scripture and Christian Ethics* (Lewiston NY: Edwin Mellen Press, 1997); James T. Bretzke, "Scripture and Ethics: Core, Context, and Coherence," ch. 5 in *Moral Theology: New Directions and Fundamental Issues*, edited by James Keating, 88–107 (New York: Paulist Press, 2004); Richard B. Hays, *The Moral Vision of the New Testament: Community, Cross, New Creation. A Contemporary Introduction to New Testament Ethics* (San Francisco: HarperSanFrancisco, 1996); Jeffrey S. Siker, *Scripture and Ethics: Twentieth-Century Portraits* (New York: Oxford University Press, 1997); and William C. Spohn, *What Are They Saying about Scripture and Ethics?*, rev. ed. (New York: Paulist Press, 1984, 1995).

Scrupulosity either sees **sin** where there is none or exaggerates the gravity of lighter venial sin, making it into serious or **mortal sin**. While almost everyone at some time may have a scruple resulting from a **doubtful** or **erroneous conscience**, serious scruples can become habitual in some individuals akin to an **obsessive-compulsive disorder (OCD)**. Pastoral treatment is often challenging, difficult, and long-term. The scrupulous person should be encouraged to remain with one confessor or counselor and to follow that person's advice, especially in avoiding confessing actions as sins that the confessor has asserted are not sins, and by not reconfessing sins that have already been forgiven. Scrupulosity is often tied in with a particularly negative and inaccurate portrayal of **God** as a harsh and demanding judge. Over time and with patience, trust, and forbearance on both the part of the scrupulous individual **suffering** and his counselor or confessor, real progress is certainly possible as some of the greatest saints in the Church, such as Ignatius of Loyola and **Alphonsus Liguori**, have suffered for a time from scruples. Recalling these saints to the individual who suffers from this disease may be of some help. *For further reading* of a traditional treatment on scruples, see Vincent M. O'Flaherty, *How to Cure Scruples* (Milwaukee:

Bruce Publishing, 1966); and for a helpful article on the distinction be-tween the superego mistaken as the voice of **conscience**, see John W. Gla-ser, "Conscience and Super-Ego: A Key Distinction," *Theological Studies* 32 (1971): 30–47. Glaser's article is also found in *Conscience: Theological and Psychological Perspectives*, edited by C. Ellis Nelson, 167–88 (New York: Newman Press, 1973).

Seal of the confessional refers to the longest standing, most sacred obliga-tion of those who hear confessions, including nonclerical translators who may assist in the sacrament when there is a language or communication barrier. These individuals are barred from indicating in any way such that someone else would then be able to surmise the identity of the penitent and the matter confessed (*CIC* #983). Nor may they use any knowledge gained from confession in any manner that the penitent might find burdensome, including in future spiritual direction, without the express prior permission of the penitent (*CIC* #984–85). This seal is absolutely inviolable, and even if divulging confessional matter should be commanded by civil law, any confessor who directly breaks the seal of confession is subject to a *latae sen-tentiae* **canonical penalty** of automatic **excommunication** reserved to the Apostolic See, while **indirect** or partial violations are subject to lesser penal-ties (*CIC* #1388). While a confessor may seek counsel from another priest or canonical expert on how to handle a particular type of case, great care must be taken that no information is indirectly provided that might reasonably al-low the other person to guess the penitent's identity. **See also** *confidentiality and secrecy* and *sacrament of reconciliation*.

Secondary ends of marriage. See *debitum, remedium concupiscientiae*, and **marriage**

Secrecy. See **confidentiality and secrecy**

Secularism is a vaguely defined philosophical theory, movement, or per-spective carrying a wide range of possible meanings. At one end of the spec-trum, secularism simply espouses letting the lay or secular part of the world play its legitimate role, free of improper control or dominance from religious authorities. At the other end of the spectrum, secularism either denies belief in **God** or proposes a sociopolitical movement to make the roles of faith and religion largely irrelevant in the public arena. A middle point on the spectrum argues for a separation of Church and state in politics and other civic spheres such that the state could not intervene in the legitimate domain of faith communities and the religious authorities likewise would not seek special privileges or to intervene in the political life of a multireligious society. Recent popes, especially **John Paul II** and **Benedict XVI**, have decried what they see as an increasing process of secularization in the world, an increase in moral **relativism**, and the diminution of the voice of religious faith in general and Christianity in particular in moral discourse, especially in Western Europe, while ultraconservatives view secularism as another face of **modernism**. **See also** *Fides et ratio* and *Veritatis splendor.*

Seduction is the deliberate act of leading another person into **sin**. Besides a serious offense against the moral order, it is additionally a sin against **charity**. Particular penalties are found in **canon law** for priests who would abuse the confessional forum of the **sacrament of reconciliation** to solicit someone to commit a sin against the Sixth Commandment, and any priest who absolves an accomplice in such a sin (except in danger of death, see *CIC* #977) will incur a *latae sententiae* of **excommunication** penalty reserved to the Holy See (see *CIC* #1378). Often the **moral manuals** treated the **casuistry** of seduction along with **scandal**, although the nature of the two terms is quite distinct, especially since under certain circumstances scandal can be unintentional and even allowed.

Self-defense. See **just war theory**

Self-preservation is a general moral duty shared by all sentient beings and expressed in the classic axiom "*primum est vivere*" ("the first duty is to live"). **Thomas Aquinas** articulated this duty in the *ST II-II*, Q. 64, art. 7, and it also has been expressed as well in a large number of moral axioms, such as "*Plus tenetur homo vitae suae providere quam vitae alienate*" ("One is required to take more care of one's own life than that of another"). These justify not only **self-defense** but also not risking one's own life in situations that otherwise would result in the death of both one's self and another person. The **manualist tradition** gave the example of a good swimmer who would be justified in repelling a drowning person who is dragging him down if it seemed unlikely that the good swimmer could save both himself and the other. Related axioms, such as "*nemo tenetur ad impossibile*" ("no one is held to the impossible"); "*impossibilium nulla obligatio (est)*" ("nothing impossible can oblige"); and "*ultra posse* (or *vires*) *nemo obligatur*" ("no one is obliged to do more than his/her ability [or strength] allows"), all stress the constant moral tradition that no one is ever obliged to do that which he considers to be a **moral impossibility**. Martin Rhonheimer, OD, in his 2009 *Vital Conflicts in Medical Ethics: A Virtue Approach to Craniotomy and Tubal Pregnancies* (117) also references this principle to support a mother's decision to terminate a pregnancy when it is reasonably foreseen that otherwise both the mother and fetus would die but that termination of the pregnancy would at least save the life of the mother (even if this could not be known with absolute certainty). Of course, the obligation to self-preservation does not prohibit or nullify acts of heroic **virtue** to save the life of another, even to the point of sacrificing one's own life, as we see in the Cross of Christ and the lives of many saints such as Maximilian Kolbe and others who risked and even knowingly offered their lives to protect other innocents, such as the innocent Jews persecuted by the Nazis during the Holocaust of World War II.

Semiwakefulness. See **advertence, culpability,** and **states of consciousness: brain death, coma, PVS, MCS, and locked-in syndrome**

Semper et pro semper and *semper sed non pro semper* is the pair of Latin axioms for **negative and positive duties**, that is, those **negative duties** or prohibitions that always are binding (*semper et pro semper*) and those positive duties or **prescriptions** that are always "true" but that allow for legitimate exceptions or **dispensations** (*semper sed non pro semper*).

Sensus fidelium (sense of the faithful) acknowledges the role that all of the faithful have by virtue of their baptism to participate in the **gifts of the Holy Spirit** (see Jn. 16:13; 1 Jn. 2:20, 27), including a practical **discernment** on Revelation and the Christian faith response in the world (see *LG* #12 and *DV* #8). This *sensus* includes both the believers' sense of their own gift of faith as well the elements of the faith itself that are professed, such as belief in the Assumption of the Blessed Virgin. While the *sensus fidelium* neither replaces nor supersedes the **magisterium**'s *munus docendi*, the Church has long recognized the legitimate role that all the baptized play in coming to a deeper understanding of the Christian faith. Both Blessed John Henry Cardinal Newman (1801–90) and **Cardinal Joseph Ratzinger (Benedict XVI)** note that in regard to the positive role of Spirit-filled *sensus fidelium* found

> in the process of assimilating what is really rational and rejecting what only seems to be rational, the whole Church has to play a part. This process cannot be carried out in every detail by an isolated Magisterium, with oracular **infallibility**. The life and suffering of Christians who profess their faith in the midst of their times has just as important a part to play as the thinking and questioning of the learned, which would have a very hollow ring without the backing of Christian existence, which learns to discern spirits in the travail of everyday life. ("Magisterium of the Church, Faith, Morality," in *Readings in Moral*

Theology, No. 2, edited by Charles E. Curran and Richard A. McCormick [New York: Paulist Press, 1980]:186)

Sequela Christi (following of Christ) refers to the **vocation** of Christian discipleship and the primary metaphor of the moral life in adopting Jesus as the Way, Truth, and Life (see Jn. 14:5–6). While related to an *imitatio Christi* (imitation of Christ), it is important to remember that this must always be done in a human way as disciples and not as pretended clones of Christ. Expressions such as WWJD (What would Jesus do?) are helpful in terms of *paranesis* or exhortation but cannot replace the harder task of moral **discernment** in making **reason**-based **prudential judgments** required in everyday living.

Serious sin. See **sin** and **fundamental option theory**

The **Sermon on the Mount** (Mt. 5–7 and parallel with the shorter "Sermon on the Plain" in Lk. 6:17–49) is often viewed as the "core" of Jesus's ethical teaching and therefore is central to **biblical ethics**. Some theologians see it as a program or mandate for everyday **Christian ethics** while others see it more as an impossible **ideal** or expression of the **Kingdom of God**'s values, which will become firmly established only at the Second Coming, and still others speak of it as a form of **interim ethic** that the early Church thought would apply for the relatively short period envisioned before the definitive Second Coming. *For further reading*, see Hans Dieter Betz, *Essays on the Sermon on the Mount* (Philadelphia: Fortress Press, 1985); Joachim Jeremias, *The Sermon on the Mount* (Philadelphia: Fortress Press, 1963); and Daniel Patte, *Discipleship according to the Sermon on the Mount: Four Legitimate Readings, Four Plausible Views of Discipleship and Their Relative Values* (Valley Forge, PA: Trinity Press, 1996).

Seven deadly sins. See **capital sins**

Seven gifts of the Holy Spirit. See **gifts of the Holy Spirit**

Sexism includes attitudes, biases, behaviors, and the application of **gender**, **sexual orientation** (sometimes called **heterosexism**), or sexual stereotypes that result in unjust discrimination or domination, usually of women and often in the broader cultural context of patriarchy. Sexism often holds that one gender is somehow superior to the other, and **feminist ethics** in particular critiques sexism. As with any form of unjust prejudice or discrimination, sexism is clearly sinful, but just what constitutes sexism in the concrete remains debated. Tensions around sexism are felt strongly in the insistence of noninclusive language in ecclesial documents, especially liturgical texts, in which "man" and "he" are used to denote both men and women, and in the refusal of **women's ordination**. In his apostolic letters *Ordinatio sacerdotalis* (1994, "On Priestly Ordination") and his *Mulieris dignitatem* (1988, "On the Dignity of Women"), **John Paul II** denies this charge and outlines his theology on the complementary roles of men and women in accord with the *imago Dei* and **God**'s plan for humanity in **creation**. This theme is also picked up in the **CDF**'s 2004 *Letter to Bishops on the Collaboration of Men and Women in the Church and in the World*.

Sexual abuse is a grave offense against **justice**, **charity**, and the purposes of **sexuality**. The clerical sexual abuse crisis that gained international attention in the decades from the 1990s to the present is an unparalleled **scandal** that has shattered countless lives and seriously compromised the ministry and credibility of the Church and its leaders, demoralized both priests and the faithful, and led to immense financial ramifications. According to one report, in the eight-year period from 2004 to 2012, more than $2.48 billion was paid for legal fees and damages to victims by dioceses, eparchies, and religious orders—an amount that does not include costs dating back to the first national reports from 1985 in which many more millions of dollars of secret payments were made to victims. Sexual abuse in **canon law** falls under the category of **crimes and delicts** and is considered to be a *delicta graviora* (grave delict). In partial response to the sexual abuse crisis, **John Paul II** issued in 2001 *Sacramentorum sanctitatis tutela* ("Safeguarding of the Sanctity of the Sacraments"), which established procedural norms and designated the **CDF** as the primary office for handling sexual abuse charges against priests. The **USCCB**'s **Dallas Charter** set a **zero tolerance** policy as the primary institutional response to clerical sexual abuse in the United States. Many priests have been laicized or permanently removed from ministry, and not a few have been imprisoned as well. At least one archbishop (Boston's Bernard Cardinal Law, in 2002) had to resign for the mishandling of clergy sexual abusers, and a few others have resigned because of their own sexual abuse, but most of the bishops and leaders of religious orders were not otherwise punished for lack of oversight or even knowingly reassigning serial pedophiles into other pastoral ministries. This continues much controversy as advocacy groups such as BishopAccountability.org continue to militate for bishops and religious superiors to acknowledge greater responsibility for this crisis.

Sexual ethics. See **sexuality, gender, sexual orientation, and sexual ethics**

Sexuality, gender, sexual orientation, and **sexual ethics** are the areas of considerable, yet sharply contested, views in the **history and development of moral theology and doctrine**. Sexuality, used for the first time in a Vatican-level document in the **CDF**'s 1975 *Persona humana* (see *PH* #1, 5, 9, 10, 13), is now widely accepted as basic human modality—that is, an essential way of being human—that cannot be reduced merely to a **physicalist** analysis of sexual organs but must also include **personalist** dimensions (see *CCC* #2332–33). How this modality is lived out concretely in the context of **culture** and the **natural law** will likely remain the locus of divergent and divisive discussion for years to come. Looking backward, we can note considerable progress in the acceptance, at least in theory, of the notion of sexual equality between men and women and of a distinction between biological and social understandings of gender—i.e., it is no longer accepted by most that somehow God's will ordains that women must remain only in the home to act as subservient wives and self-sacrificing mothers, that **sexism** is sinful, and that discrimination based on gender or orientation is contrary to **human dignity** and **rights**. **Leo XIII**'s 1880 **encyclical** *Arcanum Divinae Sapientiae* and **John Paul II**'s 1988 apostolic letter *Mulieris dignitatem* contain many common points, but the overall perspective on the nature and various roles of women certainly differs quite markedly; there has been a real change in the continuity of **Tradition** in this area of **feminist ethics** and many other areas. **Pius XI**'s vocabulary and tone in his condemnation of artificial **birth control** in his 1930 *Casti connubii* is not echoed in **Paul VI**'s 1968 *Humanae vitae*, even if the moral analysis of the act of **artificial contraception** is similar. Although the term "**homosexuality**" is a late-nineteenth-century neologism, most likely the Apostle Paul considered same-sex activity as a voluntary form of sexual depravity. However, both *Persona humana* and the *Catechism of the Catholic Church* acknowledge that sexual orientation is not easily or completely understood, and that for most people it is not a matter of free choice but more fundamentally established in one's sexual constitution (see *PH* #8 and *CCC* #2358). **Masturbation** was viewed by **Thomas Aquinas** as a "most grievous sin," more dreadful than incest, rape, **adultery**, **seduction**, and **fornication** (*ST II-II* Q. 154, art. 11 and 12), but today we are cautioned that in forming "an equitable judgment about the subjects' moral responsibility" about this action we "must take into account the affective immaturity, force of acquired **habit**, conditions of anxiety, or other psychological or social factors that lessen or even extenuate moral **culpability**" (*CCC* #2352). Continuity and change are likely to be the twin hallmarks in any *status quaestionis* or *quaestio disputata* connected with sexual ethics for decades to come. *For further reading*, see Michel Foucault, *The History of Sexuality: An Introduction* (New York: Random House, 1978); Lisa Sowle Cahill, *Sex, Gender and Christian Ethics* (New York: Cambridge University Press, 1996); Charles E. Curran and Richard A. McCormick, eds., *Readings in Moral Theology No. 8: Dialogue about Catholic Sexual Teaching* (New York: Paulist Press, 1993); Kevin Kelly, *New Directions in Sexual Ethics: Moral Theology and the Challenge to AIDS* (London: Geoffrey Chapman, 1998); Susan E. Parsons, *Ethics of Gender* (Boston: Blackwell, 2001); and Todd A. Salzman and Michael G. Lawler, *Sexual Ethics: A Theological Introduction* (Washington, DC: Georgetown University Press, 2012).

"Signs of the times" is used by **Vatican II**'s *Gaudium et spes*, "Pastoral Constitution on the Church in the Modern World," for **discernment** in "scrutinizing the signs of the times and of interpreting them in the light of the Gospel," which requires a positive openness to the world in order to "recognize and understand the world in which we live, its explanations, its longings, and its often dramatic characteristics" (*GS* #4). Although often associated with Vatican II's call for *aggiornamento* (renewal), the dynamic of interpreting God's signs is found throughout scripture (see Dt. 4:32–36; Jn. 14:16–17, 26; 16:12–15) and is tied with discernment of the Holy Spirit's promptings, which must be carefully distinguished from the **Zeitgeist** (German, "spirit of the age") so as not to sacrifice the gospel to an improper accommodation of contemporary **culture** or **political correctness**.

Simony is the temporal trading, buying, or selling of spiritual goods such as the sacraments, **indulgences**, or ecclesiastical offices or favors. The **manualist tradition** classed simony as a serious violation against **divine law** requiring **restitution**. A particular difficulty addressed by the Holy See, such as Benedict XIV's 1741 *Quanta cura* down to **Paul VI**'s 1974 *Motu proprio firma in traditione*, concerns Mass stipends and support of the clergy, which run the risk of either actual abuse or a misunderstanding as simony leading to **scandal**, on one hand, but which also help the faithful in the legitimate support of the Church's spiritual and temporal ministries (see *CIC* #945–58).

Simul iustus et peccator (at the same time justified and a sinner) refers to **Augustine**'s doctrine of **original sin**, which held that while baptism wipes away the sin, some stain or residual effects remain, especially in the form of **concupiscence**. Martin Luther interpreted this doctrine, especially in light of his understanding of justification by faith (*sola fide*), to emphasize the total gratuity (*sola gratia*) of salvation on God's part to sinful humanity, which under its own power could never hope to live a truly righteous life and please **God**.

Sin is ultimately an offense against **God**, but as **Thomas Aquinas** observed, "We do not offend God except by doing something contrary to our own good" (*SCG* #3, ch. 122; see also *CCC* #1849–50). Sin is a mysterious power, as the Apostle Paul anguished in Romans, that defies both our complete understanding and our ability to conquer unaided on our own. Yet **justification by faith** assures us we can be freed from its concrete power over our daily lives and from our final destiny as well if we accept Christ's offering of saving grace. Catholic **Tradition** has posited two species of sin, mortal and venial, although as Thomas Aquinas noted, real sin is mortal (death-dealing) and venial sin is sin by **analogy** only (*ST I-II* Q. 88; see also 1 Jn. 5:16). In the strict sense mortal sin is the definitive rupture of a person's saving relationship with God, and if the person should die unrepentant in the state of mortal sin, he would condemn himself to hell. Three conditions must simultaneously present for mortal sin: (1) grave matter of the moral object and (2) **sufficient knowledge** followed by (3) **sufficient consent** (see *CCC* #1857). "Knowledge" here means moral knowledge, not just merely academic knowledge that could be measured in a true/false test. In other words, someone must truly see the heinousness of a seriously immoral action and still willfully choose to do it for these criteria to be met. All sin can be forgiven by **absolution** in the **sacrament of reconciliation**, which is the ordinary means to absolve mortal sin, although mortal sin can also be forgiven though an act of perfect **contrition**. Venial sins can also be forgiven through participation in the other sacraments as well as through acts of **charity**, piety, and repentance. Serious or grave sin has gained increased usage in theological language to denote objectively grave matter that may not necessarily be mortal sin (see *RP* #17). Sins of commission and omission highlighted the fact that one can sin by not doing something one should (omission) as well as by doing something wrong (commission). Social sin is a concept originally from **liberation theology** but is now widely acknowledged as a manifestation of **structural evil** that involves collective human agency (see *FC* #9) but going beyond the traditional paradigm of individual acts of personal **culpability**. *For further reading*, see James T. Bretzke, "Sin and Failure in a Morally Complex World," ch. 7 in *A Morally Complex World* (Collegeville, MN: Liturgical Press, 2004), 191–208; Josef Fuchs, "Structures of Sin," ch. 4 in *Moral Demands and Personal Obligations* (Washington, DC: Georgetown University Press, 1993), 62–73; Bernard Häring, "Sin in Post-Vatican II Theology," in *Personalist Morals: Essays in Honor of Professor Louis Janssens*, edited by Joseph A. Selling (Leuven, Belgium: University Leuven

Press, 1988), 87–107; and Patrick McCormick, *Sin as Addiction* (New York: Paulist Press, 1989). **See also** *fundamental option theory, original sin, pecca fortiter*, and *simul iustus et peccator*

Situation ethics is a loosely defined ethical theory condemned by the **Holy Office** (today the **CDF**) in the 1950s but that reappeared in the 1960s. The theory held that it was primarily the **circumstances**, or situation, along with the **intention** of the moral agent acting within those circumstances, that determined the moral **rightness** or wrongness of a particular action. The theory was popularized by the American Episcopal seminary professor Joseph Fletcher in a 1966 book of the same name. Fletcher held that **love** is the only absolute, therefore other **moral principles** could be cast aside or held to be less determinative as long as the agent sought to act in the most loving manner possible. The book's appendix presents several concrete cases that Fletcher felt illustrated how the love principle may seem to conflict at times with other seemingly **absolute moral norms**.

The most discussed of these cases was called the "sacrificial **adultery**" of Frau Bergmeier, a German picked up at the end of World War II by an advancing Soviet Army patrol. Her husband was already a prisoner of war in England, and she had three children to care for at home. She came to know that pregnant prisoners were released by the Soviets as medical liabilities, and with the help of a "friendly Volga German camp guard," she was impregnated and eventually released and reunited with her whole family back in Berlin. Fletcher states that the child born of this union was loved more by the rest of the family since in their view that child had done the most to achieve their reunion. Fletcher concludes the case with two questions: (1) should the family be grateful to the Volga German camp guard; and (2) had Frau Bergmeier done a "good and right thing"? It is unknown if this was an actual case, and Fletcher himself does not explicitly answer his own questions, although in the context of situation ethics theory advanced in his book, it would seem an affirmative answer should be given.

This case provoked considerable ecumenical discussion among Protestant and Roman Catholic ethicians who were divided in their own responses to Fletcher's questions. In addition to the many practical difficulties in the moral **discernment** of determining what the "most loving response" would entail, we would add the problem of unforeseeable and unintended consequences of the actions of both Frau Bergmeier and the Volga camp guard. How would they know with reasonable certainty how their own families might react? What if their relationship developed in a different direction from their initial intent, and so on? In addition to these, the primary issues debated among ethicians revolved around an understanding of adultery: was it a violation of an absolute moral norm found in the **Decalogue**, or would this be a **virtually exceptionless norm** or perhaps an instance of *lex valet ut in pluribus* (the law applies in most [but not all] cases)? These questions further involve understandings of the objective moral order and especially **intrinsic evil** as well as the key **goodness and rightness distinction**. The classic Protestant tradition would hold that this might be an example in which Luther's notion of *pecca fortiter* (sin boldly) would lead us to put our trust in **justification by faith**, and the classic Catholic position would stress the concepts of **erroneous conscience**, possibly due to Frau Bergmeier's **invincible ignorance** in her complex and desperate situation. *For further reading* that arose regarding these themes, including a further essay by Fletcher, see Gene H. Outka and Paul Ramsey, eds., *Norm and Context in Christian Ethics* (London: SCM Press, 1968).

Slander is the deliberate harming of another person's reputation by spreading false or distorted information about her. It is a violation of the Eighth Commandment of the **Decalogue** against **lying** as well as a potentially serious **sin** against **charity**. See the fuller treatment under **calumny and defamation**.

The term "**slippery slope argument**" is often used in debate or rhetoric to warn that if a particular course of action is taken or adopted, more serious, perhaps unforeseen, consequences are likely to occur, much like starting down a ski slope and then careening out of control halfway down. Logically, this mode of argument is by itself neither self-evidently true nor false since much depends on the probability that the negative consequences would in fact occur if the proposed action were taken. For example, a commercial airplane could crash, but since statistics show this to be a very safe form of travel, invoking the slippery slope against all air travel would be problematic. On the other hand, electing to go over Niagara Falls in a barrel would seem foolhardy, even if some individuals have survived this trip. Slippery slope arguments are found fairly frequently in moral discourse, such as *HV* #17: "consider how easily this course of action [use of artificial **birth control**] could open wide the way for marital infidelity and a general lowering of moral standards." In brief, and in absence of other arguments, the slippery slope suggests caution; upon deeper reflection one may then decide to proceed or not.

Sloth. See **capital sins**

Sobrino, Jon, SJ. See **liberation theology**

Social encyclicals and social teaching from the papal **magisterium** date from **Leo XIII**'s 1891 *Rerum novarum* continuing up to (at this writing) **Benedict XVI**'s 2009 *Caritas in veritate* (*Charity in Truth*). Other key social encyclicals include **Pius XI**'s 1931 *Quadragesimo anno* (*"Fortieth Anniversary"* [of *Rerum novarum*]) written in the throes of the Great Depression and critiquing the excesses of **socialism**, **communism**, and **capitalism**, and calling for an economic order grounded in the **common good** and based on cooperation, **solidarity**, and **subsidiarity**. **John XXIII**'s 1961 *Mater et magistra* dealt with just wages, aid to developing nations, and the responsibility of all Christians to work for a more just world, and his 1963 *Pacem in terris* tackled the challenges of building world peace in the context of the Cold War. **Paul VI** built on this theme in his 1967 *Populorum progressio* by linking peace with the establishment of a more just order, followed by his 1971 apostolic letter *Octogesima adveniens*, which analyzed new problems such as urbanization, workers, the roles of women, youth, media, ideology, and so on. **John Paul II**'s 1981 *Laborem exercens* stressed that humans are the subject of work and never objects and supported anew the rights of workers to unions and collective bargaining. His 1987 *Sollicitudo rei socialis* (1987) addressed issues of globalization and economic and political divisions in the world, and his *Centesimus annus* (1991) commemorated the one hundredth anniversary of *Rerum novarum* and condemned **communism** as well as aspects of **capitalism** that exacerbate oppression of the poor and pay insufficient attention to the **common good**. **Benedict XVI**'s 2009 *Caritas in veritate* grappled with a wide range of social problems including globalization, the economic order, **ecology**, energy, and the environment as well as demographic tensions, **relativism**, **solidarity**, and many others. Benedict affirmed that while the "Church does not have technical solutions to offer and does not claim 'to interfere in any way in the politics of States' (*PP* #11)" its mission is to search for and proclaim the truth in its social doctrine (*CV* #9). *For further reading*, see Edward DeBerri and James Hug with Peter J. Henroit and Michael S. Schultheis, *Catholic Social Teaching: Our Best Kept Secret*, 4th ed. (Maryknoll, NY: Orbis Books: Center for Concern, 1985, 2003).

Social Gospel. See **Rauschenbusch, Walter**, and **WWJD?**

Socialism is an economic system or a political philosophy that espouses common ownership or state control over the means of production and the delivery of many key social services, such as education, health care, economic planning, and so on. It would be incorrect to identify all forms of socialism with **communism**, and while some totalitarian and materialistic aspects of socialism have been condemned by the Church from the time of **Leo XIII**'s 1891 **encyclical** *Rerum novarum* onward, it would be incorrect to assert that socialism as such is today so regarded by the **magisterium**. Indeed, many of the more recent documents on Catholic **social encyclicals and social teaching** from a wide variety of organs of the magisterium, including recent encyclicals such as the 1987 *Sollicitudo rei socialis* and the 1991 *Centesimus annus* by **John Paul II** as well as **Benedict XVI**'s 2009 *Caritas in veritate*, outline economic policies in service of the **common good** that bear greater resemblance to socialist policies than to many contemporary forms of **capitalism**. **Liberation theology** also seeks to correct the abuses of capitalism found in oppressive social and economic structures and thus often promotes socialism as a more just economic and political system. In many parts of the world there are political parties identified with Christianity or Catholicism, such as Italy's Christian Social Democrats, that also espouse socialism within a democratic system of government. **Thomas Aquinas** maintained that **private property** was not an absolute right but only a relative right justified by a legitimate concern for public order and stewardship of material goods in a fallen world (see *ST II-II*, Q. 66, art. 2).

Socialization is the process by which an individual, by about the age of six or seven, becomes enculturated in a particular culture, integrating that culture's language, norms, customs, ethos, and so on. **See also** *culture and inculturation*.

Social sin and structural evil. See **liberation theology**

Social teaching. See **social encyclicals and social teaching**

Sociopath is the psychological term for one instance of a serious antisocial personality disorder characterized by the American Psychiatric Association's 4th edition of the *Diagnostic and Statistical Manual* as "a pervasive pattern of disregard for, and violation of, the rights of others that begins in childhood or early adolescence and continues into adulthood." Effective treatment of this disorder is notoriously difficult and so the condition raises a number of unresolved questions for moral theology revolving around **conscience**, moral responsibility, and **culpability** for one's actions that had never been treated in the **moral manuals**. **See also** *culture and inculturation* and *socialization*.

Sola scriptura, *sola fide*, *sola gratia*, *solus Christus*, and *soli Deo gloria* (scripture, faith, grace, Christ, and glory to God alone) are the five hallmarks of classical Protestantism held in contrast to a belief that Catholic theology espouses salvation through a form of Pelagianism, **supererogation**, or **works righteousness** as well as in practices associated with the sacraments and sacramentals, **indulgences**, and the like. *Sola scriptura* rejects both the notion of **Tradition** as separate source of revelation and the role of the hierarchical **magisterium** as guardian and sole authentic interpreter of the **deposit of faith**. Rather, it holds that the Bible contains all the divine truths necessary for salvation and that every Christian has equal access and insight into **God**'s revelation. **Biblical ethics**, rather than emphasis on **reason** and the **natural law**, marks **Protestant ethics** as contrasted with Catholic moral theology. *Sola scriptura* in turn leads to *sola fide*, or justification by faith, and relies heavily on the soteriology found in Paul's letter to the Romans, which was interpreted as opposing reliance on a life of good works, pious practices, and grace conferred through reception of the sacraments for redemption. *Sola gratia* is the divine side of *sola fide* in that God's grace would be freely given to those who had faith in Christ alone (*solus Christus*) as the redeemer and savior of all humankind. There is no other mediator between God and ourselves, which rejects the Catholic understanding of the ministry of the sacramental priesthood and the **magisterium**'s *munera* to teach, govern, and sanctify in the Church. Instead, Protestant theology stresses the priesthood of all believers. Finally, the capstone hallmark, *soli Dei gloria*, stresses that honor should be paid to God alone, that respect be given to saints, and that the *obsequium religiosum* accorded to the hierarchy is misplaced. See also *ecumenism and ecumenical ethics*, *pecca fortiter*, and *simul iustus et peccator*.

Solidarity is a key principle in recent Catholic **social encyclicals and social teaching** popularized by **John Paul II** and continued by **Benedict XVI** (occurring thirty-nine times in his 2009 *Caritas in veritate* alone). Going beyond superficial sentimentalism, solidarity works against an ethos of individualism and calls Christians to sustained engagement for the **common good** in social and political life. **Liberation theology** also stresses solidarity in a real commitment evidenced in a **preferential option for the poor** undertaken especially to alleviate **structural evils** of poverty and oppression.

Sollicitudo rei socialis, **John Paul II**'s 1987 **social encyclical** "On the Social Concern of the Church," written shortly before the collapse of the Soviet bloc, commemorated the twentieth anniversary of **Paul VI**'s *Populorum progressio*, which was "directed towards an authentic development of man and society which would respect and promote all the dimensions of the **human**

person" (*SRS* #1) and critiques the disparity of uneven economic development in the world, such as between the Northern and Southern Hemispheres (*SRS* #14), and the polarization caused by the East versus West political tensions (*SRS* #20), and calls for arms reduction (*SRS* #24) before outlining a more comprehensive view of authentic human development (*SRS* #27–34) and including a section titled "Theological Reading of Modern Problems (*SRS* #35–40) that underscores the need for **solidarity** and a reading of the **signs of the times** in light of the Church's **social teaching**, which "is not a 'third way' between liberal **capitalism** and Marxist collectivism, nor even a possible alternative to other solutions less radically opposed to one another: rather, it constitutes a category of its own . . . [whose] main aim is to interpret these realities, determining their conformity with or divergence from the lines of the Gospel teaching on man and his **vocation**, a vocation which is at once earthly and transcendent; its aim is thus to guide Christian behavior" (*SRS* #41). The pope also explicitly called for a **preferential option for the poor** that must be translated into concrete action (*SRS* #42–43).

Sources for moral theology. See **fonts of moral theology**

Sovereignty (divine). See **divine sovereignty**

Special assistance of the Holy Spirit (to the **magisterium**). See **charism of office**

"Species of moral act" as used by **Thomas Aquinas** is that which determines or distinguishes the moral meaning of one type of act from another. "*Finis enim dat speciem in moralibus*" ("the end gives the species in moral matters") is the expression that appears many times in his works. Here it is the "*finis*" as "end," "object," or "goal" of the moral action that is essential in determining the act's moral meaning, or "species." **See also** *finis operis and finis operantis*, and *fonts of morality*.

Speculative reason in Thomas Aquinas denotes the function of *recta ratio* (**right reason**) to come to correct judgments about **moral principles** in the abstract. In his *Treatise on the Natural Law* (*ST I-II*, Q. 94), Thomas contrasts speculative reason with **practical reason** in this way: "the speculative reason is busied chiefly with the necessary things, which cannot be otherwise than they are, its proper conclusions, like the universal principles, contain the truth without fail." Thus, the first principle of the **natural law**, ***bonum est faciendum et prosequendum et malum vitandum*** (the good is to be done and fostered and evil avoided) is universally true but is also an abstraction that is grasped and known through our power of speculative reason. To say this principle is an abstraction does not mean it does not exist but rather it exists in a way that still must be put into practice. For example, what does it mean to "foster the good" in this or that particular concrete situation? Should we give to this charity or that one? Answering these sorts of questions requires practical reason that is exercised through making a **prudential judgment**. Thus, one person may decide to donate to Habitat for Humanity and another gives instead to Oxfam. Each is using both speculative and practical reason in coming to a concrete decision on how best to respond to the universal moral principle of aiding the poor, but their individual decisions and actions are not the same.

State of grace and state of sin. See **fundamental option theory** and **sin**

State of life. See **vocation**

States of consciousness: brain death, coma, PVS, MCS, and locked-in syndrome describe a spectrum of altered, reduced, or nonconsciousness states. Brain death occurs when all measurable brain activity ceases; brain death is irreversible and is now widely accepted as constituting physical death. Coma (*koma*, κῶμα, Greek for deep sleep) is a state of prolonged nonawareness or unconsciousness (e.g., more than six hours) in which a person cannot be awakened, does not respond normally even to painful stimuli, does not experience normal sleep/wake cycles, and is incapable of initiating any voluntary actions. PVS (persistent/permanent vegetative state) patients have apparent sleep/wake cycles but no awareness of their environment and do not respond to physical stimuli. The term "PVS" is employed differently around the world, but by current definition in the United States, it is irreversible. MCS (minimally conscious state) patients exhibit minimal behavioral evidence of self or environmental awareness. Locked-in syndrome patients are awake and aware of themselves and of their environment but have a sharply circumscribed ability to produce voluntary behavior such as speech or movement, but they sometimes move their eyes or blink to signal "yes" or "no" responses to questions posed by others. Since documented cases exist of recovery from a coma, MCS, and locked-in syndrome, even after several years, **ANH** (artificial nutrition and hydration) is normally considered **ordinary means**. Since medical opinion holds no reasonable hope of any recovery in PVS cases, such as **Terri Schiavo** (d. 2005), there is a division of opinion in the *status quaestionis* over termination of medical care such as ANH. Is it a withdrawal of ordinary means constituting **euthanasia**, or is it simply removing artificial blockage to the completion of the dying process by discontinuing **extraordinary means**? *For further reading*, see James T. Bretzke, "A Burden of Means: Interpreting Recent Catholic Magisterial Teaching on End-of-Life Issues," *Journal of the Society of Christian Ethics* 26, no. 2 (Fall/Winter 2006): 183–200; James T. Bretzke, "A Burden of Means: An Overlooked Aspect of the PVS Debate," *Landas* 18, no. 2 (2004): 211–30; John Paris, James Keenan, and Kenneth Himes, "*Quaestio Disputata*: Did John Paul II's Allocution on Life-Sustaining Treatments Revise Tradition?" *Theological Studies* 67 (2006): 163–74. **See also** *vitalism*.

Status quaestionis. See **quaestio disputata and status quaestionis**

STDs (sexually transmitted diseases) or **STIs** (sexually transmitted infections), formerly called venereal disease (VD), include a number of infections and diseases from herpes to **HIV/AIDS**. While some STIs can also be transmitted through infected needles as well as through childbirth and breastfeeding, the nature of these maladies increases the need not only for a life of **chastity** but also for effective sexual education and greater responsibility among those infected or at risk for infection to prevent or at least minimize the possibility of another person becoming infected through practices of **safe sex**. Such practices are a locus of considerable moral debate (*status quaestionis*) regarding the precise nature of the moral act and **intention** (*finis operis and finis operantis*) underlying the prevention measures as well as the legitimate application of other **moral principles** such as the **lesser evil** (*minus malum*).

Stem cells. See **bioethics** and *Dignitas personae*

Sterility. See **reproductive technologies**

Sterilization has been generally, though not absolutely, forbidden in the Church's **Tradition**. As a **direct** method of **birth control**, sterilization has consistently been condemned (see *CC* #68–71, *HV* #14, *EV* #91), however, other practices resulting in sterilization have been countenanced. Settled **casuistry** has always allowed a total hysterectomy for medical health reasons, including the removal of a cancerous uterus in pregnancy, and this principle has been confirmed numerous times by the **magisterium** (see *ERD* #53). A quite different case that had a contraceptive effect similar to a **vasectomy** was the centuries-long practice of creating *castrati* for the Sistine Choir, which continued up to the papacy of **Leo XIII** (1878–1903). Justification for this practice employed versions of the **double effect principle** and **proportionate reason**, arguing that the "good effects" of preserving musical excellence for the papal choir outweighed the bad effects of permanent sterilization and loss of sexual function by the young men—a form of moral reasoning since condemned as **consequentialism** in the papal **ordinary magisterium** (see *VS* #75). A more recent case from the 1960s concerns nuns in the war-torn Belgian Congo who apparently were given ecclesial permission from some Vatican office to take birth control to avoid possible conception from rape. Although there has been neither confirmation nor denial from the Vatican, this exception has been referenced several times since, for example, by Spanish bishop Juan Antonio Reig Pla of Segorbe-Castellon, who said in January 2011 that nuns facing the danger of rape could use the pill as "**self-defense** against an act of aggression" as this "changes the nature of the moral act [*finis operis*]," from an illicit attempt to "go against conception." A more frequent case concerns tubal ligations (uterine isolation or tubectomy) for women who are medically advised that a future pregnancy could put their physical health at serious risk, or that the pregnancy itself could not be successfully carried to term. The *quaestio disputata* focuses on the interpretation of the *finis operis* of the surgery—that is, would a tubal ligation in this instance be an illicit act of **contraception** or a licit form of **prophylaxis** to prevent future health risk and possible termination of pregnancy? Although no further argumentation was added, the **CDF** *Responsum ad dubium* "On Questions Concerning Uterine Isolation and Related Matters" (July 31, 1994), replied that even in these cases a tubal ligation could not be performed, but that a hysterectomy "to counter an immediate serious threat to the life or health of the mother" is allowed. This answer produces the conundrum of a potential case in which a tubal ligation to prevent a pregnancy is deemed illicit but a later hysterectomy of a pregnant woman to save her life (but resulting in the death of her fetus) is permitted. To date, this particular conundrum has not been further addressed by the magisterium and remains a point of ongoing debate. *For further reading*, see the various articles and magisterial documents in the section "Sterilization" in Charles E. Curran and Richard A. McCormick, eds., *Readings in Moral Theology No. 8: Dialogue about Catholic Sexual Teaching* (New York: Paulist Press, 1993), 169–220.

Structural evil. See **liberation theology**

Suárez, Francisco, SJ (1548–1617), was a Spanish philosopher and theologian who wrote on both the **natural law** and human law. Contrary to **Thomas Aquinas**, Suárez did not believe *epikeia* was a **virtue** that sought perfection of the **law**; rather, it was a **dispensation** given by the lawgiver under conditions when the law became either impossible or excessively burdensome to follow.

Subjectivism. See **relativism and subjectivism, emotivism, intuitionism,** and **postmodernism**

Submission of the will. See *obsequium religiosum*

Subsidiarity as outlined in **Pius XI**'s 1931 **social encyclical** *Quadragesimo anno* is "a fundamental principle of social philosophy, fixed and unchangeable, that one should not withdraw from individuals and commit to the community what they can accomplish by their own enterprise and/or industry" (*QA* #79). This means that decisions, policies, and their implementation ought to be handled at the lowest practical level since this level would more likely be better informed about the concrete needs and realities of the situation and able to deal with them more effectively than at a much higher level. It is not to be confused with anarchism or a denunciation of the legitimate role of **authority** and governmental structures.

Suffering in Christian theology is linked to the problem of evil (**theodicy**) as well as to our redemption from **sin** won by Christ's passion and death. While suffering should never be considered "good" in itself, the Catholic **Tradition** holds that human suffering can have a redemptive nature when accepted in union with Christ's own suffering or acknowledged as consequences for our sins as well as the sins of others. Tragically, over the centuries, many oppressed people were enjoined to accept their earthly sufferings patiently without protest in the hopes of reward or reversal of fortunes in heaven (see the parable of Dives and Lazarus in Lk. 16:19–31). **Liberation theology** and **feminist ethics** have justly critiqued this misuse of the concept of redemptive suffering. **John Paul II**'s 1984 apostolic letter *Salvifici doloris*, "On Salvific Suffering," gives an extended reflection on the Christian understanding of suffering and redemption. **See also** *anger*.

Sufficient consent. See **sufficient knowledge and sufficient consent**

Sufficient knowledge and sufficient consent are the two subjective elements that, along with the objective element sinful matter (ranging from "grave" to "light"), when taken together are necessary for an **actual sin** to be committed. The **manualist tradition** also used the terms "full knowledge" and "full consent." While the principle is the same, the word "full" seems to raise the bar higher for sin to be committed, since very few people achieve either absolutely full knowledge or full consent in their **moral acts**. Sufficient (or full) knowledge means "moral" knowledge rather than mere academic knowledge, in other words the sinner must truly see or know that the act being contemplated is actually sinful in itself, and then with moral **intention** decide to do it freely even with this knowledge. For example, the Church has traditionally held that attendance at the Sunday Eucharist is a serious obligation, and while many young people may "know" they should go to Mass, it may well be that they do not actually see their absence as truly sinful. Factors such as these, including bad **habits** or **ignorance**, that diminish either the knowledge or the **freedom** required for consent would correspondingly diminish the **culpability** for the sinful actions as well. **See also** *ex toto genere suo (grave)* and *fundamental option theory*.

Suicide and assisted suicide can be seen as a violation of the **Decalogue**'s Fifth Commandment and traditionally was also viewed as a serious lapse of the duty of **self-preservation**, a lack of hope, and as a rejection of God's **divine sovereignty** by taking unto the person herself the disposition of life that is reserved to **God** as the Creator and author of life (see *CCC* #2280–81). For this reason, in the past a victim of suicide was denied Christian burial, although there was some **casuistry** around the distinction between **direct** or voluntary suicide and **indirect** or involuntary suicide. **Canon law** included **impediments and irregularities** for those who unsuccessfully attempted suicide, and some of these remain in the 1983 *Code of Canon Law* (see *CIC* #1041). Today we understand far better the serious psychological issues, pain, and **suffering** that underlie most, if not all, attempts at suicide, and the pastoral response of the Church accords such individuals Christian funerals and extends to their loved ones compassion and support (see *CCC* #2282–83). Two other types of suicide likewise are condemned by the Church. Suicide as a form of protest against injustice additionally fails the standard of **proportionate reason** for causing such grievous harm or **evil**, and suicide as **euthanasia** likewise is not a morally licit response even to long-term intractable pain, which should be addressed through **palliative care** instead (see *CCC* #2277). Here it is important to make the proper determination between **ordinary and extraordinary means** in health care, as noted by the *Catechism of the Catholic Church* (see *CCC* #2278) and **John Paul II**, in his 1995 *Evangelium vitae* #65: when medical treatment is considered extraordinary, it may legitimately be terminated. However, so-called **assisted suicide**, whether through **PAS** (physician-assisted suicide) or with the aid of someone else, remains morally unacceptable in itself, and those who participate in giving such illicit aid could be viewed as constituting **formal cooperation with evil**.

Summum Bonum (highest good) for humans is God, which for humans is realized in the **beatific vision** (see *CCC* #1028). This telos or "end" of our nature therefore gives a proper orientation to our understanding of beatitude, happiness, and our particular moral choices (see *CCC* #1718–29). **See also** *bonum* and *contra naturam*.

Supererogation (Latin, *supererogatio*, "going beyond what is asked") is commonly understood as an act of **virtue** that exceeds the demands of moral duty (**deontology**). This aids development of moral **character** and holiness through the performance of good works, such as choosing a **vocation** that gives up **marriage** to live out a life of Christian perfection in the **evangelical counsels** (poverty, **chastity**, and obedience). The theology of **indulgences** held that acts of supererogation likewise added to the spiritual treasury of the Church, which could then be applied as satisfaction for the temporal punishment due to one's sins as well as to those of other repentant sinners. Protestant theology traditionally rejected this view as being another example of **works righteousness**.

Surrogate motherhood is associated with **reproductive technologies** in which a third party carries to term a fetus that is not her own child genetically.

Suspension. See **canonical penalties**

The *Syllabus of Errors* accompanied **Pius IX**'s 1864 **encyclical** *Quanta cura*, which condemned a number of "modern errors" including freedom of speech, **religious liberty**, the separation of Church and state, and indifferentism. The *Syllabus* did not claim to be "new" teaching but rather a compendium of previous papal pronouncements organized into ten sections with eighty propositions that were to be held as condemned. Several of these contested positions eventually fell into **desuetude** or were even reversed by later teachings of the **magisterium**, such as **Vatican II**'s *Dignitatis humanae*, "Declaration on Religious Liberty," which declared religious freedom a fundamental **human right**. The *Syllabus of Errors* represents a high-water mark of papal teaching **authority** and is seen by some as evidence for **historical development of doctrine** in light of **ultramontanism** or overreaching of ecclesial teaching claims, while others regard the *Syllabus* as a golden age in which firmer and clearer moral guidance was given by the magisterium. **See also** *classicist and historical worldviews* and *modernism*.

Synderesis and syneidesis are two Greek terms related to the **faculty of conscience** that come from variant spellings of συνείδησις (*syneidesis*) found in the Greek New Testament. Scholastic theologians and **Thomas Aquinas** believed the variants referred to two different aspects of conscience, namely as a **habit** and as an act of moral judgment done through **reason**. Latin translated (and combined) the Greek terms as *conscientia* ("knowing with"), from which comes the word "conscience."

The Synod of Bishops, established by **Paul VI** after **Vatican II**, is a triennial collegial assembly of representatives from the various episcopal conferences that convenes to discuss a common theme of interest or urgency to the Church. After the synod concludes, the pope writes an apostolic exhortation on the topic of the meeting, such as **John Paul II**'s 1981 *Familiaris consortio*, "On the Christian Family"; the 1984 *Reconciliatio et paenitentia*, "On Reconciliation and Penance"; and the 1988 *Christifideles laici*, "On the Vocation and the Mission of the Laity." Other synods bring together bishops of a certain geographical region, such as the Synods of America (1997), Africa (1994, 2009), and a series for Europe, Oceania, and Asia organized in conjunction with the 2000 Jubilee Year. The 1985 Extraordinary Synod treated the reception of Vatican II and called for the creation of a new *Catechism of the Catholic Church*, which was promulgated by John Paul II in 1992.

T

Tariff penances. See **sacrament of reconciliation**

Teleologism is the expression used by **John Paul II** in *VS #75* to critique forms of **consequentialism, utilitarianism**, and **proportionalism** for deriving the morality of an action solely from its outcomes, and thus effectively denying (in the pope's view) moral **absolutes** and **intrinsic evils**. Teleologism should not be equated with **teleology**, though, and the expression seems to be something of a papal neologism.

Teleology (Greek, *telos* [τελος], meaning "end" in the sense of goal, rather than terminus), is one of two major approaches to moral reasoning (the other being **deontology**) that begins with a consideration of the "nature" of the person as human or some aspect of the person (often called a **faculty**). Teleology then evaluates a given moral action in terms of fostering or obstructing the end or goal (its *telos*) of that nature or faculty. Intrinsic teleology as developed by **Thomas Aquinas** considers the ends or consequences of an action in order to discover the moral **rightness** or wrongness of the given action in terms of what promotes the person's *Summum Bonum*, which is God. This understanding of teleology differs from the extrinsic teleology of **consequentialism** since intrinsic teleology always looks at the consequences in respect to the proper nature or the **human person**, or to the authentic goal of a given human faculty. For example, the proper moral goal of speech is communication of the truth, and anything that would intentionally obstruct or counter that goal, such as a lie or *locutio contra mentem*, would be *contra naturam* and morally wrong. Teleology also stresses moral striving and development as seen in the growth of **character** and **virtue**. See also *gradualism, teleologism, utilitarianism,* and *Veritatis splendor.*

Temperance, from the Latin for "moderation," is the one of the four **cardinal virtues** that helps maintain proper balance and control over our **appetites**, desires, and **passions**. Temperance should not be equated with **abstinence** or **asceticism** alone.

Temple (cult) prostitutes. See **Holiness Code**

Temptation. See **concupiscence, occasions of sin, sacrament of reconciliation**, and **sin**

Ten Commandments. See **Decalogue**; see also *covenant*

Tenenda. See *credenda* and *tenenda*

Testem benevolentiae nostrae, the 1899 apostolic letter of **Leo XIII** to Baltimore's cardinal James Gibbons warned against the heresy of Americanism, which purportedly promoted anticlericalism, individualism, and the rights of **conscience** and free press over the legitimate **authority** and oversight of the Holy See.

Theodicy is the subdiscipline of theology that deals with the problems associated with **evil, sin**, and **suffering**. See also *liberation theology*.

The **theological virtues** are faith, hope, and **charity. Thomas Aquinas** termed these particular virtues "theological" since they have **God** as their proper object, are directed to Him, and are **infused** or given directly by God through sanctifying or "habitual" grace (see *ST I-II*, Q. 62). They are distinguished from the acquired virtues, such as the **cardinal virtues** or intellectual virtues, which humans can perfect through the powers of **reason** and perseverance with the special aid of God's grace.

The **theology of the body** was used by **John Paul II** for his writings on **sexual ethics**, especially **marriage**, coming from a series of 129 speeches given during weekly general audiences between September 1979 and November 1984 and whose themes were incorporated in a number of his other writings. Much of the material privileged an approach of **personalism** over the traditional **physicalism**, although usually interpreted in a **deductive** rather than **inductive** manner. *For further reading*, see John Paul II, *Man and Woman He Created Them: A Theology of the Body*, translation, introduction, and index by Michael M. Waldstein (Boston: Pauline Books and Media, 2006).

Theology of compromise. See **Curran, Charles**; and **gradualism**

Theonomy (Greek, "God's law"). See **heteronomy and theonomy, divine law, divine command ethics**, and *Lex aeterna*

Thomas Aquinas (1225–74) was a Dominican friar often called the Doctor Angelicus, Doctor Communis, or Doctor Universalis because of his immense, widespread, and lasting influence as a teacher (doctor), philosopher, and theologian. Studying in Paris under Albertus Magnus, he went on to develop a system of thought (sometimes called **Scholasticism** or Thomism) in major works such as the *Summa theologiae* ("Summary of Theology," which contains his main work on moral theology and the **natural law**), *Summa contra gentiles* (literally, "Summary against the 'Gentiles' [nonbelievers]), and *Commentary on the Sentences of Peter Lombard* that remain today the bedrock of Catholic systematic and moral theology. His appropriation and adaptation of **Aristotle** was originally considered quite progressive and even regarded with suspicion in some quarters but has proved to be an early example of what today might be called a positive attitude toward **culture and inculturation**.

Thomism. See **Thomas Aquinas**

Tolerance is the **moral principle** of **discernment** in **prudential judgment** on how best to respond to situations of objective **evil** of which one disapproves but where one also lacks the effective power or means to rectify them. Therefore, one can only "tolerate" the continued existence of this evil or unjust situation. While some consider this passive acceptance a form of **compromise with evil**, the **manualist tradition** usually distinguished between these two. Jesus's Parable of the Tares (wheat and weeds, Mt. 13:24–30) is the biblical *locus classicus* of this principle and reminds us that ultimately it is **God** who is the final arbiter and guarantor of **justice**. While in the past the Church's position that "error has no rights" limited the exercise of tolerance only to those situations in which Catholics lacked the political power to enforce Church teaching, **Vatican II**'s *Dignitatis humanae* significantly revised that interpretation in declaring that all people have an inherent right to **religious liberty**—even the right to choose to worship a false religion (*DH* #2–3). **See also** *zero tolerance*.

Torture is condemned by *Gaudium et spes* (#27) and *Veritatis splendor* (#80) as an **intrinsic evil**, although regrettably it is still practiced today by governments under euphemisms, such as "enhanced interrogation techniques" for waterboarding, and in the past was even condoned by the Church as a legitimate response to heresy. Today torture is condemned both in international law (such as the United Nations Universal Declaration of Human Rights and the Geneva Conventions) and in the domestic laws of many countries. Calling a terrorist a *hostis humani generis* (enemy of the human race) provides no legitimate exceptions to the **proscription** against torture or the requirements of *ius in bello* conduct in **just war theory**. See **also** *tyrannicide*.

Totality (principle of, *pars propter totum*) allows that the "part" can be sacrificed under certain **circumstances** for the good of the "whole" (see *ST II-II*, Q. 65, art. 1). In the **manualist tradition** the part/whole relation and the corresponding **proportionate reason** were narrowly interpreted in a **physicalist** manner, for example, one could amputate a gangrenous limb when there was no other possibility to save the individual's own life. However, organ donations to save another person's life were not sanctioned under this principle since the "part" sacrificed (e.g., a kidney) would not benefit the "whole" of the donor's body. Such actions were viewed as a form of self-mutilation and **intrinsically evil**. **Thomas Aquinas** used the **totality principle** more broadly to justify **capital punishment**, sacrificing an individual who could be "excised" for the good of the whole community, including for heresy (see *ST II-II,* Q. 64, art. 2 and *ST II-II* Q. 11, art. 3).

Interpretation of the totality principle clearly has undergone significant **development of moral doctrine**. Though seemingly forbidden by *CC #71*, today organ donations are no longer considered intrinsically evil but an act of **charity**. Jesuits **Arthur Vermeersch** and **Gerald Kelly** developed this point in their **casuistry**, and **Pius XII** in an **occasional allocution** of May 14, 1956, confirmed the morality of a corneal transplant. *ERD* #30 approves of organ donations, and **John Paul II**, in an Italian occasional allocution of August 2, 1984, to the Association of Italian Blood and Organ Donors spoke approvingly of the "finality" (*finalità* [*finis operis*]) of the "noble and meritorious act of donating blood or organs to brothers and sisters (*fratelli*) in need," which shows true "generosity" and "human **solidarity**."

Others, such as **revisionist moral theologian Louis Janssens**, interpret the totality principle in terms of **personalism**, concluding that a complete moral evaluation of an act "must consider the whole action with all its components, and examine whether or not this totality is promotive of the person and his or her relationships, namely in the totality of the person's dimensions" (Janssens, "Personalism in Moral Theology," in *Moral Theology: Challenges for the Future. Essays in Honor of Richard A. McCormick, SJ,* edited by Charles E. Curran [New York: Paulist Press, 1990]: 95). The **Pontifical Commission on Births** also used this **personalist** interpretation of the totality principle to justify a couple's decision to choose **artificial contraception**, although, as noted, this particular application was rejected in **Paul VI's encyclical *Humanae vitae***.

Tradition, with a capital "T," was commonly held before **Vatican II** as virtually a separate font of revelation, transmitted through the apostolic and patristic authors, and the **magisterium**. Vatican II's *Dei Verbum* declared that while scripture and Tradition were both to be venerated (see *DV* #9), scripture alone ultimately functions as the *norma normans non normata*. Tradition plays an important role in handing on the spiritual heritage of the Church to both new members and successive generations but, like scripture, must also be continually retranslated, reread, and reinterpreted within the context of a believing, worshiping, and acting faith community of disciples. Otherwise, tradition may become what church historian Jaroslav Pelikan calls the "dead faith of the living." Constancy of Tradition is certainly an important testimony to the wisdom of the community, but assessing this "constancy" can be difficult. For example, historian John Noonan notes regarding **birth control** that while the condemnation of **artificial contraception** was relatively "constant," the reasons given and the concomitant issues involved have changed so much throughout the centuries that it is problematic to conclude that "what" has been "constantly taught" in fact represents precisely the same issue in the same contexts, with the same judgments based on the same biology, the same **moral norms**, and so on. The **inseparability principle** used extensively by **John Paul II** to condemn artificial contraception is a quite recent addition to the debate not found in the "constancy of Tradition." *For further reading*, see John T. Noonan Jr., *Contraception: A History of Its Treatment by the Catholic Theologians and Canonists* (Cambridge, MA: Harvard University Press, 1965, 1986); Bernard Hoose, *Received Wisdom? Reviewing the Role of Tradition in Christian Ethics* (London: Geoffrey Chapman, 1994); and John E. Thiel, *Sense of Tradition: Continuity and Development in Catholic Faith* (New York: Oxford University Press, 2000).

Transhumanism is a movement that promotes the improvement of human nature, especially in its biological area, going beyond the limitations and imperfections currently found in the human condition. Biotechnology aids this process, and while certain aspects of correcting and improving human limitations are admirable, as a whole this movement suffers from the same weaknesses found in the earlier eugenics movement and would also fall under the same condemnations of certain **reproductive technologies** found in the **CDF**'s instructions, *Donum vitae* (1987) and *Dignitas personae* (2008).

Trent. See **Council of Trent**

Truth and truthfulness in the **Decalogue**'s Eighth Commandment is required as moral **duty** (**deontology**) both to **God**, the author of truth (*co-*

ram Deo), and to our fellow humans in society (*coram homnibus*). Any intentional violation, such as lying, defined in the **manualist tradition** as *locutio contra mentem*, is *contra naturam* to the proper end of the **faculty** of speech, namely the communication of the truth. However, considerable **casuistry** was developed, such as **mental reservation**, that justified exceptions to literal truth-telling in certain situations, especially those requiring **confidentiality and secrecy**.

Tubal ligation (uterine isolation). See **sterilization**

Tubal pregnancy is another name for **ectopic pregnancy**.

Tubectomy (uterine isolation). See **sterilization**

Tutiorism, closely related to **rigorism**, holds that in cases of a *dubium* or **doubtful law**, or in debate among experts or sources, one should always follow the "safest" or strictest opinion. This theory was countered by **probabilism**, which held that in cases of such doubt or disagreement one could in good conscience follow a "probable" opinion on the basis of a sufficiency in terms of arguments or experts. **Probabiliorism** was a middle view between probabilism and tutiorism, which held that in instances of doubt or debate one should only choose the "more probable" view. At the other extreme was **laxism**, which set the bar so low that as long as some **authority** or arguments existed for the loosest opinion, one could legitimately adopt it. However, laxism had few if any actual supporters, so it was used primarily to illustrate counterpositions to tutiorism or probabilism. See also *epikeia, Jansenism, legalism, lex dubia non obligat, quaestio disputata,* and *Voluntarism*.

Tyrannicide, the killing of an unjust ruler, was much discussed in the Middle Ages, and an analogous debate has arisen in more recent times in applications of the **just war theory**, **torture**, **capital punishment**, and to some extent **liberation theology**'s critique of **social sin and structural evil**. **Thomas Aquinas** (see II Sent., d. XLIV, Q. ii, a. 2), **Francisco Suárez** (see (Def. fidei, VI, iv), and many other theologians of the time held that private individuals had a presumptive right to remove a *tyrannus in titula*, that is, one who had unjustly usurped the ruling power, if there were no other reasonable means of effectively redressing the serious offenses against the **common good**. More sharply debated was the case of a *tyrannus in regimine*, a tyrant who nevertheless did come to power legitimately. Some theologians held removal from office, especially by homicide, of any legitimately installed ruler violated the **natural law**, while others, including Aquinas (see

ST II-II, Q. 42, art. 2) and Suárez (see Def. fidei, VI, iv, 15), maintained that this would be legitimate in cases of extreme tyranny when no other safe and realistically successful means were available. Some also argue tyrannicide includes assassination of a so-called ***hostis humani generis*** ("enemy of the human race," such as a terrorist leader). However, the very real possibility of **rationalization** in abusing even an unjust ruler's **human rights** is not inconsiderable, and for this reason **torture** is labeled an **intrinsic evil** that can never be practiced even in extreme cases.

U

Ultramontanism originates from the term *"ultra montes,"* which means looking "beyond the mountains" (the Alps) to Rome for answers or intervention in any contested matter. Today it is usually employed pejoratively of **infallibilism** or of those who overaccentuate the powers of the Vatican or the papal **magisterium**. **Vatican I**'s 1870 definition of papal **infallibility** in *Pastor aeternus* and the expression *Roma locuta causa finita* are seen as high-water marks of ultramontanism, while the principle of **subsidiarity** and **Vatican II**'s *Christus Dominus*, "Decree on the Pastoral Office of Bishops," the increased role of national and regional episcopal bishops conferences, and the growth of **ecumenism** are all seen as ecclesial counterbalances to the dangers that can arise from excessive concentration of **authority** in just one region or office. **See also** *obsequium religiosum.*

Unions. See *Rerum novarum,* and **social encyclicals and social teaching**

Unitatis redintegratio is the **Vatican II**'s "Decree on Ecumenism." **See also** *ecumenism and ecumenical ethics.*

Unitive dimension of marriage. See **inseparability principle** and **marriage**

Universal moral norms are those that bind absolutely every time and in every place and situation. Violations of such norms are **intrinsically evil**. **Thomas Aquinas** in his *Treatise on the Natural Law* lists as the foundational universal moral **precept** *"Bonum est faciendum et prosequendum, et malum vitandum"* ("The good is to be done and fostered, and evil avoided"), which is known through **speculative reason**. "Speculative" for Thomas does not mean "possibly true" but rather always true or universal and derived from abstract reasoning. For example, in Euclidian geometry a three-sided polygon whose internal angles equal 180° is necessarily and universally a triangle. While universal moral norms have no legitimate exceptions, not every moral norm is universal: if there is an exception to a particular norm, then it cannot be universal. For example, while we could posit as a universal norm that students must study in a given course, it would be a problematic universal to demand they attend each and every class without fail, because there are a number of **circumstances** that could provide a legitimate excuse from attendance, such as a family emergency, illness, transportation breakdown, and the like. For this reason Thomas says there is another type of moral norm (called **middle axioms** by some moralists) that is generally true but that admits legitimate exceptions (*lex valet ut in pluribus*, "the law holds in most [but not all] cases"). **Discernment** of these norms incorporates **practical reason** with speculative reason to come to a **prudential judgment** about what should be done. In this process Thomas observes that the more we descend to concrete application, there is a corresponding loss of universal applicability due to the factors of **contingency and fallibility**. Thus, **concrete material norms** have a more provisional character when contrasted with universal norms: "But as to the proper conclusions of the practical reason, neither is the truth or rectitude the same for all, nor, where it is the same, is it equally known by all" (*ST I-II*, Q. 94, art. 4). Since it is difficult for humans in one time and place to foresee every other possible set of circumstances for all other times and places as they seek to formulate concrete absolute universal norms, some moralists prefer the term "**virtually exceptionless norms**" to refer to moral norms that seem to be universal but that perhaps may have some unforeseen legitimate exceptions that arise later on. **See also** *situation ethics*.

Unjust aggressor. See **just war theory**

USCCB, the United States Conference of Catholic Bishops (renamed in 2001 to replace the **NCCB**, the National Conference of Catholic Bishops, founded in 1966), is the organ of the United States Bishops Conference, which is composed of all active and retired US bishops. It meets in plenary sessions twice a year, electing as officers for three-year terms a vice president who usually, but not always, is subsequently elected president. The USCCB maintains a website (www.usccb.org) and a number of offices and committees, including one on doctrine that on occasion publishes critiques of theologians or individual works. In the past the USCCB published a number of important **pastoral letters** on a range of social issues, but these have decreased significantly since the promulgation of **John Paul II**'s 1998 apostolic letter *Apostolos suos*, which decreed that bishops conferences per se did not possess a separate teaching **authority**. Henceforth its teaching documents require either unanimous consent of all voting bishops present or a *recognitio* (confirmation) by the Holy See. Two USCCB documents that remain quite important in the ethical arena are its *Ethical and Religious Directives for Catholic Health Care Institutions* (*ERD*, 5th ed., 2009) and the pastoral letters released or confirmed in advance of the four-year presidential elections, such as the 2007 *Forming Consciences for Faithful Citizenship*, which was slightly modified and reconfirmed in 2012.

Usury and interest-taking is an example of the **history and development of moral theology and doctrine**. Up until the Industrial Revolution usury was defined as any taking of interest and was condemned by several church councils and theologians (including **Thomas Aquinas**) as an **intrinsic evil**. Today this teaching is no longer held, and even the Vatican bank charges interest on loans and gives interest on deposits. Usury in the sense of exorbitant interest charged for a loan remains a grave evil and an affront against **distributive justice**, even if the usurious loan is part of **contract justice**. *For further reading*, see John T. Noonan Jr., *The Scholastic Analysis of Usury* (Cambridge, MA: Harvard University Press, 1957).

Uterine isolation (tubal ligation). See **sterilization**

Utilitarianism is a form of **consequentialism**, which is skeptical of **natural law** moral **absolutes**. Instead, utilitarianism holds that the choice to maximize the greatest good or happiness for the greatest number of people constitutes morality. Utilitarianism and consequentialism also oppose **deontological** prescriptions (things that must always be done) and proscriptions (things that may never be done). Influential proponents of utilitarianism include English philosophers Jeremy Bentham (1748–1832) and John Stuart Mill (1806–73), while contemporary philosophers such as Princeton's Peter Singer (b. 1946) continue to advocate this theory. What constitutes the "greatest good for the greatest number" is judged somewhat differently according to act utilitarianism and rule utilitarianism. Act utilitarians look primarily at a calculus of the benefits and burdens predictable from a certain course of action, whereas rule utilitarians call for the added consideration of how longer-term consequences of a certain course of action becoming a "rule" might have on the calculation of the benefits and burdens. For example, if a racist mob were threatening to burn down a ghetto unless the sheriff were to release to them an African American prisoner, act utilitarians could judge this prisoner's release to the mob as morally justified since doing so might spare the ghetto denizens the mob's murderous rampage, thus constituting their greater good and happiness. However, a rule utilitarian might argue that giving in to the mob's demands could create the loss of respect for the rule of **law**, which down the line has far more deleterious effects for society than if the sheriff had handed over the prisoner. Neither act nor rule utilitarians have been able to answer to general satisfaction how one protects the **human rights** of the minority in the greater good calculus, and the denial of an objective universal moral order leads to the theory's condemnation by most Catholic moral theologians and the **magisterium**, for example, in **John Paul II**'s 1993 *Veritatis splendor* (see *VS* #74–75; 106).

Utopia (Greek, "no place") is the other-worldly paradise and the title of Thomas More's famous 1516 book on **ideal** government. It is contrasted with **dystopia**, a political state that is repressive and totalitarian. However, this side of God's kingdom we can never have total perfection. While a vision of an ideal future can be helpful to move us toward working for a better world, we also will always have to live in the real world that involves **tolerance** and even **compromise with evil**. **See also** *interim ethic*, *liberation theology*, and *Zielgebot*.

V

Vasectomy is the **sterilization** of the male's **capacity** for **procreation**, which can be used as a form of **birth control**. **See also** *marriage*.

Vatican I (December 8, 1869; adjourned on October 20, 1870, at the outbreak of the Franco-Prussian War) was the twentieth ecumenical council of the Church and the first held since the **Council of Trent**. Its constitution, *Dei Filius* ("Son of God"), on the Catholic faith confronted rationalism, materialism, and atheism, but the council is most noted for its definition of papal **infallibility** in *Pastor aeternus* ("Eternal Pastor"), "The Dogmatic Constitution on the Church of Christ." Some thought this would render future councils superfluous since the pope could pronounce infallibly on all matters of **faith and morals** (*de fide vel moribus*) without recourse to the **authority** of an ecumenical council. **See also** *extraordinary magisterium*.

Vatican II, the twenty-first ecumenical council of the Church and most important ecclesial event since the sixteenth-century **Council of Trent**, was opened by **John XXIII** on October 11, 1962, and after four sessions was closed by **Paul VI** on December 8, 1965. The council produced sixteen documents: four constitutions (***Dei Verbum***, ***Lumen gentium***, *Sacrosanctum concilium*, and ***Gaudium et spes***), three declarations (including ***Dignitatis humanae***), and nine decrees (including ***Optatam totius*** and ***Unitatis redingratio***). As with any authoritative text, a proper **exegesis** and **hermeneutics** is required, paying attention to the drafting discussions and contexts in an integral manner especially avoiding cherry-picking or **proof-texting**. *For further reading*, see Karl Rahner, "The Abiding Significance of the Second Vatican Council," *Theological Investigations*, vol. 20 (London: Darton, Longman and Todd, 1981): 90–102, originally published as "Towards a Fundamental Theological Interpretation of Vatican II" in *Theological Studies* 40 (1979): 716–27, and also published in *Vatican II: The Unfinished Agenda, A Look to the Future*, edited by Lucien Richard, with Daniel Harrington and John W. O'Malley (New York: Paulist Press, 1987), 9–32; Giuseppe Alberigo, ed., *History of Vatican II*, 5 vols. (Maryknoll, NY: Orbis, 1995–2006); Massimo Faggioli, *Vatican II: The Battle for Meaning* (New

York: Paulist Press, 2012); and John O'Malley, *What Happened at Vatican II* (Cambridge, MA: Belknap Press, 2008).

Vehemens horror ("vehement horror") dates back to the sixteenth century to describe the subjective fear or extreme distaste for a certain treatment that would constitute a real psychological personal **burden** for an individual, possibly transforming an otherwise **ordinary means** procedure such as an amputation or blood transfusion (e.g., for a Jehovah's Witness) into **extraordinary means**. This concept remains valid in **AHCD**s and end-of-life decisions to forgo medical treatment.

Venereal disease (VD). See **STDs/STIs**

Venial sin. See **sin**

Veritatis splendor ("Splendor of the Truth"), **John Paul II**'s 1993 **encyclical** "On Fundamental Moral Theology," begins with a reflection on the nature of **goodness** and morality using the "call of the rich young man" in Matthew 19:16–21 before turning to perceived major challenges to Catholic moral teaching including moral **relativism**, the lack of acceptance of the **divine** and **natural law**, and resistance to the **magisterium**'s **authority** to teach **concrete material norms** proscribed as **intrinsic evil**. The encyclical also condemned the theories of **consequentialism, utilitarianism, proportionalism**, and **fundamental option**—especially for the latter's treatment of **mortal sin**. Some scholars question whether the portrayals of proportionalism and fundamental option are fully accurate, wondering instead if the condemnations represent simply possible misunderstandings of these positions. *For further reading*, see, for a positive reception of the encyclical, J. A. DiNoia, and Romanus Cessario, eds., *Veritatis Splendor and the Renewal of Moral Theology* (Princeton, NJ: Scepter Publishers, 1999), and for a more critical reception, see Joseph Selling and Jan Jans, eds., *The Splendor of Accuracy: An Examination of the Assertions Made by Veritatis Splendor* (Grand Rapids, MI: Eerdmans, 1994).

Vermeersch, Arthur, SJ (1858–1936), was a Flemish canonist and professor of moral theology at Rome's Pontifical Gregorian University (succeeded by Francis Hürth). His *Questiones morales de justitia* detailed **casuistry** on a number of topics, although he is most remembered for his help in the drafting of **Pius XI**'s 1930 **encyclical** *Casti connubii*, which severely condemned any form of artificial **birth control**.

Vice (Latin, *vitium*, "fault, blemish, defect, or imperfection"), like **virtue**, is an acquired **habit** formed by repeated actions that in this case leads one to **sin**. The habitual nature of vice can reduce but not completely remove personal **culpability** for those sins committed under the force of the vice. In traditional moral theology, the sinful vices were often linked with specific sins (e.g., the **capital sins**) and also contrasted with their opposing virtues so that the bad habit could be overcome by practicing the corresponding virtue, such as correcting **pride** with **humility** (see *CCC* #1865–66). Even though sin committed through vice is removed and forgiven by **contrition**, by acts of **penance** and **charity**, or by the **sacrament of reconciliation**, these still do not automatically remove the negative habit, so special attention must be given to the improvement of moral **character** through a life of virtue.

Vice list is a rhetorical device often found in biblical literature that gives illustrative examples of negative moral living. Appropriate interpretation of these vice lists is an important task for **exegesis, hermeneutics,** and **biblical ethics**. An example is 1 Corinthians 6:9–10: "Fornicators, idolaters, adulterers, male prostitutes, sodomites, thieves, the greedy, drunkards, revilers, robbers" (*NRSV*). At first glance this list seems to function as an indication of **God**'s final judgment, but the point of this vice list is to include most, if not all, of us. Even if some might not be guilty of some of the sexual sins, it would be harder to avoid completely the charge of having been at times "greedy" or a "reviler." Here Paul's larger purpose is to call everyone to **conversion**, as is made clear in the next verse: "And this is what some of you used to be. But you were washed, you were sanctified, you were justified in the name of the Lord Jesus Christ and in the Spirit of our God." As with any biblical passage, a vice list should not be taken out of its context or used as **proof-texting** to confirm a judgment made on other grounds (e.g., that all fornicators, etc., are irremediably destined for damnation). A *lectio continua* that brings us into contact with all of the Bible can be helpful to correct such problematic interpretative tendencies.

Vidal, Marciano, CSsR. See **liberation theology**

Vincible and invincible ignorance. See **ignorance** and **conscience (erroneous)**

Virtually exceptionless norm, a term preferred by some moralists, such as **Richard A. McCormick, SJ** (though he did not invent the term), to denote **moral norms** traditionally understood as moral **absolutes** and whose transgressions are **intrinsic evils**. "Virtually exceptionless" is not meant to introduce either **relativism** or **laxism** into the objective moral order but rather to acknowledge the epistemological limitation of fully knowing in advance with **concrete material norms** every possible **contingency** that would govern the **circumstances** or, to a lesser extent, the **intention** in each and every action that is prohibited as a moral absolute. For example, while **direct abortion** is absolutely prohibited in the abstract, is the termination of nonviable fetal life such as in the case of an **ectopic pregnancy** likewise absolutely prohibited? Virtually all moralists today accept termination of an ectopic pregnancy, so the use of the term "virtually exceptionless norm" might suggest that this formulation is both more accurate and more helpful in moral **discernment** than terminology such as moral absolutes or intrinsic evil.

Virtue (Latin, *virtus*, meaning "manliness, excellence, worth, goodness, courage"). See **habit and virtue, virtue ethics, cardinal virtues, infused knowledge and infused virtues**, and **theological virtues**

Virtue ethics focuses on the moral agent, especially in terms of his **character**, rather than concentrating on the "**rightness**" or "wrongness" of individual actions. Addressing the question "what ought I to be(come)?" grounds and comes before answering "what ought I to do in this situation?" **Virtues** and **vices** thus go beyond the acquisition of mere **habits** and actually help the construction of the individual's moral identity. Since every moral agent lives in a community and a web of social relationships, these factors likewise furnish important considerations in virtue ethics analyses. In addition to whether an action is "right," virtue ethics asks questions about how the various relationships are strengthened, cared for, maintained, and so on. *For further reading*, see Joseph J. Kotva Jr., *The Christian Case for Virtue Ethics* (Washington, DC: Georgetown University Press, 1996); Daniel Harrington and James F. Keenan, *Jesus and Virtue Ethics: Building Bridges between New Testament Studies and Moral Theology* (Kansas City, MO: Sheed and Ward, 2002); and Daniel Harrington and James F. Keenan, *Paul and Virtue Ethics* (Lanham, MD: Rowman and Littlefield, 2010).

Vitalism, a putative **moral principle** that holds that because life is absolutely sacred, we must do everything to preserve biological human life at all costs, as seen in a cultural and technological ethos, which holds that everything that can be done to save or prolong a life should therefore be done. However, this **rigorist** view is not the Roman Catholic moral tradition. As **John Paul II** expressed well, while human "life is sacred from the moment

of conception to natural death," this earthly life still has a "relative character" and "is not an 'ultimate' but a 'penultimate' reality" (*EV #2*). **See also**
advance health care directive; *autonomy (bioethical principle)*; *euthanasia*;
ordinary and extraordinary means; *PAS*; *PEG tube*; *PVS*; *probabilism and
probabiliorism*; *rigorism*; *Schiavo, Terri*; *Summum Bonum*; *tutiorism*; and
lex valet ut in pluribus. **For further reading**, see *CIC #2278*, and Pope John
Paul II's "Address to the Participants in the 19th International Conference of
the Pontifical Council for Health Pastoral Care," November 12, 2004.

Vocation (Latin, "call") denotes the unique role each person plays in the
world. In the pre–**Vatican II** Church the term was usually reserved for those
who entered clerical or religious life. Practice of the **evangelical counsels** of
poverty, **chastity**, and obedience, leading to "Christian perfection," helped
create a de facto "higher" class of professional Christians. However, Vatican
II stressed that every Christian has a universal call to holiness (see *LG* ch.
5), and other conciliar documents, especially *Gaudium et spes*, highlighted
the special roles that married couples, parents, and the laity play in the world
that cannot and should not be done by the religious. Thus, vocation is better
seen in the original New Testament vision outlined by Paul in his theology of
the Mystical Body and the many gifts (or **charisms**) given by the Spirit for
the good of the whole community (see 1 Cor. 12: 3–31; Rom. 12: 6–8). This
broader understanding of vocation has been continued in the contemporary
magisterium, such as with **John Paul II**'s 1988 *Christifideles laici*, "On the
Vocation and the Mission of the Laity," and in the various **social encyclicals**.
See also *discernment*.

Voluntarism in political philosophy is akin to libertarianism and holds that
most human associations should be voluntary in nature, and no one should
ever be coerced into joining or participating in an action or collective she
does not desire. In sociology voluntarism refers to the type of social activism
that one joins freely, like Bread for the World or Oxfam. In theology the term
has a more complex and quite different meaning. Here Voluntarism is closely
intertwined with **nominalism**, which holds that since moral **universals** cannot confidently be discovered through **reason**, morality is viewed as simply
obeying **God**'s omnipotent will (*voluntas* in Latin) and the commandments
that **divine sovereignty** "legislates" for us. A problematic aspect here is the
understanding of the grounding of both morality and moral **goodness**—that
is, something is good only because God so wills it—with moral goodness
then predicated on simple obedience. Law itself, rather than the values the
law is designed to uphold, becomes the ultimate and supreme norm of the
moral **rightness** of human action. Standing in considerable tension with Vol-

untarism is **Thomas Aquinas**'s understanding of the exercise of reason in **conscience** and **free will** to **discern** God's own true will expressed through the *lex aeterna* and the **natural law** leading us more deeply into the *Summum Bonum* (God as supreme good) of human life. *For further reading*, see Josef Fuchs, "Our Image of God and the Morality of Innerworldly Behavior," ch. 3 in his *Christian Morality: The Word Became Flesh*, 28–49 (Washington, DC: Georgetown University Press, 1987).

W

War. See **just war theory** and **pacifism**

WCC. See **World Council of Churches**

Wealth. See **capitalism, common good, distributive justice, property rights, social encyclicals and social teaching**, and **socialism**

White privilege is a relatively recent term that marks the special advantages given to whites over nonwhites, especially in terms of special prerogatives, **dispensations**, or exemptions not extended to members of other races. **Affirmative action** programs seek to restore the balance of **justice** distorted by this bias that often arises from **racism**. See also *liberation theology* and *political correctness*.

Will. See **free will and freedom**

William of Ockham (c. 1288–c. 1348), a Franciscan medieval philosopher/theologian closely identified with the theories of **nominalism** and **Voluntarism**, is also associated with the so-called *lex parsimoniae* (law of parsimony) or "Ockham's Razor," which suggests that when confronted with competing hypotheses or positions that otherwise seem equal, one should choose the one that is more succinct, economical, or "parsimonious" in its supporting argumentation, especially in introducing the fewest new assumptions.

Wisdom. See **gifts of the Holy Spirit**, and **prudence and prudential judgment**

Womanist theology is a form of **liberation theology** both allied with and in tension with **feminist** and black theology (see, for example, **James Cone**) by prioritizing the experiences of African American and other women of color, such as **mujerista theology**. The term "womanist" was coined by Alice

Walker. Prominent womanist theologians include Katie Cannon, M. Shawn Copeland, Jacquelyn Grant, Renita Weems, and Delores Williams.

Women's ordination, although explicitly forbidden by the Roman Catholic **magisterium**, is allowed in several other Christian denominations and remains hotly debated, often cast as a **human rights** and **gender** issue, especially in **feminist ethics**. See also *Lambeth Conference* and *Ordinatio sacerdotalis*.

Work. See *Laborem exercens* and **social encyclicals and social teaching**

Works of mercy are based on the **virtue** of compassion, the building of community, and the practical desire to alleviate the **sufferings** of others. These are divided into two categories, spiritual and corporal, each having seven different works. The spiritual works are instructing the ignorant; counseling the doubtful; admonishing sinners; patiently bearing wrongs; forgiving offenses gladly; comforting the afflicted; and praying for the living and the dead. The corporal works are feeding the hungry; giving drink to the thirsty; clothing the naked; giving shelter to the homeless; visiting the sick; ransoming captives; and burying the dead.

Works righteousness is an expression used in classic Protestant theology to condemn views such as Pelagianism or semi-Pelagianism, that personal salvation can be merited through **legalism** or our personal efforts and good works rather than through **justification by faith alone** (*sola fide*). Examples of works righteousness in the Protestant perspective include Catholic sacraments, **indulgences**, and the Catholic teaching on the necessity of good works to match Christian faith. See also *pecca fortiter*.

World Council of Churches (WCC) is a worldwide **ecumenical** organization founded in 1948 and based in Geneva representing 349 global, regional, national, and local Christian churches; it aims to foster better unity, witness, and service. Member churches send delegates to international assemblies held at various places around the world every seven to eight years. The WCC has a number of standing commissions, such as the Justice, Peace, and Creation Commission, to foster ongoing dialogue and action in intervals between the assemblies. While the Roman Catholic Church is not a member of the WCC, it works closely with it on a number of levels and sends observers to major WCC gatherings. The Vatican's Pontifical Council for Promoting Christian Unity nominates a number of members to the WCC's Faith and Order Commission and collaborates with some other ecumenical bodies on the regional and national levels. **See also** *ecumenism and ecumenical ethics.*

Wrath. See **anger** and **capital sins**

WWJD? (What would Jesus do?) is a question popular among evangelicals since the 1990s to guide all ethical decisions. A follow-up motto "answered" the WWJD question: *FROG* (Fully rely on God). The motto comes from Protestant minister Charles Sheldon's1896 novel *In His Steps: What Would Jesus Do?* and from a 2010 movie, *WWJD*, based on an updated version of Sheldon's novel. In the novel a group of congregants volunteers to make every daily decision for the following week in response to the WWJD question. The newspaper editor, for example, refuses to publish a sports account of a boxing match since he believes Jesus would not do this. The experience profoundly changes the congregants' lives and leads them to embrace the Social Gospel ministry spearheaded by **Walter Rauschenbusch**. While greater focus on Jesus and his Gospel values is laudable, the WWJD movement has a number of practical and theological difficulties. Many complex contemporary issues, such as adult stem-cell research or macroeconomics, do not easily find answers from this question. Even more basic questions still need requisite attention to the **exegesis** and **hermeneutics** of **biblical ethics**, especially to avoid **proof-texting** or an overly simplistic *sola scriptura* approach.

X

Xenophobia, an unsubstantiated fear of "foreigners," often surfaces in **racism**, which in modern times has consistently been condemned by the Church.

Y

Yoder, John Howard (December 29, 1927–December 30, 1997), a Mennonite biblical ethicist with a doctorate under **Karl Barth**, espoused a radical Christian **pacifism** while rejecting what he and his former University of Notre Dame colleague **Stanley Hauerwas** termed **Constantianism**, by which Christianity inappropriately seeks to accommodate itself to the contemporary **Zeitgeist** of secular political and cultural values. Yoder stressed the normativity of the New Testament **biblical ethics**, developed in his 1972 *The Politics of Jesus*. This gives a political reading of the cross of Christ that allows that, while Jesus did not give biblical rules requiring literal obedience, he did proclaim a social ethic directly applicable to our contemporary world. Yoder argued that the role of Christians is not to take over society but simply to follow Jesus Christ and be his church—even if that should lead to persecution or disdain, since the final vindication comes in the resurrection and the full coming of the **Kingdom of God**. In the 1990s sexual misconduct allegations against Yoder led to his being disciplined by the Indiana–Michigan Conference of the Mennonite Church, to which Yoder was eventually reconciled the year before his death.

Z

Zalba, Marcelino, SJ (1908–2009), was one of the last pre–**Vatican II** theologians of the **manualist tradition**. He had a distinguished teaching career first in his native Spain at the University of Deusto in Bilbao (1941–62) and then at the Pontifical Gregorian University in Rome until his return to Loyola, Spain, in 1990. As a member of the **Pontifical Commission on Births** he was one of the four who formulated the so-called Minority Report (along with fellow Jesuits **John Ford** and Stanislas de Lestapis and the Redemptorist Jan Visser), which argued against any change in the Church's long-standing teaching on **birth control**. Father Zalba's particular view in this regard centered on **Tradition** and the **special assistance of the Holy Spirit** to the **magisterium**, which led him to argue that the Catholic teaching on this matter was unchangeable and had to be correct since any modification would de facto support the **Anglican Communion**'s 1930 **Lambeth Conference** acceptance of birth control, falsely suggesting that the Holy Spirit was more present in that schismatic sect than in the Roman Catholic Church. Father Zalba also held opinions that proved to be at variance with some of the eventual teachings of Vatican II, such as the theoretical acceptability of slavery and **torture** under certain conditions (e.g., when practiced by the Church for serious motives) and the belief that the magisterium could bind **consciences** under the pain of **mortal sin**, which he advanced as another reason the Church could never change its teachings on birth control, since in the past the Church had sent people to hell for practicing this.

Zeitgeist is a German term that literally translates as "spirit of the age" understood in a pejorative sense, akin to an exaggerated **secularism**, cultural **relativism**, or **political correctness**. Likewise, Paul's polemic delivered in 2 Corinthians 4:4 condemns those blinded to **God**'s Word by the spirit of this age (literally the "god of this eon"). Zeitgeist is contrasted with reading the **signs of the times** (see *GS* #4, 11), which aims at Gospel **discernment** of what the Spirit is helping to make possible in the world today.

A **zero sum game** (in economics) is based on the premise that the world's **wealth** is static and fixed; therefore, whatever is gained by one party necessarily results in a corresponding loss by another. For example, a ten dollar payment to another (taxes, charitable contribution, payment for goods or services) renders the payor ten dollars poorer and the payee ten dollars richer. This economic view supported the Church's former condemnation of any form of **interest-taking** as immoral **usury**, but **capitalism** demonstrates that new wealth can be created; therefore, widespread use of the zero sum game is a misleading economic principle.

Zero tolerance policies seriously punish any violation of established rules, even if the violation were a one-time offense, and regardless of accidental mistakes or mitigating **circumstances**. For example, in schools such policies are formulated to discourage possession of banned items such as drugs, alcohol, cell phones, and weapons. In response to the **sexual abuse** crisis the **USCCB**'s **Dallas Charter** permanently removes from ministry any individual against whom a credible accusation of sexual misconduct with a minor has been substantiated. Criticisms of zero tolerance policies center on what can be viewed as an excessive punishment for even minor infractions and as the failure to take into sufficient account all of the circumstances around the infraction. **See also** *crimes and delicts* and *tolerance.*

Zielgebot (German, "fulfillment command") strives to realize as far as possible an **ideal** while recognizing that no ideal can ever be completely fulfilled this side of the eschaton.

Selected Bibliography

Bretzke, James T. *Bibliography on Scripture and Christian Ethics*. Studies in Religion and Society series, vol. 39. Lewiston, NY: Edwin Mellen Press, 1997.

———. *Consecrated Phrases: A Latin Dictionary of Theological Terms*. 3rd ed. Collegeville, MN: Liturgical Press, 1998, 2003, 2013.

This book-length dictionary compiles, translates, and explains the meaning of a large number of Latin terms employed in the various branches of theology: moral, biblical, canon law, systematic, liturgical, and historical.

———. *A Morally Complex World: Engaging Contemporary Moral Theology*. Collegeville, MN: Liturgical Press, 2004.

This book deals with methodology and moral discourse, natural law and moral norms, scripture and ethics, conscience, sin and moral failure, and pastoral applications.

———. *A Research Bibliography in Christian Ethics and Catholic Moral Theology*. Lewiston, NY: Edwin Mellen Press, 2006.

Childress, James F., and John Macquarrie, eds. *The New Dictionary of Christian Ethics*. Philadelphia: Westminster Press, 1967, 1986.

Curran, Charles E., and Richard A. McCormick, et al., eds. *Readings in Moral Theology*. 16 vols. Mahwah, NJ: Paulist Press, 1979–2011.

This ongoing topical series of readings across the liberal–conservative Roman Catholic spectrum began in 1979 with the first volume, *Moral Norms and Catholic Tradition*, and is currently up to the sixteenth volume, *Virtue*.

Geaves, Ron. *Key Words in Christianity*. Washington, DC: Georgetown University Press, 2006.

This very brief book includes dictionary-type entries of vocabulary used in both Roman Catholic and Protestant theological circles.

Green, Joel B., ed. *Dictionary of Scripture and Christian Ethics*. Grand Rapids, MI: Baker/Brazos Press, 2011.

This is an encyclopedic work on a wide spectrum of ethical topics, including many that would not normally be found in other works on biblical ethics.

Hauerwas, Stanley M., and Samuel Wells, eds. *The Blackwell Companion to Christian Ethics*. Malden, MA: Blackwell Publishing, 2004.
Hauerwas and Wells look at Christian ethics through the lens of worship, contending that worship is what should shape the moral life of Christians.

McFarland, Ian A., David A. S. Fergusson, Karen Kilby, and Iain R. Torrance, eds. *Cambridge Dictionary of Christian Theology*. Cambridge: Cambridge University Press, 2011.

O'Collins, Gerald, and Edward Farrugia. *A Concise Dictionary of Theology*, rev. and exp. ed. New York: Paulist Press, 1991, 2000.
Short entries in this work cover both historical and theological terms used in Roman Catholicism.

Parrinder, Geoffrey. *A Concise Encyclopedia of Christianity*. Oxford: Oneworld Publications, 1998.
Parrinder's short dictionary-type entries span a wide spectrum of terms and figures found in Christianity; the work also includes a timeline.

Richards, Larry. *The Zondervan Dictionary of Christian Literacy: Key Concepts of the Faith*. Grand Rapids, MI: Lamplighter/Zondervan, 1987.
Brief encyclopedia-type entries are written from an evangelical Protestant perspective.

Roberti, Francesco Cardinal, and Msgr. Pietro Palazzini, eds. *Dictionary of Moral Theology*. Trans. from the Italian 2nd edition under the direction of Henry J. Yannone. London: Burns & Oates, 1962.
This classic dictionary of moral theology is an excellent resource for definitions and short encyclopedic articles of a wide variety of moral terms, although obviously in the spirit of the pre–Vatican II manualist tradition.

Schweiker, William, ed. *The Blackwell Companion to Religious Ethics*. Malden, MA: Blackwell Publishing, 2004.
This work considers the teachings of world religions.

Sparks, Richard C. *Contemporary Christian Morality: Real Questions, Candid Responses*. New York: Crossroads Publishing Company, 1996.
Sparks offers one hundred answers to frequently asked moral questions.

Stoeckle, Bernhard, ed. *Concise Dictionary of Christian Ethics*. New York: Seabury Press, 1979.

Tubbs, James B., Jr. *A Handbook of Bioethics Terms*. Washington, DC: Georgetown University Press, 2009.